SINGULAR VISION

SINGULAR VISION

The Founding of the
Catholic Church Extension Society of Canada
1908 to 1915

MICHAEL POWER

NOVALIS

© 2013 Novalis Publishing Inc.

Cover design: Blaine Herrmann
Layout: Audrey Wells

Published by Novalis

Publishing Office
10 Lower Spadina Avenue, Suite 400
Toronto, Ontario, Canada
M5V 2Z2

Head Office
4475 Frontenac Street
Montréal, Québec, Canada
H2H 2S2

www.novalis.ca

Library and Archives Canada Cataloguing in Publication

Power, Michael, 1953-
    Singular vision : the founding of the Catholic Church
Extension Society of Canada, 1908-1915 / Michael Power.

Includes bibliographical references and index.
Also issued in electronic format.
ISBN 978-2-89646-533-0

    1. Catholic Church Extension Society of Canada--History.
2. Catholic Missions in Canada--History. 3. Burke, Alfred
E. (Alfred Edward). I. Title.

BV2195.P69 2013   266'.271   C2012-906636-2

Printed in Canada

We acknowledge the financial support of the Government of Canada through the
Canada Book Fund for business development activities.

5 4 3 2 1   17 16 15 14 13

CONTENTS

Acknowledgements 6

Preface, *by Father Philip J. Kennedy, President, Catholic Missions in Canada* 8

Introduction 10

1. The Boat Ride 15

2. Father Alfred Edward Burke 31

3. Organization of Church Extension, 1908–1910 46

4. The Crusade Begins 69

5. Ukrainian Catholics: The First Wave, 1891–1914 80

6. Church Extension's Ukrainian Crusade, 1908–1915 99

7. The Women's Auxiliary of Toronto, 1910–1915 131

8. McEvay, Burke and the French 152

9. An Interlude, 1911–1912 168

10. Showdown with Archbishop Neil McNeil, 1913–1915 181

11. An Assessment of Father Burke's Presidency 219

Endnotes 227

Bibliography 257

Index 263

ACKNOWLEDGEMENTS

M y grateful thanks go to a small army of people. Some of them I have known for many years and count as friends and colleagues; some of them I have never met except through correspondence, but count them as colleagues in the collaborative effort of conjuring up the past. Without these people I could not have conducted my research and written this book:

Father Philip J. Kennedy, president of Catholic Missions in Canada, for his support, patience and understanding, for his timely translations of Latin- and French-language documents and for his reading and correcting the manuscript

Father Edward J.R. Jackman, OP, of the Jackman Foundation, for the Foundation's generous financial support of this project

John Burtniak, for copy editing the manuscript and making many helpful suggestions for improving the quality of the text

Joe Sinasac of Novalis Publishing, for his enthusiastic reception of the story and for publishing the book

Professor Mark McGowan of the University of St. Michael's College, the first historian of Church Extension, for reading the manuscript

The many archivists, librarians, diocesan chancellors and researchers, for their assistance in locating and copying primary documents: Marc Lerman, Gillian Hearns and Andrea D'Angelo of the Archives of the Roman Catholic Archdiocese of Toronto; Loutitia Eason of the

Archdiocese of Oklahoma City; Éloi De Grâce of the Archdiocese of Edmonton; Gloria Romaniuk of the Ukrainian Catholic Archeparchy of Winnipeg; Yolande Comeau of the Archdiocese of St. Boniface; Julie Reid of the Centre du patrimoine, Saint-Boniface, Manitoba; Diane Kelly of the Archdiocese of Keewatin–Le Pas; Yvette Gareau of the Diocese of St. Albert; Carol Hollywood of the Diocese of Calgary; Sylvia Best of the Diocese of Peterborough; Diane Lamoureux of the Grandin Archives; Father Art O'Shea of the Diocese of Charlottetown and biographer of Father A.E. Burke; James Lambert of Divisions des archives de l'Université Laval; Debra Majer of the Diocese of London Archives; M.C. Havey of the Archives of the Edmonton-Toronto Redemptorists; Jennifer Peco of the Archdiocese of Vancouver; Betty Sears of the Peterborough Public Library; Noel McFerran of the John M. Kelly Library of the University of St. Michael's College; Francis Handrahan of the Public Archives and Records Office of Prince Edward Island; Karen Ball-Pyatt of the Kitchener Public Library; Arthur G. McClelland of the London Public Library; Jeff Beattie of Mount Hope Cemetery; Anna Reczynska, historian from Poland; Patria Rivera of Catholic Missions in Canada; Karen Lemiski of the Basilian Fathers Museum in Mundare, Alberta.

Theresa Power, for her work on the *Catholic Register* microfilm and for dealing with Library and Archives Canada

Kathleen Power, for reading the manuscript and acting as my guardian angel. *Deo Gratias*!

PREFACE

A century of growth in missionary enterprise, one that continues to exist and grow to this day, deserves a quality historical account. This volume presents the history of our own missionary society at its birth and through its early days.

As it happens, the account makes for an engaging story. In 2008, when we celebrated the 100th anniversary of Catholic Missions in Canada – known at the beginning and during most of its history as The Catholic Church Extension Society of Canada – many of us thought it would be an opportune time for the production of a history. However, circumstances kept us from that task, and our present chosen historian was occupied on a different work. In 2008, then, we had to be satisfied with a small booklet-sized effort that I wrote and produced myself with the office staff of Catholic Missions in Canada, entitled *Home Missions in Canada: The Beginnings*. It is more of a commemorative publication than a history. It is replete with photographs, old and new, to give as complete a picture as I could of the historical sweep of the Society. It served its purpose but is now out of print and therefore unavailable.

How fortunate we were to find Michael Power, the author of *A History of the Roman Catholic Church in The Niagara Peninsula 1615–1815* (published in 1983), *Servants of All: A History of the Permanent Diaconate in the Archdiocese of Toronto 1972–2007* (published in 2010), and many other historical books, articles and reviews. Michael is well known for his ability to probe the evidence of hidden and long-forgotten correspondence and literary papers and make connections within the subjects of his pursuit, to arrive at clear conclusions.

Most of this present account concerns certain personalities, not always showing their best sides, yet all the characters in this endeavour of Home Missions had one aim in mind – that of bringing the message of Jesus Christ to the far reaches of a vast country, and sustaining the Word of God and the structures of the Church everywhere the people lived and settled. How this aim was accomplished is revealed in the pages of Michael Power's readable account.

Knitted together, and dealt with in sufficient length, are the simultaneous stories of the Oblates and other orders of missionary priests and sisters, and the relationships within a group of stolid bishops. Of special importance are the accounts of the establishment of the Ukrainian Catholic Church in this country, and the difficulties that arose between English- and French-speaking Church leaders. The work of the many women who served Catholic Missions at home, the Women's Auxiliary, is remembered and extolled.

Although Catholic Missions in Canada is now occupied with assistance to missions in Labrador, some Eastern dioceses and the northern Territories, the great thrust of The Catholic Church Extension Society of Canada in 1908 and for many decades thereafter had been westward from the Society's headquarters in Toronto. The movement of missionary interest and monetary funds and chapel materials was mostly to the Western provinces, and to the bishops of these young territories, who made sure that their missionary personnel were properly provided for as they preached the Gospel to all.

This history of the first years of the now-great Society is well presented by Michael Power, and it will serve as a fine illustration of the efforts of the Church members to build up God's Kingdom, and as a dependable reference for the vibrant life of the Canadian Church at the beginning of the twentieth century.

(Rev.) Philip J. Kennedy
President
Catholic Missions in Canada
8 August 2012

INTRODUCTION

S even years in the corporate life of an organization that is more than one hundred years old may seem too brief, and therefore too insignificant, to deserve a scholarly book-length treatment. But the opening years in the history of the Catholic Church Extension Society of Canada, from June 1908, when it was established, to August 1915, when its first president reluctantly resigned in a storm of controversy, were anything but insignificant. Those first years were absolutely vital to the formation and direction of the Society, particularly in the establishment of a solid foundation for the first-ever Catholic organization in Canada dedicated to the oftentimes confounding business of Catholic home missions. Church Extension's primary mandate was to convince Catholics in the more established dioceses of Eastern Canada that much of Canada was still missionary territory and that their co-religionists in the missions were poor and isolated and desperately needed their help on an ongoing basis. It was quite a struggle to build and outfit chapels, to educate seminarians, to recruit Latin Rite and Eastern Rite priests, and to sponsor schools and convents. The whole enterprise of Church Extension rested on a lively faith, a desire to do good works, and a steady stream of small donations from a large pool of Catholics committed to home missions. Their generosity was the "widow's mite" multiplied thousands of times and dutifully recorded, week by week, in the Extension news section of the *Catholic Register*.

The founding years of the Society are also the most exciting in Church Extension's story. They were one part visionary, one part practical and one part soap opera. There was plenty of ambition, misunderstanding, turmoil, false starts, pleas for assistance and ongoing battles in the press and from the pulpit against the religious and social enemies of tens of thousands of recently arrived Catholic immigrants from the multicultural Austro-Hungarian Empire. This was a chapter in the history of the Church in Canada begging to be written in detail.

At the same time, one wonders how the Society survived the behind-the-scenes bickering and contentious debate over who was in control of the board of governors – the bishops or the laity – and who exactly was in charge of the Society's overall direction and daily operations, via the three-man executive committee: the president, who was appointed by the pope, or the chancellor, who was the archbishop of Toronto? Who held the levers of power and control in this canonically erected Pontifical Society, the priest-president or the archbishop-chancellor whose episcopal city served as Church Extension headquarters? It made for an interesting contest of wills, which was duly played out and meticulously recorded on the pages of the *Minutes* of the meetings of the board of governors and in volumes of intense and hair-splitting correspondence worthy of a nineteenth-century potboiler. The historical record on which this book is based is bursting with letters and telegrams and official directives filled with opinions, charges, counter-charges, negotiations and face-saving manoeuvres.

At the end of its first seven years, the Society not only emerged intact from its self-inflicted wounds but also righted itself so that it could continue, uninterrupted, its vital apostolic work, which it did ever more vigorously and far more intelligently. The Society was able to achieve success because everyone on both sides of the fence, even during the worst of the quarrelling, wanted it to succeed. It would have been a major calamity for Catholics in mission territory if the Society had collapsed. Such an outcome would have been a humiliation from which the Church in Canada would have taken a generation or more to recover, especially in view of the seemingly never-ending triumphs of the two leading Protestant home mission societies. They were always flush with money and had no trouble spending it.

The dramatis personae of our story is impressive – a real cast of Catholic characters at the opening of the twentieth century, including two popes, the Vatican secretary of state, several cardinal protectors, two apostolic delegates to Canada, archbishops and bishops, Canada's first Ukrainian eparch (bishop), the Metropolitan of Lviv, who paid a historic visit to Canada in 1910, various religious communities, and the gifted and energetic president of the Women's Auxiliary. And we must not forget to mention those Catholic judges, industrialists, canal and tunnel builders, financiers, factory owners and journalists who, as members of the board of governors, donated $30,000 to the Society at its inception. By investing in Catholic home missions, these governors lent to the Society a vigorous persona of professionalism, political connections and social standing. They were called upon for the benefit of their fellow Catholics, who were expected to participate in Church Extension's work, and for Canadian society as a whole. These men meant business. They were rich and successful. As members of the Catholic elite, they knew a great deal about fundraising and when to play the Catholic card in a largely Protestant milieu. Unfortunately, the leading layman on the board, who happened to be the chief justice of the Supreme Court of Canada, did not know when to play his cards in the presence of the archbishop of Toronto and was forced to fold his hand and follow his ally, the president of the Society, out the door.

The most important members of our cast of characters, however, were two priests from Prince Edward Island: Father Francis C. Kelley and Father Alfred E. Burke. Father Kelley was Father Burke's former altar boy. As a young priest on loan to a parish in Michigan, he founded the Catholic Church Extension Society in the United States in 1905. The original concept of Catholic home missions was his brainchild. Father Kelley was also one of the founders of Church Extension in Canada, in 1908, along with Archbishop Donato Sbarretti, OFM, the apostolic delegate to Canada; Archbishop Fergus Patrick McEvay of Toronto; Monsignor Alfred A. Sinnott; Father John Kidd; Sir Charles Fitzpatrick, the chief justice mentioned above; and, of course, Father Burke.

Now, there would have been no Church Extension in Canada had it not been for the collaboration of Sbarretti and McEvay, and there would have been a much diminished lay presence on the board of governors had Sir Charles not been a member from the outset. But to Burke is accorded the "singular vision" of the title of this book. Burke was the visionary. He was a fearless political animal, the driving force on the ground. It was his infectious charisma that attracted wealthy Catholics to the board and carried the Society during its early days. He was the midwife to the birth of a Catholic missionary spirit in Canada. This was no small accomplishment. From the well-managed inculcation of this missionary spirit among Catholics there flowed a more inclusive understanding of the Church Universal in Canada and many good ideas and plans for action that allowed Church Extension to take on a corporate life that was bigger and stronger than any clash of personalities in the board office.

But if Burke was the visionary – and every new organization needs one – he was not a very practical president. Aside from the purchase of the *Catholic Register*, and turning it into a steady and effective voice of Church Extension, Burke did very little to move the Society beyond its initial euphoria. Indeed, the *Register* was central to Burke's downfall. The sober and careful administration of the Society was short-circuited because Burke, a frustrated journalist, spent an inordinate amount of time as editor-in-chief of the newspaper, and in his self-appointed role as arbiter of Catholic opinion on public matters, he managed to insult and malign those he understood to be his enemies, in particular French-speaking Catholics.

And when it came to soap operas, there was no one more adept than Burke at spinning out the drama as soon as he understood that his departure from Church Extension was all but inevitable. The first significant misfortune to befall Burke was the death in 1911 of Archbishop McEvay, his patron, protector and kindred spirit. The second was the appointment in 1912 of Archbishop Neil McNeil to the See of Toronto. McNeil had little time for the flamboyant and outspoken Burke, who enjoyed too much independence as a priest for McNeil's liking. Burke had become an albatross and an embarrassment whose behaviour generated criticism from his fellow clergy. Burke had to go. In the end, he was eased out with a Church honour and a pastor's salary.

As sad and as graceless as Burke's exit was, we must keep in mind that while he was president, from 1908 to 1915, Church Extension had invented itself as an indispensable spiritual lifeline to a multitude of far-flung Catholic communities, many of which had no chapel or church or resident priest. These communities in need were located mainly in the Archdiocese of St. Boniface in Manitoba, the Diocese of Prince Albert in Saskatchewan, and the Diocese of St. Albert in Alberta (later the Archdiocese of Edmonton). Of interest is the fact that the Ukrainian Catholic Church, which acquired its own eparch in 1912, was the leading beneficiary of the Society's fundraising efforts. Ukrainian Catholics received so much attention because, even though they were the largest in number of recently transplanted Catholic communities, they were judged by the Society to be the most vulnerable to proselytizing and poaching. That the Latin Rite Church Extension was able to connect with and nurture Eastern Rite Ukrainian Catholics, despite differences in language, liturgical ritual and cultural customs, speaks volumes about Burke's genius and determination to have Church Extension serve every constituency of home missions in Canada. That desire to serve also extended to numerous parishes and missions in the interior of British Columbia, in northern Ontario, in the Eastern part of Québec and the Gulf of St. Lawrence and in western Newfoundland.

Today, Catholic Missions in Canada continues the work of Father Alfred E. Burke's "singular vision," and is the living embodiment of the hopes of Church Extension's founders. Canada remains mission territory in so many places, and Catholic Missions is busier than ever bringing spiritual comfort and material sustenance to numerous isolated islands of the Catholic faith.

Michael Power
Welland, Ontario
16 July 2012

CHAPTER 1

THE BOAT RIDE

T he Catholic Church Extension Society of Canada was founded on 25 June 1908, as the Richelieu & Ontario Navigation Company steamer *Tadoussac* was passing down the St. Lawrence River, from Quebec City to Chicoutimi. It was an unlikely setting to launch what became, over time and much experimenting, a great Catholic enterprise that is still flourishing more than a century later in numerous parishes and mission posts throughout Canada. Church Extension's work, once commenced, has continued uninterrupted, despite two world wars, the Great Depression, periodic economic downturns, changes in leadership of the Society, and the ever-evolving face and needs of the Church in Canada. The missionary spirit among Canadian Catholics, long cultivated and encouraged by Church Extension (known since 1999 as Catholic Missions in Canada), remains to this day vibrant, generous and productive.

However, since the setting of the Society's establishment was so unusual, at least in historical hindsight, the earliest accounts of the events that brought the founders together on a river steamer, and the substance of their numerous conversations on board, often vary in essential details and, as a result, can be misleading and confusing. The accounts also contain several errors of fact that need to be addressed.

These are the result of enthusiasm, fallible memories and a desire to add a touch of the incredible or fantastic – a very Catholic exercise of the imagination – to what was essentially a straightforward story of like minds that agreed to take the Church in Canada on a new path of missionary activity.

The founders were seven in number: two archbishops, four priests and one layman. They were Archbishop Donato Sbarretti, OFM, apostolic delegate to Canada from 1902 to 1910; Archbishop Fergus Patrick McEvay, installed as archbishop of Toronto on 17 June 1908; Sir Charles Fitzpatrick, chief justice of the Supreme Court of Canada; Monsignor Alfred Arthur Sinnott, secretary to the apostolic delegate in Ottawa; Father Francis Clement Kelley, founder, in 1905, and president of the Catholic Church Extension Society of the United States of America; Father John Thomas Kidd, secretary to Archbishop McEvay; and Father Alfred E. Burke, at the time pastor of Sacred Heart parish in Alberton, Prince Edward Island.[1] Their coming together was unlikely mere coincidence.

Missing from this otherwise impressive assemblage were members of the French-speaking clergy of any description. None were present to participate in the discussion and ensuing decision to organize Church Extension, which was intended by the founders to become a Canada-wide movement. Although their absence was unintentional and regrettable, it was nonetheless an organizational blunder and diplomatic oversight that no number of subsequent appointments of French-Canadian prelates to the board of governors, or Church Extension's early achievements in the pursuit of its missionary mandate, would be able to ameliorate. The exclusion of the French wing of the Church from the Society's founders came to be seen by many of the French-speaking clergy, in particular by the Québec hierarchy and its ally in Western Canada, Archbishop Adélard Langevin, OMI, of St. Boniface, Manitoba, as an insult and a threat. At the first instance of disagreement over the role of the French language in the destiny of the Church in Western Canada, discord and division rose up within the ranks of the governing body and episcopal supporters of Church Extension.

Of the seven founders of Church Extension, three were from Prince Edward Island: Father Kelley, Father Burke and Monsignor Sinnott. Kelley had been one of Burke's altar boys at St. Dunstan's Cathedral in Charlottetown. Although Burke was the elder of the two men by eight years and had remained on the Island, while Kelley had moved to the United States, Kelley never forgot Burke and considered him a model of the clerical dynamo that he wished to emulate in his own priesthood. When Kelley wanted a priest to take charge of Church Extension in Canada, he looked no further than Burke. Kelley also crossed paths with Sinnott when Kelley, a theological student, was serving as an examiner for the class in elementary Latin at St. Dunstan's College, also in Charlottetown. One of the pupils he quizzed was a very young Arthur Sinnott. Kelley never forgot him. This was the same Sinnott who, as secretary to Archbishop Sbarretti, was instrumental in convincing the apostolic delegate to take up the cause of Church Extension. The support of Sbarretti – which could never have been presumed – was essential to the formation of Church Extension in 1908. Although the Canadian version of the Catholic world could be very small, there were enough people in it who were "ambitious for the higher things" (1 Cor. 12:31).

There are five sources – four published and one unpublished – for the narrative of the boat ride. The earliest is a story that appeared on the front page of the *Catholic Register* of 19 November 1908. The article had no by-line but was sent from Chicago, the headquarters of Church Extension in the United States, in the lead-up to the First American Catholic Missionary Congress that took place there later in November. Fathers Kelley and Burke surely provided the information. The article opened with a brief biography of Archbishop McEvay, giving him prominence in the story, and mentioned the names of all seven founders. Kelley had gone to Québec to receive an honorary degree from Laval University (l'Université Laval), which explains *his* presence on the boat, and he and Burke were surprised to learn that Sbarretti, McEvay, Fitzpatrick, Sinnott and Kidd were also on board. One evening, when the four priests were discussing Church Extension, Burke said, "I would gladly take up the work if I could secure one Canadian

Archbishop and one great Canadian layman to back me."[2] Quite un-expectedly, Fitzpatrick appeared on deck and one of the priests said, "There is your layman, and your Archbishop is below."[3] Burke was chosen to approach Fitzpatrick and McEvay and ask for their support. They promptly gave it to him; a meeting of the seven then took place and Church Extension in Canada was born before the boat docked at Chicoutimi. Sbarretti did not come up in the discussion.

The second source is another article. Father Burke wrote it for the *Catholic Register* of 7 January 1909. Oddly, for someone who was a central participant, Burke made no reference by name to either Father Kidd or Monsignor Sinnott, the two secretaries. He did refer, however, to a clerical messenger. It could only have been Sinnott, secretary to Sbarretti, because in his article Burke located Kelley and Sbarretti (in a compartment below deck discussing Church Extension) and McEvay, Fitzpatrick and himself (on deck but not together). Burke was alone when he was summoned by the messenger to meet Kelley and Sbarretti. The story continues:

> Sbarretti and Kelley: "Dr. Burke, we are fully convinced that Church Extension should be undertaken at once in Canada, and that you should undertake it."
> Burke: "This is so sudden; but if I could get an Archbishop and a Catholic layman of position and influence, I would try."
> Sbarretti and Kelley: "Both are here. The Archbishop of Toronto is out there on deck and so is Sir Charles Fitzpatrick. Go and secure them."[4]

The third source is also from Burke, written in his unmistakable and difficult-to-decipher handwriting.[5] It is the only entry in a two-page *Minute Book of the Catholic Church Extension Society of Canada.*[6] Despite its brevity, this document is quite informative. It is the only source that provides a specific date for the organization of Church Extension and that names the steamer and its approximate location on the St. Lawrence River when the founders agreed to set up the Society. The *Tadoussac* was then steaming between Quebec City and Murray Bay (La Malbaie). The *Minute Book* records the names of the seven founders and the nine members of the first board of governors;

it mentions aims and objects of Church Extension, as presented by Father Kelley, but it does not list them; and it notes that the apostolic delegate was honorary chairman of the board and that Father Burke was president and managing director.

There is no date on the *Minute Book* to indicate when Burke wrote it. But that is not critical. What matters is that Burke did not attempt to embroider the basic facts. This makes the *Minute Book* so much more informative and reliable than the *Catholic Register* accounts of 1908 and 1909 and (not surprisingly) more credible than the two remaining sources for the boat-ride story, both of which were written by Father Kelley in two autobiographies, published in 1922 and 1930.[7]

In each instance, Father Kelley wanted his readers to believe two things: that he and Father Burke were on the steamer together soon after their reception of honorary doctorates in theology from Laval University, as part of the ceremonies marking the university's three hundredth anniversary, and that the presence on board of Sbarretti, McEvay, Sinnott and Fitzpatrick (Kidd is absent from the story) was a matter of pure coincidence, a complete surprise and a fortuitous turn of events. According to Kelley, Burke told him earlier in 1908, in letters and personal encounters, that all he needed to institute a Canadian branch of Church Extension was one archbishop and one prominent layman.[8] On this important point, Kelley's recollections agree with the *Catholic Register* stories. What is new is Kelley's slip about correspondence and personal encounters, as if the two priests, working for the same purpose, had laid the groundwork for the moment at hand. This rubs against the allegedly chance encounter with the two archbishops and with Sinnott and Fitzpatrick just when meeting them meant absolutely everything to the Canadian conception of Church Extension.

Kelley continued his story this way. During a conversation between Burke and himself, the subject of course being Church Extension, it is Sinnott who seemingly appeared out of thin air. He joined the conversation and, amused, remarked to Kelley and Burke, "It is not necessary to go off the boat to find your archbishop and your prominent layman. The Archbishop of Toronto is on board, and Sir Charles Fitzpatrick, the Chief Justice of Canada, as well."[9] Burke seized the moment. He went and spoke to McEvay and Fitzpatrick about Church Extension and returned to report to Kelley, which made Kelley look like the linchpin of the St. Lawrence River negotiations.

What is one to make of all this? What is a more plausible story of the historical origins of Church Extension in Canada? First, there is the confusion about honorary degrees. The occasion was the tercentenary of the founding of Québec in 1608, and not the three hundredth anniversary of Laval University. Both Kelley and Burke did indeed receive honorary degrees – Doctor of Divinity – from Laval, but not on the same date.[10] Kelley received his on 25 March 1908, and Burke his on 29 May 1908. There is no evidence in the university archives to suggest that the degrees were conferred at a special ceremony in late June 1908, as implied by Kelley.[11]

So, what put Kelley and Burke on the *Tadoussac* on 25 June – along with Sbarretti, McEvay, Fitzpatrick, Sinnott and Kidd? The answer will take some time to deliver, but it rests on a reasonable belief that Kelley, Burke and Sbarretti had planned everything well in advance and met the other four founders-to-be at a rendez-vous on the *Tadoussac* in order to arrive at a formal agreement on the Church Extension proposal, and that they met on the *Tadoussac* because they, like so many other Church dignitaries, had gathered in Quebec City for the annual St. Jean Baptiste Day festival, on 24 June, made all the more special in 1908 because of the Québec tercentenary. The *Tadoussac* was taking a large Church party to Chicoutimi at the invitation of Bishop Michel-Thomas Labrecque, the local bishop. The seven founders, therefore, were together on the same steamer on 25 June for a definite purpose, using the Québec celebrations as a convenient venue for their meeting.

What, then, was the chain of events that brought the founders to the *Tadoussac*? For starters, it is necessary to recognize Father Francis Clement Kelley as the principal founder of Church Extension in Canada. It was Kelley's brainchild to establish the Church Extension Society in the United States. It was his genius to have invented the movement and machinery of Catholic home missions, using as his model the home mission movements of the Methodists, Baptists and Congregationalists.[12] And it was essentially his idea to broaden the reach of Church Extension into Canada, with a particular eye on the Church in the West.

The lone proviso to this assessment of Father Kelley's organizational genius is that someone may have prodded him into taking action in Canada and that Father Michael Francis Fallon, OMI, a future bishop of the Diocese of London, may have been that person. A member of the board of governors of the American Society, Fallon was the Canadian-born provincial of the Oblates of Mary Immaculate in the United States, a position that took him to many missions throughout North America. He also had a reputation as a high-profile player in the affairs of the Canadian Church who was not afraid to broadcast his opinions. Fallon would have had plenty of opportunities and no hesitation to tell Kelley in person his ideas about the most pressing needs of the Church in Western Canada. What those conversations might have been can be found in a letter from Fallon to Kelley, dated 16 January 1908. Fallon wanted Church Extension to provide English-speaking priests for the West to counter what Fallon saw as a debilitating French hegemony over the Church in Manitoba, Saskatchewan and Alberta.[13]

Fallon's letter came from deep within the swirling vortex of the old-style Canadian battle of French versus English. Kelley, who had been educated in Québec, appreciated Fallon's anxiety and fears, but wisely did not take up his battle cry as an appropriate *public vision* for Church Extension in Canada. He listened to Fallon but did not let him co-opt Church Extension. He visited the West and correctly concluded that Fallon's stance, even if it were the truth of the matter – and there is evidence in the ensuing Regina imbroglio that Kelley agreed with Fallon – would not be helpful to the establishment of the Society in Canada. (This was not the end of Fallon's involvement with Church Extension in Canada. See Chapter Eight.) Kelley wanted Canadian Church Extension to discover its own unique missionary mandate without any overt or official entanglements in the politics of language and religion. Time proved him right. As matters were to unfold, the Canadian Society's first priority would not be the recruitment of English-speaking priests for the West, despite the die-hard enthusiasm of its founding president, Father Alfred E. Burke, for just such an undertaking. The Society's opening campaign would be the salvation of Ukrainian Catholics, an enormously emotional and complicated undertaking that almost immediately imparted to the Society a powerful and unifying purpose necessary to its early survival.[14]

Although Father Kelley could not foresee that the mission of Church Extension in Canada would be significantly different from that in the United States, he did appreciate the practical fact that the Society would be stillborn without the official blessing of the apostolic delegate in Ottawa and, at the very least, the tacit approval of the three bishops in the West. If Kelley wanted something dearly for the Church, or from the Church for himself, he had no qualms climbing directly to the top rung of authority and asking for it. He was fearless and confident in that particular regard.

His opening move was to lobby in person Archbishop Sbarretti, the apostolic delegate in Ottawa, and Archbishop Paul Bruchési of Montréal (the interview took place in Joliette). Next, he wrote to Archbishop Langevin, on 20 November 1907, enclosing printed information on Church Extension in the United States and informing him of his interviews with Sbarretti and Bruchési. In 1895, Langevin had become not only archbishop of St. Boniface, a historic French-speaking See, but also, and more importantly, metropolitan of the ecclesiastical province of the same name. Over the years, Langevin had become the undisputed Catholic Prince of the Prairies and the Québec Church's favourite son in the West.[15] His two suffragan bishops were Bishop Émile-Joseph Legal, OMI, of St. Albert, Alberta, and Bishop Albert Pascal, OMI, of Prince Albert, Saskatchewan.[16] To Langevin, Kelley wrote:

> It has been suggested by a great many that such a work [Church Extension] should also be established in Canada. I had a talk with His Excellency, the Apostolic Delegate, a short time ago, and he favored very much the plan. The next day, I saw the Archbishop of Montreal, who said that the Bishops of the Northwest had never exposed their wants as the missions of the United States had done to those in the wealthier dioceses of the East. He suggested that if the Bishops of the Province

of Saint Boniface expressed their desire to have such a Society formed and showed the needs of it, there would be no difficulty about the rest.

A great many Canadian people are already interested in this matter and I think that if your Grace and the Bishops of your Province desire it, a work will be taken up which will mean a great deal for the Northwestern missions.[17]

Who these "great many Canadian people" were Kelley did not bother to mention. By 1907, Catholic Church Extension Society of the United States was hardly a household name in Canada or even among Canadian Catholics, the very people who should know because they would be called upon to support this new Society. Kelley was exaggerating for effect, but that apparently did not bother Langevin, who shared Kelley's letter with his suffragan bishops and replied a month later, on 20 December 1908. Langevin expressed just enough interest in Kelley's proposal to elicit an enthusiastic reply from Kelley on 23 December 1907:

> The Bishops of the maritime provinces, I believe, would be interested in the matter, and I found, from an interview with Archbishop Bruchesi – as I said to you in a previous letter – that his mind is open and his heart very willing. If your suffragan Bishops will draft a strong endorsement of the Society, at their next meeting, and urge the formation for Canada, placing such a resolution in my hands, I think I can promise you relief from the present situation. I have placed a little editorial note in our Magazine which ought to help. Recently, the Protestant churches of Toronto voted $500,000 for missions. Surely this is an example which we ought, at least, to make an attempt to follow.[18]

It was odd that Kelley did not mention the Ontario bishops, and even odder that he held out the prospect of immediate financial relief for Langevin if he and his suffragan bishops would endorse the erection of a Canadian Society. But Langevin was in no hurry to be tempted by Kelley's offer of money, no matter how much the archdiocese may have needed it. Behind the official courtesy of Langevin's initial correspondence with Kelley resided a wariness of *les irlandais*, a term of derision and contempt used by the Québec hierarchy to describe the "Irish" element in the Canadian Church. The result was a culture of mutual suspicion, with the French accusing the so-called Irish of plotting to anglicize the Church, and the "Irish" denouncing the French for their race-based nationalism.[19]

Archbishop Langevin's reaction to Father Kelley's invitation can be seen as another instance in this culture of mutual suspicion. Langevin was offended that Kelley had arrived unannounced in Regina, Saskatchewan, in 1907, and that subsequent to his visit he had told a Canadian priest in New York that Regina's first bishop needed to be an English-speaking one.[20] It was a rare moment of artless meddling for the president of American Church Extension. Kelley's indiscreet "Irish" remark about Regina found its way back to Langevin, who added it to what would grow into a litany of complaints against Father Burke and Church Extension in Canada.

While Langevin was in no hurry to continue his dialogue-by-letter with Kelley, perhaps hoping that Kelley's dream to set up Church Extension would fade away quickly and quietly in the face of his own official silence, Kelley was far from idle. He used Langevin's silence during the early months of 1908 as an opportunity to continue his lobbying of the apostolic delegate, but this time with his own point man in Ottawa. This is where Father Alfred E. Burke enters the narrative. Kelley had invited Burke to come to Chicago in March 1908 and familiarize himself with Church Extension's administration. He then directed Burke to Ottawa, where he could stop on his way home to Prince Edward Island and present Sbarretti with Kelley's plans for the launching of the Canadian branch of Church Extension. Kelley told Sbarretti all this in a letter of 13 March 1908, which preceded Burke's arrival in the city four days later, on 17 March. Kelley continued:

> If Father Burke could secure a leave of absence from his Bishop [James Charles McDonald] for a couple of years to organize the association, with your patronage as well as the act of concurrence of some of your influential Catholics, lay and clerical, a Canadian board could be constituted at once, and we would

lend every assistance to make everything progress in such a way as to shortly convince the most incredulous of ultimate efficacy and success. The indications which reach us daily from Canada and the spectacle rising up before us constantly of souls perishing on the broad plains for the Bread of Life, which we should be furnishing in some measure of adequacy, compel me to solicit anew an urgent and favorable consideration of this matter, before it is too late. I know how keenly Your Excellency feels the situation already, and can only assure you that a little extra effort – even the appearance of insistence on your part will better make for the progress of the Church in Canada than anything else we know of.[21]

Kelley mentions the date of 17 March 1908 in his 1930 autobiography. He wrote, "Something happened, on March 17th, 1908, that made the way for Father Burke a bit easier."[22] On its own, this is cryptic and vague, but Burke's correspondence can explain it. Three letters are dated 17 March 1908: two to Kelley and one (a circular letter) to a selection of Western bishops. A fourth is dated 18 March 1908 and addressed to Kelley. These four letters were written in Ottawa. A fifth letter, bearing the date of 23 March 1908, was sent to Kelley from Alberton.[23]

Much useful information can be gleaned from the four Burke/Kelley letters. Burke had interviews with Bishop McEvay in London and Michael J. Haney, an influential Catholic businessman in Toronto, before he arrived in Ottawa at eight in the morning on St. Patrick's Day. Two hours later, Burke was ringing the doorbell at the delegate's house. Intense discussions took place over the course of that day and the next. Kelley's letter to Sbarretti of 13 March 1908 was the basis upon which Burke and Sbarretti agreed on the necessity of establishing Church Extension in Canada. What follows is a summary of the highlights of the four letters:

- According to Burke, Sbarretti was bound and determined to establish Church Extension, regardless of any opposition to it that might arise among the Canadian hierarchy.

- The two men agreed that Ottawa was the preferred headquarters for Church Extension.

- Burke tried but failed to enlist the immediate support of Archbishop Joseph-Thomas Duhamel of Ottawa.[24] Duhamel was afraid that local Catholic charities and continued financial support for Propagation of the Faith would be hurt by Church Extension fundraising. He was of the opinion – later expressed to Sinnott, the delegate's secretary – that the work of Catholic societies was under the jurisdiction of each Ordinary in his own diocese. It was too early for a supra-diocesan society such as Church Extension.[25]

- Burke also failed to convince Archbishop Bruchési to be the episcopal sponsor of the society. Their meeting in Montréal was very cordial, but Bruchési argued that, except for Bishop Pascal of Prince Albert, the Western bishops had yet to signify their desire for assistance. He would say nothing more until they did.

- Burke and Sbarretti agreed that if, in the end, neither Duhamel nor Bruchési would co-operate, they would turn to Archbishop Louis-Nazaire Bégin of Québec and ask him to host the society. If he refused, Sbarretti reassured Burke that he would find a bishop.

- Bishop Pascal had indeed expressed his support for Church Extension, but not in writing. Something more formal was needed from him and the other Western bishops. Sbarretti asked Burke to compose a circular letter and date it 17 March 1908. Sbarretti would sign and send copies to Bishop Pascal, Bishop Legal and, interestingly, Bishop Augustin Dontenwill, OMI, of New Westminster (later Vancouver), British Columbia. Sbarretti invited these bishops to list their needs and to state whether they favoured the establishment of Canadian Home Missions.

- There was no mention of contacting Archbishop Langevin. He had yet to send Kelley, as requested by the latter on 23 December 1907, a resolution from Langevin and his suffragan bishops in support of Church Extension. This delayed Kelley's report to Sbarretti and prompted the apostolic delegate to remark to Burke that he expected nothing from Langevin.

By the time Burke returned to his parish in Alberton on Saturday, 21 March, he was completely convinced that Church Extension would become a reality in the near future. He had good reason to believe so. Sbarretti was in Church Extension's camp. And he stayed there, resolutely. But things did not go as planned in Ottawa. Bruchési remained cool towards the idea of Church Extension. Bégin was hardly more welcoming. He did not want to be the Society's principal patron, although in a spirit of compromise he did accept an invitation to join the first board of governors. After all, he was the archbishop of Québec, Canada's most historic diocese.

A more serious setback, however, was Sbarretti's failure to convince Duhamel that his episcopal city of Ottawa was the logical choice for Church Extension headquarters. Duhamel's answer came at the end of March 1908. Sbarretti relayed the news to Burke on 2 April. Burke could not believe it. He wrote Sbarretti on 13 April:

> Your Excellency – I am quite surprised that Mgr. Duhamel should formally refuse to permit the establishment of Church Extension for Canada, at Ottawa, especially as it could not possibly mean any drain on the resources of the Diocese and promised so much for the general well-being of Catholicity in Canada. When I left him, as I reported to your Excellency, he seemed to be in a mood to consider the claims of the organization at least, and said that he would take the first opportunity of talking it over fully with you. I felt sure too that your knowledge of the work and the promise it seemed to offer you of filling a long-felt want in Canadian Church economy, would have enabled you to overcome any little objection which he might raise. I do hope that the door is not so completely closed upon us as I might infer from yours now before Monsigneur [sic] would reconsider, one should think.[26]

But the door was closed firmly and forever. This letter from Burke to Sbarretti was imbedded in one from Burke to Kelley, written the following day. Burke concluded: "The Westerners [Langevin, Pascal and Legal] are to be awaited in any case. I am getting anxious though. Those Bishops can block any work anywhere."[27]

It was Langevin, as metropolitan, who could block, or at the very least obstruct, Church Extension's ambitions. His main weapon during the first half of 1908 was a frosty silence, despite what his suffragan bishops might have to say on the subject. One suffragan who did reply to Sbarretti's St. Patrick's Day circular was Bishop Pascal. In a letter of 5 May 1908, written by his secretary, Father H. Lacoste, OMI, Pascal outlined for Sbarretti the many needs of the Diocese of St. Albert and the reasons why he believed that Church Extension would be useful in meeting them.[28] Reception of this letter prompted Sbarretti to suggest to Langevin that he and his suffragan bishops discuss Pascal's letter at their next meeting.[29]

They may have discussed Pascal's letter, but, once again, Langevin took no action. He had other things on his mind, including a planned trip to Europe, which would consume months of his time. On his return to Canada in August 1908, Langevin was surprised to learn about the founding of Church Extension the previous June,[30] and was flabbergasted to be informed that Archbishop Bégin had accepted a seat on the Society's board of governors.[31] Sbarretti and Burke had outflanked him. Langevin would spend considerable energy during the remaining years of his episcopacy sniping at Church Extension, but to no lasting effect. His was a rearguard reaction and, like all such reactions, was bound to fail in the long term. (More will be said about Langevin's relationship with Burke and Church Extension in Chapter Eight.)

There was only one other archdiocese worth considering for Church Extension headquarters. That was the Archdiocese of Toronto. Unfortunately, the archdiocesan leadership was in a state of transition, forcing Burke to wait to make his move. Archbishop Denis O'Connor officially resigned on 4 May 1908 and was succeeded by Bishop Fergus Patrick McEvay, who had been bishop of London since 1899. (McEvay's appointment was dated 13 April 1908, weeks in advance of O'Connor's resignation. Burke may have known about McEvay's transfer to Toronto in advance.)[32]

Archbishop McEvay's installation at St. Michael's Cathedral took place on Wednesday morning, 17 June, eight days before the historic boat ride.[33] Archbishop Sbarretti, in his capacity as apostolic delegate, was in attendance for the grand and imposing ceremony. He very likely would have urged the newly minted archbishop to sponsor the

Society in the archdiocese, and McEvay, whose promotion to the See of Toronto had been arranged by Sbarretti, probably readily accepted. Some Ontario bishops had wanted Bishop David Scollard of North Bay to succeed O'Connor, but Sbarretti had the measure of McEvay and engineered his ascent in the provincial hierarchy.[34] He chose well. Archbishop McEvay would become an enthusiastic champion of the goals of Church Extension in Canada and Father Burke's principal protector in times of controversy with his French episcopal critics.

••••

We can account for the presence of all the founders on the *Tadoussac*, on 25 June 1908, except for one: Sir Charles Fitzpatrick. He would have been in Quebec City for St. Jean Baptiste day, but who invited him to the meeting on the *Tadoussac*? It was either Sbarretti or Burke, but probably Sbarretti, because he lived and worked in Ottawa and he and Fitzpatrick would have moved in the same Catholic circles in the capital. Both Sbarretti and Burke realized that Church Extension needed the active involvement of wealthy and influential Catholic laymen who enjoyed a high profile in their respective fields and were willing to spend their money and time promoting the interests of the Catholic Church in Canadian society. Sir Charles Fitzpatrick suited this role perfectly. In both politics and law, few Canadians, let alone Catholics, were his equal.

Born on 19 December 1853, in Quebec City, Fitzpatrick was educated at St. Anne's College, the Quebec Seminary (Séminaire de Québec) and Laval University, where he earned a BA (1873), an LLB (1876) and an LLD (1902). He was an *avocat* in his home province and a barrister in Ontario, specializing in criminal law. He was chief counsel for Louis Riel in 1885, and he defended Honoré Mercier, the Québec premier, in the Baie des Chaleurs scandal in 1892. He sat as a Liberal in the Legislative Assembly of Québec from 1890 to 1896 and represented the same constituency in the House of Commons from 1896 to 1906. Fitzpatrick was Solicitor General from 1896 to 1902 and Minister of Justice from 1902 to 1906. In recognition of his elevation to chief justice, he was invested as a Knight Commander of St. Michael and St. George (KCMG) in 1907.[35] Although Fitzpatrick was preoccupied by his work on the bench, he found time to take his membership in Church Extension's board of governors very seriously throughout eight years of service. From the very commencement of the Society's operations, he was a close ally of Burke and an uncompromising defender of lay interests on the board. He was afraid of no one.

••••

Let us go full circle and return to the beginning of our story. The Catholic Church Extension Society of Canada was formally organized on 25 June 1908. Although, to a large extent, its objects and its organizational structure were borrowed from its elder sister in the United States, Church Extension in Canada was, from its conception, an independent body intended to live its own unique history. Several days after the ride on the *Tadoussac*, Father Kelley and Father Burke were writing the new Society's constitution in the library of St. Dunstan's College in Charlottetown. They were assisted by Father J.T. Murphy and Father T. Curran.[36] Also on Prince Edward Island was Archbishop McEvay, who was enjoying a summer holiday. By 8 July 1908, a first draft of the constitution was ready for McEvay's inspection.[37] On 15 July, Burke was in Ottawa writing to Sir Charles Fitzpatrick. The news was good: "His Excellency the Apostolic Delegate has approved in all its main features the Constitution of the Catholic Church Extension Society and I am writing to say that arrangements will be made for a meeting of the Board of Governors as soon as I can get back from Chicago."[38] The rest of the year would be an active and fruitful one for Father Burke and Church Extension.

CHAPTER 2

FATHER
ALFRED EDWARD BURKE

A t first glance, Father Alfred Edward Burke may appear to be a most unlikely choice to conduct the daily administration of a new organization intended to harness the missionary spirit of Catholics everywhere in Canada. Up until he became the first president of Church Extension, Burke had risen no higher in the Church than pastor of a rural parish in his home diocese of Charlottetown, after twenty-three years in the priesthood. But what he lacked in clerical status and achievement, aside from his honorary doctorate in theology in 1908, he made up for with high-profile memberships in a number of associations and movements and with a well-honed reputation for imaginative ideas that stretched far beyond his home province of Prince Edward Island and preceded him everywhere on his visits throughout the country. People inside and outside the Church took note of him.

Father Burke was a peripatetic priest, a celibate celebrity who took seriously – and sometimes too seriously – his Catholic churchman-ship and his Dominion citizenship, managing to combine these two aspects of his public career in a unified persona during his presidency of Church Extension. He was ambitious and energetic, a superb organizer and a man whose Roman collar was often sufficient to persuade wealthy

Catholics to part with their money for the cause of Church Extension. Father Burke was a gifted public speaker and a flinty debater prone to controversy and mockery of his opponents. In him were the elements of the politician and the journalist. If he had not been a Catholic priest, he would have been a natural for the House of Commons. Also, he was bubbling with ideas and complaints on many fronts, and regularly turned to the letter columns of the local newspaper to air them.

Father Burke was born on 8 September 1862 in Georgetown, Prince Edward Island. He was the fourth of seven children of Captain James Burke, a descendent of Tipperary Irish, and Mary Moar, whose family originated in the Orkney Islands.[1] He attended the local school in Georgetown and studied at St. Dunstan's College for three years, from 1877 to 1880. In his final year, Burke was chosen to deliver the address on literature. From St. Dunstan's, he moved to the Quebec Seminary in Quebec City, where he studied theology for five years, earning the highest academic accolades, and was ordained a priest on 30 May 1885 by Archbishop Elzéar-Alexandre Taschereau.

Burke's inaugural assignment in the Diocese of Charlottetown was curate, or assistant priest, at St. Dunstan's Cathedral and secretary to Bishop Peter McIntyre.[2] In his spare time, he compiled historical sketches of four or five pages each of every Island parish and religious house. His research was original, extensive and reliable, but remained unpublished and relegated to the bishop's archives. He may have done this work at the command of his bishop, although this is not clear. Other assignments included assistant priest at Rustico and administrator for a year at St. Joachim's parish in Vernon River.

On 22 September 1887, Bishop McIntyre appointed Father Burke as parish priest of Sacred Heart in Alberton and of the neighbouring parish of St. Mark's on Lot 7, Prince County. Writing in 1930, Francis Clement Kelley, Burke's former altar boy at the cathedral and now bishop of Oklahoma City, speculated that Bishop McIntyre was of the conviction that "it was his business to run the diocese."[3] In other words, it appears that the young and newly minted Father Burke had offended the bishop with his own unsolicited ideas about diocesan administration. McIntyre's solution was to promote Burke to a small rural parish far away from the episcopal palace in Charlottetown. But if McIntyre, widely known as the Prince Bishop, believed that Burke would disappear quietly into the fog of a comfortable clerical obscurity, he was wrong in his estimation of his former secretary's appetite for activity.

Father Burke thrived in Alberton. There he experienced the freedom to lead his own parish and to establish himself as a Catholic priest par excellence during the twenty years of his pastorate. In a bid to elevate the level of religious life in the parish, he hired an organist and set up religious education classes for adults. He then organized tea parties, which became an annual fundraising event in Alberton, built an imposing rectory based on the mansion designs of the American architect George Baker of St. Paul, Minnesota, landscaped the parish property and beautified the local cemetery. On 12 October 1890, Bishop James Charles McDonald, McIntyre's successor, blessed Sacred Heart Church, consecrated the altar and erected the Way of the Cross.[4] Burke had turned what had been a declining and forgotten parish into a jewel of active parochial life.

In 1893, Father Burke established in his parish the Island's first branch of the Catholic Mutual Benefit Association (CMBA). Founded by Bishop Stephen Ryan of Buffalo in 1876, in Niagara Falls, New York, the CMBA provided life insurance for practising Catholic men from the ages of eighteen to fifty, contingent on a successful medical examination. Death benefits were $500, $1,000 or $2,000, depending on the premium, and were paid promptly, according to many published testimonials in Catholic newspapers. Although modest, these sums often saved many widows and their children from sliding into poverty or even destitution. The benefit could also be paid after thirty years of contributions. The CMBA established its first Canadian branch in Windsor, Ontario, in 1878, and was vigorously supported by Bishop John Walsh of London and Archbishop John Joseph Lynch of Toronto.[5] In 1904, Burke was elected a Grand Trustee of the CMBA on the first ballot at its annual convention in Toronto.[6]

Concerning temperance, another vital social concern, Father Burke had an abhorrence of any type of alcoholic drink. For him there was no such thing as temperance in alcohol. On the day of his parish tea party in July 1894, he deliberately destroyed a newly arrived whisky consignment at a local shop and was sued by the shop owner for damages to his private property. Burke was found guilty, fined eight dollars or one month's imprisonment and given a criminal record. This judgment was later overturned by another court, but only after a highly indignant Burke was persuaded to allow his lawyer to do the talking in court. Far from embarrassing him to any discernible measure, or curbing his appetite for scolding and shaming liquor merchants in public, the controversy and polemics surrounding Burke's trial only emboldened him to continue his personal vendetta against grogshops. In 1908, Father Burke became president of the Island branch of the Dominion Alliance for the Total Suppression of the Liquor Traffic.

Life insurance and prohibition were not the only two extra-parochial concerns of Father Burke. He became an avid agriculturalist, in tune with his people who, for the most part, made their living from the land. He began by instituting the Alberton agricultural exhibition in 1892. It was a masterstroke of publicity, emphasizing pride and local achievement. The exhibition's success propelled Father Burke ever deeper into public life. Over the years, he parlayed his self-taught knowledge and his inspirational presence by taking on executive positions and directorships in an impressive number of associations devoted to nearly every aspect of the Island's agricultural economy, including the Island's reforestation. At one time or another, he was president of the Fruit Growers' Association of Prince Edward Island and vice-president of the Canadian Forestry Association of Ottawa, the Pomological Society of Boston and the Maritime Bee Keepers' Association. In addition, he was a director of the Maritime Poultry Association, the Maritime Stockbreeders' Association and the Island's Winter Fair. He was involved in the Dairymen's Association and was a prime mover in the establishment of the West Prince Board of Trade in 1903.[7]

Father Burke was not a dabbling theorist in any of these endeavours. Rather, he was a genuine Renaissance man who was a quick study of the topic at hand and an authoritative proponent and defender of the aims of each of these associations and societies. He was even an experimenter in fruit-tree grafting in the rectory orchard. His numerous articles for agricultural and horticultural journals were judged to demonstrate "extensive knowledge, sound advice, and breadth of view."[8] His most notable triumph came in 1904, when he delivered a lecture in the Railway Committee Room in Ottawa on Island reforestation to four hundred people, including many Americans involved in the forestry business. Among those participating were Sir Wilfrid Laurier, the prime minister and chair of the meeting, and Earl Grey, the governor general. It was a bravura performance. Two years later, Biltmore Forest College in North Carolina awarded him an honorary doctorate.[9]

Father Burke realized that if Prince Edward Island were to flourish as an agricultural community, and to enjoy basic opportunities to diversify its rural economy, it needed a safe and secure link to the mainland. Isolation, especially during the long winter months, guaranteed continued economic stagnation. At public meetings in Emerald in 1903 and in Charlottetown in 1905, Burke spoke in favour of petitioning the Dominion government to invest in the Capes route for quicker and more reliable steamer navigation. The capes in question were Tormentine, New Brunswick, and Carleton Head, Prince Edward Island. This route needed new piers on both ends and the latest ice-breaking steamers to ensure passenger and mail service twelve months of the year. In time, the Dominion government would provide more modern steamers, but it did not proceed with the Capes route.

Father Burke's fondest desire on the question of a link, however, was to see a rail tunnel built under the Northumberland Strait. Archbishop Cornelius O'Brien of Halifax, another Islander, was the first to put forth this audacious proposal.[10] Not to be outdone, George Howlan, a Conservative senator who became lieutenant governor of Prince Edward Island, adopted O'Brien's idea, seeing in it an opportunity to make money. In 1886, he formed a company whose sole purpose was to construct a rail tunnel. In exchange for building the tunnel at his company's expense, Howlan asked the Dominion government for complete ownership of the Island's railway system and an annual subsidy to operate it.[11]

Howlan's gambit went nowhere. But that is not the point. Father Burke was a friend of both O'Brien the prelate and Howlan the politician, giving him a suitable occasion to move easily between the two supposedly separate spheres of Church and state in a matter that was entirely secular and political in nature. By endorsing the rail tunnel, and in Howlan's case proposing to build it, these two prominent Islanders conferred a resilient respectability upon it and guaranteed that the idea would not die on the Island without first having a formal hearing in Ottawa. But that hearing was not to happen for a long time.

After Howlan's death in 1901, Island leadership on the tunnel issue quietly and unofficially passed to Father Burke (O'Brien died in 1906). A mass meeting at Charlottetown on 10 March 1905 approved the selection of Father Burke and three others to head an Ottawa-bound delegation of the Island's senators and members of parliament. Their instructions were simple but daunting: to deliver a memorial to Prime Minister Sir Wilfrid Laurier, urging his Liberal government to commit to the construction of the tunnel as a matter of policy. The delegation met with Laurier and other officials on 1 April and returned to Charlottetown two weeks later to submit its report to a second mass meeting, also held in Charlottetown.

Father Burke was the principal speaker. He assured his audience that the delegation was well received by the prime minister and his minister of finance and by members of the House of Commons and Senate. Nearly everyone was sympathetic to the proposal for a tunnel. The press was also receptive. Burke claimed that a contractor was willing to build the tunnel for $10 million, with the backing of New York engineers who were ready to begin work. As well as leading the delegation to Ottawa, Burke published a pamphlet on the subject, *The Tunnel Between Prince Edward Island and the Mainland*, around the time of the 1905 meeting with Laurier. It was the published record of his convictions and feelings.

The government made no promises, although it knew that one of the main terms for the Island's entry into Confederation in 1873 – uninterrupted communication with the mainland – had yet to be fulfilled. In May, Burke took his case for the tunnel to Toronto, where he addressed the Toronto Board of Trade and the Canadian Manufacturers' Association. In July, having returned to the Island, he orchestrated a gigantic "Tunnel Tea" at Cape Traverse. That was the end of the open agitation. Two years passed. Laurier's Liberal government remained uncommitted, choosing procrastination as its preferred method of political response. Frustrated but undeterred, Burke publicly vowed to revisit the issue with Laurier in early 1907, after the CMBA executive convention in Kingston. His persistence in the matter and his loyalty to the Island earned him the moniker "tunnel Burke." For Burke and his many supporters, it was a badge of honour. But by March 1908, even Burke, the eternal optimist and hard-nosed lobbyist, had to concede that Laurier had no intention of investing in a multi-million-dollar tunnel for tiny Prince Edward Island. There was no sizeable political payoff in such an expensive and risky adventure. The idea faded away, but "tunnel Burke" did not.

Father Burke loved to travel. As attached as he was to his people in Sacred Heart parish, and to the welfare and destiny of Islanders in general, Prince Edward Island was too small a place for him to find his true public voice. He may have been a parish priest, and perhaps at times during his two decades at Alberton he may have felt fated to live the rest of his life in some backwater of the Diocese of Charlottetown, but the parochialism of his native Island could never satisfy his many pent-up ambitions or his innate wanderlust. Having been educated in Québec, Burke experienced a taste of another world. He would spend a good deal of his life dashing about in all directions, often in the service of some association, society or Island project, as we have seen, or simply because there were more worlds to experience. His appetite to travel was almost insatiable. Burke's life was the very antithesis of the vow of stability, which, happily for him, he was not obliged to take at his ordination as a diocesan priest. He preferred to be on the move.[12]

During the 1890s, for example, Father Burke seemed to be everywhere except in his parish.[13] In June 1892, he and six others left on a six-week tour of the Northwest (Manitoba and what would become Saskatchewan and Alberta), at the invitation of the Canadian Pacific Railway (CPR). At Saint John, New Brunswick, on the westward portion of the journey, this select company, which included at least two politicians, was joined by several more people and given a special car on the train, courtesy of the CPR. Although no reason for the journey was given in the only contemporary newspaper account of it, it seems that Father Burke was invited by the CPR and the Dominion government to assist in the formulation of colonization policy.[14] Burke returned to the Northwest in July 1893. His itinerary included Montréal, Ottawa and Winnipeg. The purpose of the journey was "immigration and colonization."[15] In an 1894 interview, Father Burke was asked about colonization that year. He answered: "I was up to Montreal and Ottawa on that business. It is slow this year. Low prices for wheat and the commercial depression [are] the cause. Most people fear this depression will be greater still this year."[16]

This is very intriguing, a tease for the historian, given Burke's later career at the Catholic Church Extension Society. Under his direction, and at his almost obsessive insistence, Church Extension adopted Ukrainian Catholic immigrants out West as its most urgent priority. It is a pity, then, that no report about his 1892, 1893 or 1894 findings and conclusions on immigration and colonization has been found, if one had ever been written, for Burke must have seen plenty of evidence of the first wave of Ukrainian Catholic settlers during his trips to the West.

Father Burke returned to the West in the autumn of 1895. During that visit, he preached at Immaculate Conception church in Winnipeg and spent part of his sermon addressing one of the most divisive topics of the day, the Manitoba Schools Question, which concerned repeated Catholic attempts to overturn the provincial abolition of publicly funded Catholic schools.[17] Burke had an opinion on the matter and was not shy about giving it from the pulpit or telling it to the press. He hoped that the Conservative government of Sir Mackenzie Bowell would exercise its constitutional powers to provide a reasonable solution, one that would restore minority rights and bring peace and unity to the country.

Near the end of June 1894, Father Burke attended the first inter-colonial conference sponsored by Canada and held outside Great Britain. The delegates from ten colonies, including Canada, met in Ottawa.

The British government, although unhappy with such independent proceedings, sent observers. For the imperialist Father Burke, the big story was the grand reception for the delegates on Parliament Hill, which he described in detail in an interview with *The Daily Examiner*, an Island newspaper firmly in the fold of the Conservative camp. He told the reporter: "Fifteen hundred nabobs and ladies passed the receivers in evening dress. The recollection of some of those old frights would haunt you forever."[18] Burke returned to Ottawa in December 1894 on unknown business. While there, he offered his condolences to Lady Annie Thompson, the widow of Sir John Thompson, Canada's first Catholic prime minister, who had died suddenly at Windsor Castle on 12 December 1894.[19]

Father Burke toured the Magdalen Islands, which belonged to the Diocese of Charlottetown, in the summer of 1898. To celebrate his visit, he wrote a four-part account of his trip for *The Daily Examiner*.[20] His travelogue included details about a wide range of topics: the school system, the different religious groups, the French-speaking population, the fishing industry, the various lagoons and harbours, All Right Island, Grindstone Island, Grand Entry and Byron Island. He was very thorough in his observations, treating his subject with a lightheartedness, even joy, rare in his other writings that tended to be either serious in subject matter or disputatious in tone and delivery. But the Magdalen Island articles leave an unintended impression of a rather pompous Father Burke carrying on like an important ecclesiastical dignitary instead of a parish priest from Prince Edward Island on an unofficial pilgrimage. Near the end of the final installment, he wrote: "As we pass, the people salute us most cordially everywhere, the men never failing to uncover [doff their hats] no matter how occupied at the time, the women with the grace so peculiar to the French, vouchsafing a respectful inclination of their comely heads."[21]

Father Burke's love of writing to the local press was just as strong and irresistible as his love of travel. But it was hardly in travelogues, as rewarding as that type of writing may have been for him, that he sought to make his mark in the public square, outside the sanctuary of his parish church. A duellist at heart, Burke turned to the letters page of *The Daily Examiner* to vent what can only be described as his political spleen. These letters, however entertaining they might be for today's readers who are not used to late-nineteenth-century polemics, reveal the pugnacious, peevish and partisan side of a personality that was otherwise intelligent, curious and generous in its pursuit of knowledge and the common good. Burke could be vindictive and unrelenting in his pursuit of his opponents and critics, often forgetting, as he inflicted his righteous fury on lesser beings, that he was a Catholic priest answerable to his bishop for his conduct and not some freewheeling muckraker and hack dealing in character assassination. Even by the journalistic standards of the day, which allowed for all kinds of intemperate remarks and outrageous judgments, Burke at times went to extreme lengths to skewer public figures. Craving attention and currying controversy, Burke was incapable of drawing boundaries around his opinions or reining in his anger. He had little sense of proportion.

It was one thing for Father Burke to rush to the defense of Archbishop James Vincent Cleary of Kingston, when the Toronto *Globe*, the *Montreal Star* and even *The Daily Examiner* of Charlottetown attacked the archbishop for his 1897 pastoral letter that forbade the participation of Catholics at non-Catholic marriages and funerals.[22] Or for him to challenge and denounce biased and inaccurate reporting by the Protestant press on Catholic schools and students in Québec.[23] But it was a very different matter for Father Burke to hound relentlessly and in a most partisan fashion a Liberal-appointed public servant by the name of Mr. Sharp concerning train service in West Prince County.[24] Or for him to label as a "Rotten Corruptionist" a Catholic critic who dared to contradict him in the pages of the *Patriot*, a Liberal newspaper. It seems that the critic had signed his letter with the initials "R.C." As every Islander understood, these initials meant Roman Catholic.[25] For Burke, they stood for traitor.

These two controversies took place in May and June 1900 and inevitably attracted the attention of Bishop James Charles McDonald of Charlottetown, Father Burke's ecclesiastical superior.[26] Although McDonald did not believe that any Catholic priest should be engaged in political name-calling in the press, he was willing to tolerate Father

Burke's extravagant, even eccentric, behaviour for a long time because of his standing in Island society. But the bishop could hardly be expected to tolerate Burke's outburst in the press following the funeral of George Howlan, who had died on 11 May 1901. This was the same Howlan who had been a senator, lieutenant governor and rail tunnel promoter. Over the years, he often stayed with Father Burke at the Alberton rectory, and Burke was a frequent visitor to Government House in Charlottetown. Howlan's funeral took place at Sts. Simon and Jude Church in Tignish two days after his death. Father Burke had fully expected to preach at the funeral Mass, because this had been Howlan's request, as understood by Burke's and Howlan's other friends. When Burke saw Father Martin Monaghan ascend the pulpit to deliver the sermon, he could barely control himself in front of the congregation of mourners.[27]

After waiting twelve days, Father Burke sent the following letter to *The Daily Examiner*, which was published on 25 May 1901. He lambasted not only Father Dugald MacDonald, the pastor of Tignish, but also Bishop McDonald himself. It was a monumental blunder:

Lest anyone might think that I could disregard the request of the distinguished dead, or the wishes of the friends of the late ex-Governor Howlan, I take this means of saying in reply to l'Impartial's comments, copied into your paper, that I was quite willing and ready to preach the funeral sermon at Tignish on the 13th, when, to my utter surprise and amazement, the pastor, without a word of warning, and with ulterior motive manifest, wired His Lordship Bishop McDonald to bring a preacher. This request, extraordinary in the light of all the circumstances, the Bishop acceded to. So far as I was concerned I could not take the pulpit without the consent of the pastor, or at the request of his superior, – ecclesiastical usage precluded me from doing so. But anyone could see at a glance that this was a piece of sharp practice that no pastor except the one in question would be guilty of and few bishops permit. By it the urgent request of the dead and the feelings of the living were outraged, and I was shocked beyond anything I can tell myself. Possibly the parties to the sad affair were happy; but I cannot think so.

However, I am of the opinion that this sort of thing has gone quite far enough, and if no other be found to do so I promise to see, in the future, that such conduct be properly exposed and condemned in the public press, the only effective means at hand. We have reached a point where self-respect and duty to our people call a halt, and we shall not, I hope, disregard the warning or refuse the labour it involves.[28]

By maligning a fellow priest and insulting his bishop, Father Burke gave impertinence a whole new meaning. But he did not stop there. To ensure that the public understood the meaning of his letter, he wrote a second one a week later, dated 1 June 1901, boasting that he published his letter of 25 May over his own name "with a full knowledge of the consequences."[29] This was pure bravado, a dare to his bishop to discipline him.

One person who understood the gravity of the unfolding situation facing Father Burke was Dr. P.C. Murphy, Burke's brother-in-law. Murphy wrote two letters to *The Daily Examiner*. In the first, dated 31 May 1901, he confirmed that Howlan had indeed asked Father Burke to preach at his funeral, but that the controversy, stoked by the newspaper's editorial writer, had gone too far: "The matter is regrettable from every standpoint, and in the opinion of a Catholic layman it would be well to let it drop now."[30] After Father Burke's letter of 1 June, Murphy felt obliged to deliver this scolding, in a letter of 5 June 1901:

When the pulpit of our church is made to do service in satisfying personal animosity it is time for laymen to call a halt and refuse to prolong the discussion, no matter how well-armed with incontrovertible facts. The public, Catholic and Protestant, are shocked at the whole affair, and to help prevent further scandal I am done with it.[31]

Bishop McDonald could not have agreed more with Murphy when it came to the scandal caused by Father Burke. Nothing frightens a bishop more than clerical scandal. A close second was the attitude of the Protestant majority on Catholic infighting gone public for all to witness. McDonald took action. Employing the full authority of his episcopal powers, he wrote to Burke on 7 June 1901:

The scandal caused by your public utterances in the 'Examiner' newspaper regarding the funeral services of the late Honorable Mr. Howlan, is such as must prove most detrimental to religion in the diocese of Charlottetown. It should not be necessary for me to point out to you that my solemn duty obliges me to safeguard the religious welfare of the faithful of this diocese, and by all lawful means to prevent their being scandalized in their holy faith. While I regret that it should be necessary for me to take such a step, nevertheless my sacred duty obliges me to send you the following notice, namely, that by this letter I formally prohibit you from writing correspondence or communications for the public press, or causing such correspondence or communications to be published in the public press unless you shall have previously submitted the manuscript of each and every such correspondence or communication for my approval, which approval must be obtained before any such publication. I earnestly trust that your good sense will point out to you the necessity of abiding by this order. This prohibition shall remain in force until revoked by my hand and seal.[32]

Instead of obeying Bishop McDonald, Father Burke appealed to the bishop's metropolitan, Archbishop Cornelius O'Brien of Halifax, asking him for an official opinion. As part of his appeal, Burke sent O'Brien a copy of McDonald's letter and copies of *The Daily Examiner* letters. Burke insisted that since the letters were the cause of McDonald's censure, the prohibition should be limited to letter writing. O'Brien was sympathetic to Burke's plea. Writing to McDonald on 15 June 1901, O'Brien thought that the prohibition was too inclusive:

As the wording of the prohibition is general, it not only inhibits the Rev. Mr. Burke from publishing correspondence on matters of Faith, Morality and Church discipline, but also on any and every subject historic [as well as] scientific, or even asking for tenders to erect a building etc. Of course I do not think Your Lordship intended all this – unless, indeed, you had very serious reasons unknown to me. I would therefore make the friendly suggestion that Your Lordship should restrict the terms of your prohibition to Church discipline, criticisms of his Superiors and brother Priests, and such other definite subjects as you may deem necessary.[33]

This was not the official opinion that Burke had sought. Nor was it what McDonald expected to hear from his metropolitan. O'Brien's gentle diplomacy satisfied neither party in the dispute. McDonald replied to O'Brien in a letter of 19 July 1901:

In reply to Your Grace's letter, re Father Burke, I confess that my prohibition was couched in terms, which may appear too general; but in view of the circumstances and the man, was difficult to be more definite and attain the end in view.

Father Burke, by the tone of his letters, especially in matters political, has given rise to such adverse criticism, both among Catholics and Protestants of this province, criticism which has redounded to the detriment of religion and its ministers. His last letters were simply uncalled for; and to anyone acquainted with the facts of the case, unreasonable and calumnious, and have been productive of much harm to our people.

I may say that if Father Burke wishes at any time to give the public the benefit of his scientific or historical lore, I will be but too glad to give him permission to do so, if he fulfills the condition laid down in my letter, a condition which I deem not expedient to alter, at least for the present.[34]

Following notification from Archbishop O'Brien of Bishop McDonald's letter of 19 July, in which he steadfastly refused to make any modification to his original prohibition, Father Burke asked O'Brien to render a formal judgment. O'Brien delivered it in a letter to McDonald, dated 22 August 1901. His judged that "the prohibition of June 7th 1901 should be modified by restricting it to matters of Faith, Church discipline and criticisms of Ecclesiastical Superiors and Brother Priests."[35]

Apparently, Father Burke was willing to live with this modification. But McDonald was unwilling to accept O'Brien's ruling. It was his turn to appeal. On 31 August 1901, Bishop McDonald sent a twelve-page summation of the case to Archbishop Diomede Falconio, the apostolic delegate. McDonald was careful to include copies of his correspondence with Burke and O'Brien and lengthy samples of Burke's letters to the press.

McDonald made clear his deep mistrust of Burke, characterizing him as possessing a "restless disposition" and "if any opening were left him he would find some way of continuing his old career of vituperation."[36] He listed seven reasons why his prohibition of 7 June 1901 should stand: the tone of Burke's letters was highly offensive; they produce scandal; they place the clergy "in a false position in the eyes of their respective flocks and in the estimation of the general public"; "they cause antagonism towards the Church and its clergy"; "they destroy the influence of the clergy with the faithful in the performance of the sacred ministry"; "they give the impression that a Catholic priest may be in good standing with his Church, and may at the same time speak of his fellow man with a manifest ill-will"; and if he had been "called upon to submit the above reasons to the first court of appeal, the Judgment therein given would have been different."[37]

The paper trail ends with McDonald's appeal to the apostolic delegate. But the fact that Burke's letter writing to the press ended with his letter of 1 June 1901 points to a victory for Bishop McDonald. Of course, the bishop's prohibition did not include Burke's participation in the CMBA, the rail tunnel agitation, the movement for the reforestation of the Island, temperance, and all the agricultural associations of which was a member. Nor did it restrict his penchant for travel or his reception of honorary degrees. Burke may have been deprived of a bully pulpit in the popular press, but he had other venues by which to air his views and make known his name to the public. Father Burke was as busy as ever from the date of McDonald's prohibition on 7 June 1901 to the founding of the Catholic Church Extension Society on the *Tadoussac* on 25 June 1908. Burke was probably only too happy for the opportunity to take up a new cause on a much larger stage. And McDonald, who would die in 1912, was probably relieved to see the last of Burke.

CHAPTER 3

ORGANIZATION OF CHURCH EXTENSION, 1908–1910

T here was considerable groundwork facing Father Burke and the other members of the board of governors before Church Extension would have a firm organizational foundation on which to build its vision of Catholic home missions. The board needed to approve a constitution and implement the by-laws, acquire an act of federal incorporation, convince individual Canadian bishops to support its work and, having accomplished all of the above, petition the Holy See for a charter that would bestow upon the Catholic Church Extension Society of Canada the status of a Pontifical Society. This was the big prize, since it would fortify the Society's legitimacy in the eyes of the Catholic faithful. Lastly, there was the matter of Church Extension's need to cultivate a Canada-wide following. The establishment or purchase of a newspaper by the board would be the best means to advertise and report on the work of Church Extension.

After Father Burke left Ottawa, with the apostolic delegate's blessing on the preliminary constitution for Church Extension, he travelled to the Chicago headquarters of Church Extension in the United States, as he said he would in his letter of 15 July 1908 to Sir Charles Fitzpatrick.[1] Father Burke's authority to conduct interim business on behalf of the Society derived from an operational decision of its founders to strike a provisional board of governors before they concluded their meeting on the *Tadoussac* on 25 June. In order to function as a legitimate body, the Society needed a board. Father Burke recorded the names of nine governors. They were Archbishop Donato Sbarretti, Archbishop Louis-Nazaire Bégin of Québec, Archbishop Fergus Patrick McEvay, Sir Charles Fitzpatrick, the Hon. Alexandre Taschereau (the Québec minister of public works), Bishop Charles J. McDonald of Charlottetown, Father John T. Kidd, Monsignor Arthur Alfred Sinnott, and of course Father Burke. The board, then, had four bishops, three priests and two laymen. Its first two decisions were to designate Sbarretti honorary chairman and Father Burke president and managing director.[2]

In September 1908, Bishop Joseph-Alfred Archambeault of Joliette, Québec, joined Bégin and Taschereau on the board.[3] Together they were the French face of Church Extension's governing body. Not one of these three men, however, was an active member, which suggests that the inclusion of their names was political window dressing to compensate for the absence of any French prelates or laymen in the founding of the Society. This is not to suggest that their nomination to the board was insincere, but that it might have been perceived as being too late and too obvious an attempt to present the Society as a unified Catholic effort. Archbishop McEvay had been anxious from the beginning that Church Extension have a "French Foundership" among its ranks – wealthy French-Canadian Catholics from Québec – so that the Society "could make a clear face against the world."[4] It was not to be. Bégin's commitment had been tentative ever since Archbishop Langevin had, in a letter of 21 August 1908, questioned Bégin's decision to accept a position on the board.[5] Both Bégin and Archambeault would resign as governors in November 1910 (see Chapter Eight), and Taschereau's name would disappear quietly from the roll call of board members.

The appearance of Bishop McDonald's name was also a courtesy, but for a very different reason. He was Father Burke's Ordinary and from him Burke would need an exeat from the Diocese of Charlottetown if he were to work full-time on behalf of Church Extension in the Archdiocese of Toronto.[6] McDonald duly delivered the exeat on 23 April 1909, and McEvay happily incardinated Burke into the archdiocese the following month, on 9 May 1909.[7] Bishop McDonald did not participate in board meetings.

Father Burke's first order of business in Chicago was to compose and circulate Church Extension's initial "begging letter." It was dated 31 July 1908, and because it was addressed simply to "Dear Sir," its targeted audience may have been the Catholic press, Catholic politicians and Catholic businessmen – people with influence and money. The purposes of the Society were, for the most part, practical in scope and were naturally tied to the priest-centred and sacramental nature of the Catholic faith. Its goal was to strengthen the Church in Canada, principally in the Prairie provinces and British Columbia, by providing financial assistance for the construction of churches and chapels in poor places; supplying altars, vestments and sacred vessels for the liturgy; supporting missionaries; distributing Catholic literature; and educating priests for the missionary field.[8]

It was the education of priests for the Canadian missions, however, that was uppermost in Father Burke's mind, and this became the rallying cry and central ambition of his letter. "The great need of the Northwest and pioneer districts of other provinces is for priests to take care of the people already there and already Catholic," he wrote. "Thus the Society is making its first work that of education. It is establishing a Missionary College, near St. Dunstan's, in Prince Edward Island."[9] If anyone thought that the location of the proposed college was odd, because it was at the other end of the country, Burke pointed out to his readers that the Diocese of Charlottetown was famous for producing an abundance of priestly vocations, but that far too many of the Island's clergy migrated to the United States. Canadian-educated priests who had English as their mother tongue were practically non-existent for the home missions, and there was no better place to educate a new generation of priests for Church Extension work than on the Island.

For Father Burke, and many others of his generation, the dynamics of providing the much-needed spiritual care for "the immense numbers of people now pouring into our immense new agricultural regions"[10] was rooted in a near mythological vision of priest and people united in a common effort to establish new Catholic communities within a distinctly Canadian context. According to the Catholic imagination of the day, the active presence of missionary priests among newly arrived Catholics would cause many good and lasting things to happen, not only for the Catholic faithful but also for the country as a whole – things that would help to build up the Church and to enrich the Dominion in countless ways. In the words of the *Catholic Register*, the priest "eventually brings a church, a church is a lodestone that draws about it a self-respecting and law-abiding people. These draw to themselves prosperity and the country profits by their residence."[11]

This was the Catholic ideal of religious and social progress. It inspired the founders and board of governors of Church Extension in 1908. But behind the idealism was a sense of fear: "Churches must be built and priests supplied in that vast territory which is being opened up for settlers. Now is the time to make a beginning. Ten years hence it will be too late. Catholic settlers without church or priest will be lost to the Faith."[12] Fear of losing Catholic newcomers to Protestant proselytizers (although they were not mentioned at this time) put an extra step into the marching orders of the Society as it began to organize itself in preparation for the battles to come.

Father Burke's second task while in Chicago was to finalize the society's Constitution and By-Laws for formal presentation to the board of governors in September. For this, he turned to Father Francis Clement Kelley. A polished version of both the Constitution and By-Laws, as a single document, was ready within a month, despite Father Kelley's absorption in preparations for the First American Catholic Missionary Congress. This document bears no date, but the evidence strongly suggests the summer of 1908.[13]

The Constitution was divided into six articles:

Article 1: Name
Article 2: Object
Article 3: Membership
Article 4: Administration
Article 5: Officers
Article 6: Change of Constitution

As for Article 1, the name Catholic Church Extension Society of Canada would not be changed until 1999, when it became Catholic Missions in Canada. As for the remaining Articles of the Constitution, they would remain unchanged for many decades, except in the composition of the board of governors in Article 4 and the addition of a new category of membership, in 1910, in Article 3: the Fifteen Year Members, who donated $100 in cash in a lump sum.[14] Of special interest, then, in the nascent corporate history of Church Extension are Articles 2, 3, 4 and 5.

The object of Church Extension, according to Article 2, "shall be to foster and extend the Catholic Faith in Canada."[15] This was a mission statement that would have resonated with every Catholic. So, too, would have the means. The fostering (protection) and extension of the faith would be achieved in five distinct but interrelated ways:

(a) by cultivating a missionary spirit in the clergy and people
(b) by the founding of a college for the education of missionaries
(c) by the building and equipping of chapels in pioneer districts
(d) by contributing to the support of poor missions
(e) by the circulation of Catholic literature[16]

These five were similar in wording to that describing the purposes of the Society as delineated in the circular of 31 July 1908, and were augmented by what was essentially a sixth way, although not specifically identified as such in the Constitution: "and by every other means proper to the main purpose of the Society."[17] By adding this all-inclusive provision, Church Extension gave itself the latitude it would need to adapt its strategy and tactics to circumstances unforeseen at the time of writing the Constitution. It was a wise move.

Article 2, stating the Society's objectives, was reprinted word for word in a story on the founding of Church Extension in the *Catholic Register* of 17 September 1908. Interestingly, it appeared a full six days prior to the meeting of the board of governors at which the Constitution and By-Laws were to be submitted for the board's approval.[18]

Article 3 provided four classes of membership based on monetary contribution. Founders contributed $5,000, either in a lump sum or over ten years in equal installments of $500 per year. Life Members contributed $1,000, either in a lump sum or over ten years in equal installments of $100. A second option for a Life Membership was to support one missionary student for Church Extension for a period of ten years. Dues for Annual Members, aimed at the middle class, were ten dollars per year. Contributing Members, who paid no less than fifty cents per year, were the rank and file of the Society's membership list. Moreover, "when a sufficient [number] of those are found residing in the same place they may be formed into a branch of the Society under the direction of their own officers."[19] One such branch was established in Toronto under the direction of a diocesan priest.

Article 4, on administration, listed the names of the board of governors, adding two new members to the original nine. They were the Hon. Nicholas Beck, a judge of the Supreme Court of Alberta,[20] and Michael Patrick Davis, a highly successful canal and bridge contractor who lived in Ottawa.[21] Judge Beck was a convert to Catholicism. Prior to his appointment to the board, he had worked with Archbishop Sbarretti on the rights of denominational schools in Alberta and Saskatchewan. Both Beck and Davis would work hard to promote and protect the lay point of view on the board of governors and were regular participants in its annual proceedings. This eleven-member board had four bishops, three priests and four laymen. Membership on the board of governors was limited to Founders and Life Members.[22]

Among other matters, Article 4 also referred to an executive committee: "For the transaction of business, this Board may delegate all, or any of its powers to an Executive Committee of not less than three members."[23] Real power and influence over the direction of the Society resided in this committee, which never exceeded the minimum number of three members. In addition to overseeing Church Extension's operations in between annual general meetings, the executive committee had full control over the Society's receipts and expenditures, and it was required by the By-Laws to give a true accounting of them to the full board at least once a year. Only two committee members were needed for a quorum.[24]

Article 5 dealt with the officers of the Society. They were the chairman of the board of governors, president, vice-president, general secretary and treasurer. Elected annually by the board were the chairman, vice-president and treasurer. The president, also elected by the board, would serve for a term of five years and would appoint the general secretary and any assistant secretaries as needed. The president and vice-president were the only salaried officers of the board.[25]

Next were the By-Laws. They were six in number and governed the duties of officers. They covered the following: chairman of the board of governors, president, vice-president, treasurer, auditors and temporary chairman of the board.[26] Since Father Burke was president of Church Extension from its inception in 1908 until his resignation in 1915, it is worthwhile to quote the By-Law that defined the role and duties of the president:

> The President shall have full charge of raising funds for the Society, and shall be the responsible Officer in the carrying out of all the plans of the Board of Governors. He shall have the right to engage or discharge all employees, except those appointed by the Board. He shall be responsible to the Board alone, and shall submit an annual report covering the entire work of the Society. He shall be the custodian of such funds as may be donated or set aside by the Society itself for expenses, accounting for said funds in his annual report to the Board of Governors. He shall give Bonds to the satisfaction of the Board of Governors for all moneys in his custody and perform all the duties pertaining to the office of General Manager.[27]

These expectations were straightforward, and Father Burke would meet them without fail. But that is hardly the substance of the story about Burke's presidency, in particular during his last three years, when dissension on the board nearly brought Church Extension to ruin. There was nothing in the By-Law on the position of president (or in any other By-Law or, for that matter, in any other part of the Constitution) that could have opened the door to the nasty quarrel among board members that preceded Father Burke's exit from Church Extension in 1915. The By-Law was not the problem. Rather, it was the failure of the board of governors to amend the By-Law concerning the president's roles and duties when the board appointed Burke as editor-in-chief of the *Catholic Register* in November 1908. By failing to insert an amendment that would have made Burke accountable to the board for his direction of the *Register*, whether through a lack of foresight or outright naiveté, the board inadvertently handed over to Burke the next best thing to total freedom in his editorials and his selection of stories for the newspaper. Such an obvious omission in governance proved disastrous.

His work finished in Chicago, Father Burke returned to Ottawa. Writing from the office of the apostolic delegate, he called a meeting of the board of governors for 24 September 1908. This was subsequently changed to 23 September. For the meeting, Burke travelled from Ottawa to Toronto in the company of Sir Charles Fitzpatrick.[28]

The board of governors of Church Extension met in the library of Archbishop McEvay's "palace." The *Minute Book* does not record the names of those governors present, but it does show a board establishing a governing structure so that Church Extension could commence its mission. It was a very productive meeting. The board adopted without amendment the Constitution and By-Laws, elected the officers of the Society, appointed three members to serve on the executive committee, and, having decided to situate the society's headquarters in Toronto, set in motion the purchase of the *Catholic Register*. The officers were:

Patron: Archbishop Donato Sbarretti, the apostolic delegate
Chairman of the Board: Archbishop Fergus McEvay
President: Father Alfred E. Burke
Vice-President: Bishop Joseph-Alfred Archambeault
Treasurer: Eugene O'Keefe of Toronto[29]

Eugene O'Keefe was the wealthiest Catholic in Toronto and a major benefactor of the archdiocese's numerous charitable endeavours. But he declined the position of treasurer due to his age – he was nearly eighty-three years old – although he gladly donated $5,000 to become a founder of the Society and a member of the board. (In 1913, O'Keefe gave the astonishing sum of $400,000 to the construction of St. Augustine's Seminary in Toronto.[30]) In lieu of a treasurer, Father Burke was "authorized to sign all cheques and transact all business required of the Treasurer, together with his duties of president and General Managing Director."[31] With this additional responsibility, Burke effectively became the major-domo of Church Extension and by default the most influential member of the executive committee.

The executive committee was composed of Archbishop McEvay, Father Burke and Sir Charles Fitzpatrick. It was this committee that appointed Burke as temporary treasurer and hired Hugh Kelly of the law firm Foy & Kelly to act as the Society's solicitor. Kelly remained in this role until his elevation to the Supreme Court of Ontario in 1911, a position he held until his retirement in 1937.[32] But his judgeship did not preclude involvement in the Society's affairs. He was elected to the board in November 1910.[33]

During the time that Kelly acted on behalf of Church Extension, he was the guiding hand in the Society's application for federal incorporation. This was the next step in the Society's efforts to build a firm legal basis on which the Society could operate as a legitimate corporate body in all the provinces and territories of Canada. "An Act to incorporate the Catholic Church Extension Society of Canada" (Act of Incorporation) was given Royal Assent on 19 May 1909.[34] Besides detailing the powers of the Society to acquire, hold and dispose of real estate, the Act addressed the following matters: incorporation (the board of governors) and corporate name, objects of the Society, provisional directors (they were McEvay, Archambeault, Burke and Fitzpatrick), location of the head office (Toronto), branches of the Society, the By-Laws and membership.

No longer on the board of governors were two of its original founders: Archbishop Sbarretti and Monsignor Sinnott. New to the board were Bishop Émile-Joseph Legal, OMI, of St. Albert, Alberta, and four additional laymen: Michael John O'Brien, Michael John Haney, George Plunkett Magann and George C.H. Lang. In total, there were sixteen board members: five bishops, two priests and nine laymen. This was the first time that laymen were in a majority.

Bishop Legal (1840-1920) became one of Church Extension's most fervent supporters and defenders during its earliest years. A native of France, he was ordained on 29 June 1874, joined the Oblates of Mary Immaculate on 19 August 1879 and took his perpetual vows at Lachine, Québec, the following year. After parochial work in Plattsburgh, New York, and in Montréal, and a spell of English-language studies in Buffalo, New York, he was dispatched to the Oblate missions in the West, where he spent the remainder of his ministry and life. For many years, Legal lived among the Peigan Blackfoot at Fort Macleod and Pincher Creek and the Blood Blackfoot at Cardston and Stand Off. He was a teacher, architect, carpenter, doctor, cook and even gravedigger.[35] On 17 June 1897, Legal was consecrated coadjutor bishop with the right of succession to the Diocese of St. Albert. He succeeded to the See when the venerable Bishop Vital-Justin Grandin, OMI, died on 3 June 1902. Ten years later, when the diocese of St. Albert was divided into the Archdiocese of Edmonton and the Diocese of Calgary, Legal became the first archbishop of Edmonton, on 30 November 1912.

Michael John O'Brien was a millionaire railway contractor and mine owner from Renfrew, Ontario. He made a name for himself as the builder of the $40,000 Renfrew Opera House, which opened on 17 March 1909, and the donor of a silver cup for competition to the National Hockey Association in 1910.[36] Michael John Haney of Toronto was a civil engineer and a railway and canal contractor who built the railway tunnel under the Detroit River linking Windsor, Ontario, and Detroit, Michigan. He was a director and president of several companies, was closely involved with the Catholic Mutual Benefit Association, and donated $5,000 for the construction and equipment of the science hall at the University of Ottawa.[37] George Plunkett Magann, also of Toronto, was a railway contractor and owner of extensive timber rights in Ontario and the United States.[38]

Coincidentally, he was the proprietor of the *Catholic Register*. When Archbishop Sbarretti attended the installation of Archbishop McEvay in Toronto, he visited several well-known Catholic institutions in the city. Placed at his disposal was an automobile owned by Magann.[39] O'Brien, Haney and Magann became key and active players on the board, forming in essence a "lay block" in alliance with Sir Charles Fitzpatrick, often lining up behind Father Burke, the president.

George C.H. Lang lived in Berlin (Kitchener) and was the owner of the Lang Tannery, a business begun by his father, Reinhold. He was a high-profile member of his parish church and an avid supporter of the local separate school board. He was active in city and county politics and would serve on the board from 1909 to 1918.[40]

Curiously, although the word "Catholic" appears in the title of the Act, it is missing from the body of the Act. This is particularly strange in the section of the Act that details the objects of the Society. It reads:

> The objects of the Society are religious and charitable and are designed to foster, extend and diffuse the blessings of Christianity and useful knowledge, and to promote and support Christian missions and missionary schools throughout Canada, and to erect, maintain and conduct churches, cemeteries, schools, colleges, orphanages and hospitals in any of the provinces of Canada or its territories.[41]

According to Church Extension's 1908 Constitution, the sole object of the Society was "to foster and extend the Catholic Faith." This is very specific and obviously Catholic, in stark contrast to the Act's generic description of the Society's mission. It was so general in its recourse to the words "Christianity" and "Christian" that it could have applied to any Protestant home missionary society in Canada. No one at Church Extension was bothered by this. In all likelihood, Hugh Kelly or Sir Charles Fitzpatrick advised the board that this was the way such legislation governing incorporation was written and could be ignored in carrying out the primary objective of the Society, which was the extension of Catholicism in Canada by distinctly Catholic means in accordance with the practices and traditions of the Catholic Church.

When the board of governors convened for its Annual General Meeting on 6 April 1910, it conducted its business for the first time according to the federal Act of Incorporation. The entire text of the Act was reprinted in the *Catholic Register*. This was followed by the publication of the 1908 By-Laws and an assortment of lists: the election of officers, the board of governors, the auditors and the Society's solicitor. McEvay, Burke and Fitzpatrick continued as the executive committee. Its composition would not change until the death of McEvay in 1911 – he was replaced by the new chancellor, Archbishop Neil McNeil – and would not change again until the resignations of Burke and Fitzpatrick in 1915.[42]

The next step was to petition the Vatican for the canonical erection of the Catholic Church Extension Society of Canada into a Pontifical Society. Father Kelley wanted Father Burke to accompany him to Rome in February 1909 to establish contacts with those members of the Curia who would be most able to help their respective Societies gain this valuable recognition from the pope. In a letter to Burke of 5 January 1909, Father Kelley wrote:

> My reason is that the interests of your organization and ours, are identical. I am going because the Archbishop [James Edward Quigley of Chicago] wants the Society canonically erected, and it strikes me that the weakness which he sees in our Society is in yours, as well. He says that a change of Archbishops might mean harm to the Society and that the better plan is to have Rome give us full standing. I know it would be a sacrifice for you to go now, but I am only going to stay about six weeks and I strongly advise you to take the trip.[43]

Burke replied that he could not even think of going, that the time was not overly propitious.[44] It was a question of having too many start-up duties in Toronto, in particular the editorship of the *Register*. But Kelley persisted:

> With regard to the Roman matter, I will put my views in as short a form as I can.

We have discovered ourselves, after three years work, just where the most vulnerable point is, viz: in the fact that the Society depends absolutely upon the Bishop or Archbishop in whose Diocese it is located. The Society for the Propagation of the Faith has not this difficulty, as it is governed by Laymen, who, of course, are not under the authority of the Bishop.

If a new Archbishop came to Chicago tomorrow and was opposed to the Society, he could send me into a Parish, have O'Brien follow me; put Ledvina back in Indianapolis, Landry in Ogdensburg and Roe in Peoria and the Society would go to pieces....

Now, you are just beginning up there and you have been very successful. You will find exactly the same condition that we are facing in a small way and you are facing it now, on account of the condition of languages in Canada and the fact that you must educate English speaking Priests, especially, you are going to have more. If you have troubles today, be sure that they won't be a patch on what you have three years from now.

You had better build your fences strong enough and you can do it by coming to Rome and making a fight for what you want. The thing to get is Canonical Erection.

You may think that now is a propitious time to stay at work in Canada, but let me say that if you find it difficult to go now, you will find it a thousand times more difficult in three years. As you go on your duties will increase, as mine have increased. I could have left three years ago, easier than I can today, but it will not take much of your time. We can leave about February 6th on an Express Steamer, transact the business in a few weeks and be back again. We will have letters so strong that we can open every door and your presence with me will strengthen my cause and mine will strengthen yours. Now, please do not let small considerations come into play in this matter. All of your rich men will be in Toronto waiting for you when you get back and you will come back with a stronger appeal than ever.[45]

The references to "troubles today" and "three years from now" and the need to "build your fences strong enough" were perceptive and prescient on the part of Kelley. By 1913, Burke was in all sorts of trouble with Neil McNeil, the new archbishop of Toronto, and he was able to save himself from an ignominious dismissal only because canonical erection afforded him the kind of safety net that Kelley believed (rightly, as it turned out) that Burke might need.

For a man who loved to travel but had never been to Europe, let alone Rome, Burke was not persuaded by Kelley's every argument and blandishment. He was going to stay put in Toronto and let Kelley conduct Church Extension's lobbying in the Roman labyrinth. In lieu of Burke's presence, Kelley asked for (and presumably received) authorization from Church Extension's board of governors to represent the Canadian Society. Kelley described the objectives of his mission to Rome, in a letter of 20 January 1909:

> I am going to ask for Canonical Erection of the Society with a Cardinal Protector. I suppose we could have the same Cardinal for both Organizations. I do not know what will be demanded, but I suppose an annual report must be sent to Rome and it is possible that the Board of Governors will have only the nomination of the President and the actual selection will be left to the Holy Father. Of course, this is only a matter of form, as whoever was nominated would be selected. You may be sure, I will do what I can for you, as well as for ourselves.[46]

Father Kelley did not return to Chicago until 6 May 1909. He spent the greater part of his time discussing Society affairs with Cardinal Raphael Merry del Val, the secretary of state, who in all likelihood coached him in the process whereby both Societies would submit their respective petitions to the pope.[47] For Church Extension in Canada, this entailed the painstaking production of a Latin version of Church Extension's 1908 Constitution (the first Constitution), in conjunction with American Church Extension. Together, officials from the two Societies would produce near-identical Latin constitutions. Any differences between them were in details that pertained exclusively to each Society: for example, the composition of their respective boards of governors.

To this end, a delegation from the American Society, consisting of Bishop Peter J. Muldoon, auxiliary bishop of Chicago, Father Kelley, president, and Ambrose Petry, a wealthy supporter of Church Extension in the United States, attended the board of governors meeting in Toronto on 22 June 1909. The board and the American delegation discussed the conditions and terms of this "Roman Constitution," and the board delegated to Father Burke the responsibility of drawing up the document, having it signed by the proper authorities in the Society and forwarding it to the Holy See through the apostolic delegate in Ottawa.[48] This was a large assignment. It took Father Burke nine months to complete it.

The Latin Constitution was ready for the board's consideration at its Annual General Meeting of 6 April 1910.[49] The members gave their approval and sent it to Archbishop Sbarretti in Ottawa, who was on his way to Rome for his *ad limina* visit.[50] The Constitution was signed by Archbishop McEvay, as chairman of the board, Father Burke, as president, and Monsignor Kidd, as secretary. It was also signed in a separate column by the executive committee: McEvay, Burke and Fitzpatrick.

There were now two constitutions for the Catholic Church Extension Society in Canada: the 1908 English-language Constitution, and the 1909 Latin-language Constitution. Since the Latin version was not a translation of the English-language one but a much more detailed document, which included a provision giving the chancellor of the Society the right to suspend the president for just cause until the next meeting of the board of governors, it was in effect a different constitution. It was this constitution that was given to Sbarretti for official presentation to Pius X. If the pope accepted the Latin Constitution, the English-language one would have to be amended to conform to it. If the pope withheld his approval of the Latin Constitution, the English-language one would remain de facto in force for the practical management of the Society.

As early as January 1910, well before the Latin Constitution for each Society was agreed upon, Father Kelley was again urging Father Burke to go with him to Rome to form a unified front in the presentation of their respective Latin constitutions to Cardinal Merry del Val. Kelley feared that Archbishop Diomede Falconio, OFM, the apostolic delegate to the United States who all along had been hostile to Church Extension, might torpedo the project at the Vatican.[51] Falconio was no Sbarretti, who had been a founder and ardent supporter of Church Extension in Canada. The worst-case scenario, in Kelley's fervent imagination, was that the pope would give his blessing only to the Canadian Society. Such an outcome would be a crushing blow, an irony too great to endure.

Kelley wanted Burke to accompany him on the *Carpathia* on 31 March 1910, and proceeded to bombard him with a series of letters that reveal how desperate he was to have Burke with him in Rome.[52] But Burke refused. He did not want to miss the forthcoming annual general meeting – his absence would have been pure folly – and he had no desire to upstage Sbarretti, who was thoroughly determined to deal with the Canadian petition on his own. Any upstaging would have been an unforgivable blunder. Although Burke did not want Sbarretti to present the Canadian petition separate from the presentation of the American petition, and was hoping that Kelley would go to Ottawa with him "to see the Delegate and talk the whole matter over,"[53] he was in no hurry to offend a close ally. Burke accepted Sbarretti's intervention as a coup, a real privilege, for Church Extension.

Kelley, however, persisted:

My idea is that you should let the Delegate take the petition and settle it, if he wants to; then you come with me and we will be there just at the time they are considering it. You can notify the Delegate that in your capacity as "A.E. Burke" you are going to take a trip to Rome on the 31st of March, and you will be glad to call on him when you get there. I would like very much to have you and we can do a lot over there. You may be sure that the Canadian petition will not be granted until ours is on file and considered. Somebody will take care of that. Keep all this under your hat and make up your mind to come on March 31st.

We will go to Austria-Hungary together and the American ambassador will see that we have a letter from the Emperor, himself, which will get us all we want so far as the Ruthenians are concerned.[54]

Not even the prospect of a side trip to Austria-Hungary on behalf of Ukrainian Catholics was enough to change Burke's mind. So frustrated was Kelley by Burke's steadfast refusal that he wrote him:

I suppose that I will have to grin and bear it, since you won't come with me. You are making a mistake, and an awful mistake, to give over control of your affairs to anyone outside the Board…. I fail to see how your going to Rome would effect [sic] the matter in any way, except favorably.[55]

The Latin Constitution that Sbarretti took to Rome was a fourteen-part document that covered every aspect of the organization and governance of the Society, including new material on diocesan directors, field secretaries and auxiliary departments.[56] Membership of the board was expanded once again, this time from sixteen to nineteen with the addition of Sir Thomas Shaughnessy of Montréal and Hugh and James McSloy of St. Catharines, Ontario. Shaughnessy, who was later created 1st Baron Shaughnessy, was the extraordinarily wealthy and powerful president of the Canadian Pacific Railway. But the inclusion of his name was another example of Society window dressing.[57] "He had little or no interest in philanthropy or social causes," according to one of the baron's biographers. There is no evidence from the "Minutes" of the meetings of the board of governors that he ever attended a meeting or offered an opinion on any aspect of the Society's work.[58]

The wealth and social standing of the McSloy brothers was derived from their joint ownership of the Canada Hair Cloth Company in St. Catharines and later the Cataract Hair Cloth Company in Niagara Falls, New York.[59] Typical nineteenth-century capitalists, they lived close to their place of business. They were prominent citizens of St. Catharines and faithful members of St. Catherine of Alexandria parish. While

James seems to have played little or no part in the Society, Hugh McSloy's name appears as a member of the board at its meeting of 6 April 1910 and several times in the *Minute Book* thereafter.[60]

The composition of this, the fourth, board of governors during the first year of Church Extension's existence, was now five bishops, two priests and twelve laymen. This number of laymen eventually gave rise to a belief among several of them that Church Extension was a lay organization independent of the control of the Church hierarchy.

Sbarretti took to Rome not only the Latin Constitution but also a copy of the 1909 Act of Incorporation, so that Vatican authorities would know that Church Extension was in compliance with civil laws, and a compilation of extracts from letters of commendation from five archbishops, sixteen bishops and two Québec monsignors.[61] Father Burke had solicited these letters from the hierarchy. To ensure a healthy number of positive replies, he had included in each request a copy of the Apostolic Benediction on the Society that Cardinal Merry del Val had sent to Archbishop McEvay on 3 December 1908.[62] The tactic worked.

On 9 June 1910, Pope Pius X issued an Apostolic Brief, "Allata nuper ad nos," by which he formally constituted the Catholic Church Extension Society of Canada, in the process recognizing it as a Pontifical Society. The pope appointed Cardinal Sebastian Martinelli as the Society's cardinal protector in Rome; he made Archbishop McEvay (and his successors as archbishop of Toronto) Chancellor of the Society, whose chief task was to conduct the business of Church Extension with the assistance of the board of governors; and he ordered that

> the selection of the President be made from three candidates to be designated for this purpose by the Board of Governors, and that the names of these candidates be sent through the intermediary of the Cardinal Protector, to this city. We decree further, that the President of the Society thus nominated by the Holy See shall retain office for a term not longer than five years.[63]

Since the Society was now a Pontifical Society, the president would be a papal appointee, making his tenure as president independent of the archbishop/chancellor.

Pius X asked that the Society adhere to its purpose: "To turn all your zeal solely and exclusively to the good of the citizens who dwell within the limits of the Dominion."[64] He also asked that the Society work in complete harmony with two other societies, The Propagation of the Faith and Holy Childhood, and to solicit the assistance and support of bishops and priests. He declared that St. Philip Neri was the Society's heavenly patron and detailed the different indulgences that members could earn.[65]

Strangely, Pius X made no reference to the Latin Constitution in his Apostolic Brief. Our understanding of this oddity comes from Kelley, in a letter to Burke dated 27 November 1914:

> The Constitution in question [the Latin Constitution of 1910] was submitted by me to His Holiness, and submitted by the late Archbishop McEvay on behalf of the Canadian Society to His Eminence, the Cardinal Secretary of State. The whole matter, (of both Societies) was decided by His Holiness, Pope Pius X himself, in an audience granted to me on the evening of May 1st, 1910. His Holiness informed me, personally, that he did not think it wise to approve of the Constitution, for the reason that it went into too many details, which would be embarrassing to a young Society likes ours, bonding us to make no changes. He pointed out that the Societies were too young to know the exact laws they would require, and as they were established in strenuous countries like the United States and Canada, a certain amount of leeway should be allowed. Instead of approving of the Constitution, he issued instead an Apostolic Brief, fixing the headquarters of each Society, the method of securing a Chancellor and the method of nominating Presidents. In addition, he granted the spiritual favors already conceded to the American Society, to Canada.[66]

The upshot of Kelley's recollection of his papal audience was that the Latin Constitution of 1910, having been put aside by Pius X, had no standing in either civil or Church law for Church Extension in Canada. The functioning document was the 1908 English-language Constitution.

Although the Apostolic Brief was dated 9 June 1910 and Cardinal Merry del Val's covering letter to Archbishop McEvay bears the date 13 June 1910,[67] the Brief did not reach Toronto until the second week of July, prompting the Society, in its letter of thanks to the pope, to mistakenly refer to the Brief of 21 July 1910.[68]

McEvay wrote his thanks to Archbishop Sbarretti, Cardinal Merry del Val and Cardinal Martinelli all on the same day, 25 July 1910.[69] The Brief was a source of immense satisfaction to McEvay. To Sbarretti, his close collaborator on the founding of Church Extension, he wrote:

> No person knows as well as Your Excellency the unreasonable opposition from several people in the commencing of this Society, and the numerous obstacles placed in the way of its progress. Now however Rome has spoken and the cause is finished, as far as the work itself is concerned. It only remains for us who are engaged in so necessary a labor to double our efforts and to prove as far as we can our worthiness of the confidence placed in us by the Holy See.[70]

McEvay mentioned no names of those who had opposed the formation of the Society and had placed obstacles to its progress, but it is safe to say that he must have had Archbishop Langevin of St. Boniface and Archbishop Bruchési of Montréal in mind when he wrote this letter. To Martinelli in Rome, who had visited Toronto and Kingston during the time when John Walsh had been archbishop of Toronto, McEvay reminded the Society's cardinal protector that because of "changing conditions and the opening up of new lands to colonization and the influx of many and strange peoples, we are entering upon the threshold of a still greater development"[71] in the history of the Church in Canada.

Father Burke wrote his own letter of acknowledgement to Cardinal Merry del Val on 11 June 1910.[72] It was very formal and flattering, at times verging on the obsequious. It was reprinted six months later in the *Catholic Register*.[73] Catholic readers would have been familiar with the tone and style. Writing to Sir Charles Fitzpatrick in a chatty and intimate letter of 22 July 1910, Burke was ecstatic about the Brief:

> ... the Holy Father has issued a beautiful Brief constituting the Society canonically, according to our petition, standing to our back in everything that we do, giving us a Cardinal Protector in Rome, raising the Archbishop here to an Apostolic Chancellor, and making the office of the President of consequence in the country. You can read the whole Brief in the translation and in the original, and I think that you will marvel with me at the generosity of Rome, and will say that no other institution so short lived, in the history of the Church, has secured such commendation and such indisputable backing for the future. Those people who have been showing their narrowness and unfriendship shall now have to wheel around and get behind us in the work which we have to do. I am sure that you have had a great deal to do with this, and we are very grateful indeed.[74]

The board of governors held a special meeting on 19 November 1910, at which "The new Papal Constitutions and By Laws were then adopted, Clause by Clause."[75] This one-line item in the "Minutes" is uninformative and confusing. By "Papal Constitutions" the board must have meant the Latin Constitution of 1910. An examination of the special meeting of the board, published in the *Catholic Register* in seven parts between 22 December 1910 and 2 February 1911, makes this clear:

> Accordingly at ten o'clock on Saturday, the Nineteen day of November, a full meeting of the Society took place under the Presidency of the Chancellor, the Most Rev. Fergus Patrick McEvay, archbishop of Toronto, when after the reading and confirming of the minutes of the previous meeting, the following Constitution and By-Laws were formally adopted, and a resolution carried, moved by the Rt. Hon. Sir Charles Fitzpatrick, and seconded by Governor George Lang, that anything not contained in the English Constitution and By-Laws, which is found in the Latin Constitution and By-Laws submitted to and approved by the Holy See, a copy of which is

included in this Report, be now adopted and enacted as part of the Constitution and By-Laws of the Society, and that the said Constitution and By-Laws are hereby amended accordingly.[76]

But Pius X had put aside the Latin Constitution and instead issued his Apostolic Brief. The board, therefore, apparently approved a Constitution that was not in force, by virtue of a decision of the pope, and by giving its approval believed that it had amended the 1908 English Constitution. But Father Kelley, for one, was convinced that this Constitution, regardless of what the board believed it had done at its meeting of 19 November 1910, was never officially amended.[77] Also, the board increased the number of By-Laws from six to twenty-two to conform to the Latin Constitution.[78] The By-Laws dealt with membership, administration, meetings, corporate seal, officers, chairman, president, vice-president, the general secretary, treasurer, executive committee, bank account, auditors, temporary chairman and changing of by-laws. One can only assume that the board intended to conduct its corporate life according to this set, and no other set, of By-Laws.

Another item of business at the 19 November 1910 meeting was the appointment of a committee consisting of Archbishop McEvay, Sir Charles Fitzpatrick and Michael John Haney to submit a terna of names for the office of president of Church Extension to Cardinal Martinelli. The committee chose Father Alfred E. Burke as "Most Worthy," Monsignor Arthur A. Sinnott as "More Worthy," and Father Hugh J. Canning, a priest of the Archdiocese of Toronto, as "Worthy." Burke's nomination as president was never in doubt.[79]

In a handwritten note of 19 December 1910, written in English, Cardinal Martinelli informed Archbishop McEvay that Father Burke had been appointed as President of the Catholic Church Extension Society of Canada.[80] Enclosed with the note was the official notification from Cardinal Merry del Val, dated two days earlier.[81] McEvay informed Burke by letter on 2 January 1911.[82] The appointment made Father Burke one of the most influential members of the Catholic clergy outside of Québec. He had achieved a status and a profile that were greater than anything he had acquired while he was a parish priest in the Diocese of Charlottetown and an unofficial advocate of the interests of Prince Edward Island. The entire Dominion was now his stage.

• • • •

In his Brief constituting Church Extension as a Pontifical Society, Pius X listed the many good works already undertaken by the Society. One of them was the newspaper *Catholic Register and Canadian Extension*. At its meeting of 23 September 1908, the board of governors initiated the Society's purchase of the *Catholic Register* with the aim of converting its offices at 119 Wellington Street West in Toronto into the Society's headquarters. But this would take a large sum of money. George Plunkett Magann had been the owner of the paper for the past three years. To facilitate the Society's purchase, Magann, Michael John O'Brien and Michael John Haney each donated $5,000 and became Founders. For the price of $10,000, the Society purchased the printing plant, subscription lists and the paper's standing in the Catholic community.[83]

In the paper's lead editorial on 12 November, Magann announced the transaction.[84] Within two weeks, the executive committee reported confirmation of the purchase to the board of governors.[85] Before the end of 1908, the board made Father Burke editor-in-chief of the *Catholic Register*. In early 1909, he hired Father Joseph T. Roche, another Islander, to serve as associate editor.[86] Beginning in January 1909, the masthead of the paper was changed to *Catholic Register and Canadian Extension*, to reflect the paper's mission to promote and defend the work of Church Extension.

Shortly after the Society bought the paper, Father Burke wrote to Sir Charles Fitzpatrick that he was "afloat on the sea of Journalism."[87] It was a moment of jubilation for the frustrated journalist. Little did Burke, or anyone else on the board, realize that his editorship of the newspaper would sink him and come close to destroying Church Extension.

CHAPTER 4

THE CRUSADE BEGINS

T wo years prior to the successful completion of the organization of the Catholic Church Extension Society, Father Alfred E. Burke, with the approval of Archbishop McEvay and the board of governors, gave Church Extension a religious and social mandate that was to define to a large degree not only Father Burke's presidency but also the main mission of the Society well into the 1930s, many years after Burke had departed from the scene. To kick-start Church Extension into action, in 1908, when the Society was barely five months old, Burke decided to make it the vehicle for a modern-day crusade. Burke knew what he was doing. A crusade is a vigorous movement that rises as a body united by a shared set of beliefs and ideals to recover what once belonged to it or, in some instances, to prevent something precious from falling into the hands of a perceived enemy. And every crusade, whether religious or secular, and regardless of motivation or objective, needs a cause, a rallying cry, to stir the faithful into action.

Church Extension's crusade, of course, was a Catholic one, and for its central cause Father Burke chose the salvation of the souls of tens of thousands of Ukrainian Catholic immigrants in Western Canada. It was a brilliant opening move for the Society, revealing Burke at his strategic best. Ukrainian Catholics were members of the Byzantine

(Eastern) Rite in full union with Rome. They acknowledged the pope as head of the Universal Church in the same way that Roman Catholics of the Latin Rite did. Burke realized that this fact alone should be enough to attract the sympathetic attention of his Catholic readership. It did not. But in due time and with plenty of prompting and cajoling from Burke and his Western correspondents, in the pages of the *Catholic Register*, and from church pulpits, Catholics in Eastern Canada came to understand that these Ukrainian newcomers were just as Catholic as they were *and* were in desperate need of chapels and priests. Put simply, they were sheep without shepherds, vulnerable to proselytizers of all sorts.

In Father Burke's mind, what began as a misfortune of circumstance – few Ukrainian Catholic priests were willing or able to accompany their people to Canada – might turn into a tragedy of colossal proportions if not addressed immediately by the Church in a concerted and organized fashion. On his own initiative, Burke gave Church Extension a mandate to save Ukrainian Catholics from Protestant poachers. Time, however, was not on the side of either Ukrainian Catholics or the Society, which explains why Burke's crusading campaign to protect them from the hands of heretics and charlatans became so shrill and hysterical. At stake was nothing less than the preservation of the faith and identity of Ukrainian Catholics, and, in Burke's mind, a golden opportunity for English-speaking Catholics to take control of the destiny of the Church in Western Canada. It did not matter to Burke if Catholics in Eastern Canada had ever heard of Ukrainian Catholics or to what extent they knew anything about the newcomers' peculiar home-country politics, native language, "strange" customs and garb, Byzantine liturgy and unusual looking church buildings. Rather, what was paramount was to keep them firmly within the fold of Canada's Catholic family.

Father Burke commenced his crusade at the First American Catholic Missionary Congress, a three-day conference in Chicago that began on 15 November 1908.[1] The Congress was the idea of Father Clement Francis Kelley and was designed by him to consolidate the position of Church Extension in the United States by broadening episcopal support of American Extension and advertising its work and accomplishments. The Congress attracted sixty bishops and also Archbishop Diomede Falconio, OFM, the apostolic delegate to the United States who acted as papal legate. The Congress published its entire proceedings in a handsomely produced and illustrated book edited by Father Kelley.[2] A Canadian contingent was present at the Congress. It consisted of Archbishop McEvay, Bishop Legal, Sir Charles Fitzpatrick, Father Kidd, Monsignor J.E. Meunier, administrator of the Diocese of London, and Father Burke.[3] Father Kelley hoped that Archbishop Bégin of Québec would attend, but apparently he did not.[4] Archbishop Sbarretti, the apostolic delegate to Canada, gave his support to the Canadian delegation, but he does not seem to have gone to Chicago. Perhaps two apostolic delegates at the same Congress was one too many. The legendary Oblate missionary Father Albert Lacombe was present in the sanctuary of Holy Name Cathedral on Sunday morning, 15 November. Also at the Congress was Father Joseph T. Roche, the first vice-president of Church Extension in the United States. On this occasion, Roche must have met Burke, who invited him to come to Toronto as assistant editor of the *Catholic Register*.

Archbishop McEvay preached a Sunday evening sermon at Holy Name Cathedral, taking for his text Luke 10:2: "The harvest indeed is great, but the laborers are few. Pray, therefore, the Lord of the harvest that He may send laborers into the harvest." McEvay devoted his entire homily to the necessity of the Catholic priesthood in the life of the faithful, placing extra emphasis for this occasion on the indispensable role of the priest in the lives of immigrant populations. But there was a priest shortage. He believed that Canada needed at least 300 priests to meet the spiritual needs of the thousands of foreign-born people who were pouring into the country each year:

> What organization is able to deal with these people in a satisfactory manner, to speak their language, to understand their customs, to make allowances for their peculiarities and their nationalities, to train them in their own language, as far as possible and as necessary, to be law-abiding citizens and Christians. There is only one power that can do that and that

power belongs to the members of the priesthood of the Church of Jesus Christ.[5]

Bishop Legal spoke at St. John the Baptist Church in Chicago. He chose a more inclusive theme, telling his American audience that "The Christian spirit is of necessity a missionary spirit, because it comes from the Faith, and Faith must be a living and active faith, which must go always to develop and propagate."[6] Mission work was meant for every Catholic. "This sentiment," he continued, "has given birth to the Church Extension Society, a society organized for the propagation of the Faith, but organized on the broad and wide basis of American principles and American enterprise."[7] In order to succeed, the Society had to be a "gigantic organization worthy of the sacred cause and of American energy."[8]

Sir Charles Fitzpatrick gave a speech to the Knights of Columbus. The focus of his discourse was the state of the Church in the Canadian West. He estimated that a million people lived between the Great Lakes and the Rocky Mountains:

> Now that population of a million, excluding the English and French speaking Catholics, is made up to the extent of almost one-fifth of Lithuanians, Galicians, Poles, all Catholics; but Catholics without practically any religious assistance whatever. There is our problem. To provide for the necessities of the present, and, moreover, to provide for the necessities of the future.[9]

Father Burke was secretary of the Congress's committee on resolutions and, along with Father Kidd, a deacon of honour to Archbishop Falconio. Burke delivered a spirited talk on the mission of Church Extension in Western Canada. He addressed two pressing needs: for a special band of priests to serve Catholic immigrants in the home missions and for a missionary college for the home missions. It was the unprecedented number of these immigrants in the West – their ranks steadily increasing year after year – that initially inspired the establishment of Church Extension in Canada in the first place. Now was the time to act.

Those pioneer people have a special claim upon us. They are our brothers, descended, for the most part, by a common lineage, redeemed by the same tremendous sacrifice, subject to the gentle yoke of the Gospel and well disposed to receive of the Church's beneficent ministry. They are often deprived of all the blessings that [that] inestimable ministry affords and largely because those whose lines are cast in pleasanter places, those with all the advantages of complete religious service, those to whom the goods of the world have come abundantly that they might be used wisely to procure the greatest good, refuse to recognize their responsibilities and forget that it is more blessed in God's admirable way to give than to receive, and therefore neglect their duty to them and leave them alone to famish: "And there passed that way a Samaritan."[10]

Who were these pioneers? Burke had two groups in mind. The first group was comprised of "our Catholic people of English tongue in rural districts."[11] These were the people who were descended from a common lineage. They were a known quantity. The second, and much larger, group was a very different story:

We cannot afford longer to resist the cry, either, of the strange peoples of our faith – Catholic, and submitted to the Holy See – which are pouring into our country without any pastors of their own. Within the last few weeks an earnest appeal on behalf of ONE HUNDRED AND FIFTY THOUSAND RUTHENIANS of this class has been made to the Church in Canada, especially to the French bishops. These people have been the victims of religious and political proselytizers to an incredible extent since they reached America, and this through the agency largely of missionary societies. Just think what the preservation of such a body of people as this would mean to us! Think of the organized efforts of the sects to bring about this result! Think of the immense sums of money they spend to effect it! And all this time we stand idly, and let me add criminally, negligently by, and permit them to do their work unrestrained.[12]

This was the first time in the history of the Catholic Church Extension Society of Canada that Burke or anyone else associated with the Society had referred directly in print or in correspondence to the predicament of Ukrainian Catholics. And in taking up their cause, Burke was defining Church Extension's most pressing priority. He was bullish on saving the Ukrainians and chomping at the bit to do battle with the Protestant missionary societies that had been luring away Ukrainians since at least 1903. Burke was clearly agitated and anxious. The core message of his address at the Congress resurfaced in a news item in the *Catholic Register* of 7 January 1909. It estimated that the number of Ukrainian Catholics ranged from 120,000 to 150,000 and contended that forces were conspiring against the faith of tens of thousands of Ukrainian Catholics who had settled in Western Canada.[13] This was the first of numerous and alarming stories on Ukrainian Catholics to appear in the official newspaper of Church Extension.

Father Burke next took his concerns about Ukrainian Catholics to the Duke of Norfolk. Henry Fitzalan-Howard, the 15th Duke, was the premier Duke and hereditary Earl Marshall of the United Kingdom. He was also the leading Catholic layman of his generation in the English-speaking world. Not since the days of Sir Thomas More had a Catholic played such a prominent role in English public life. He was postmaster general in Lord Salisbury's cabinet, a champion of Catholic education and a founder of the University of Sheffield. He was a confidant of four popes, an emissary of Queen Victoria to the Vatican, and a designer and builder of many notable Catholic churches in England.[14] Norfolk had attended the Pontifical High Mass on the Plains of Abraham, on 25 July 1908, which was the liturgical high point of the Québec tercentenary celebrations.[15] He may have met Sir Charles Fitzpatrick on that occasion, for it was Norfolk who had asked Fitzpatrick for information on Church Extension, and it was on Fitzpatrick's invitation that Burke wrote his memorandum to the duke in April 1909.

Father Burke had a great deal to relate to Norfolk about the organization, ambitions, needs and problems of Church Extension as it commenced its missionary work. The memorandum was a lengthy and frank communication, parts of which were meant to remain private.

Paragraph six dealt with the Ukrainians. Their hardships were many; they were without clergy and thus vulnerable to the blandishments of energetic and well-funded Protestants:

> The service afforded ecclesiastically is in all cases inadequate, in many cases amounting to almost complete abandonment; and we shall lose our people by the thousands, tens of thousands, if something satisfying cannot be done. The Protestant Societies are seducing the young Ruthenians into their schools and colleges where their Faith is undermined and they are perverted; and entering the ministry of the sects, [they] attempt to pervert in turn their own people. In Brandon college [in Winnipeg] alone there is now sixteen of these Ruthenian youths intended for this sad work. The same proselytizing is going on all around, but it is not so glaring as in this case, but perhaps more fatal on this account. If we could get some few priests from any of the Colleges you name – Rome, Lisbon, Mill Hill – who would be willing to go over to the Ruthenian Rite, they could save those people religiously and conform them to English moods in a comparatively short period.[16]

Father Burke's speech to the Missionary Congress in Chicago was a good start to his "Ukrainian crusade," taking place on a large public stage, but his audience was mainly American Catholics. While they repeatedly applauded Burke during his speech, they were absorbed in the work of their own Society and most likely looked upon Canada as little more than an interesting sideshow. The Duke of Norfolk, meanwhile, was an important listening post, but he was only an audience of one. His opinions might be treasured because of his rank and standing, but his influence on the Canadian Catholic scene was miniscule at best. Now that Burke had made Church Extension not just another charitable organization but a crusade with a cause, and had initiated the call to arms on behalf of Ukrainian Catholics, in the Society's own newspaper, the *Catholic Register*, what he really needed at this critical juncture in the life of the Society was a chance to present the Society's mission to the Canadian bishops as a body. His opportunity came during the First Plenary Council of Canada.

It had been the custom for the archbishops of Canada to meet once a year to discuss matters pertaining to Church and society. The First Plenary Council of Canada, as its name makes clear, was the first time in the history of the Canadian Church that the entire hierarchy gathered in solemn convocation to discuss the most pressing problems then facing the Catholic people and to take action via voting on resolutions put forth by members of the assembly. The Council took place in Quebec City, opening on 19 September 1909 and closing on 1 November, All Saints' Day. In attendance were six archbishops, twenty-one bishops, three auxiliary bishops and four vicars apostolic. Each archbishop had two theologians, and each bishop had one. In all, there were some 250 prelates and priests who made up the Council.[17]

Was Father Burke in Quebec City at the time of the Council? Evidence from his correspondence with Archbishop Adélard Langevin shows Burke staying at the Chateau Frontenac in Quebec City at least from 3 October, the date of his letter to Langevin, to 12 October, the date of Langevin's reply.[18] On the day that Burke received Langevin's letter, he wrote a lengthy letter to Archbishop Sbarretti, the Apostolic Delegate, stating Church Extension's willingness to recruit and support a chaplain for Catholic immigrants at two ports of entry: Québec in the summer and St. John, New Brunswick, in the winter.[19] Burke was a busy man, as usual. Other evidence, however, this time from Burke's correspondence with Archbishop McEvay, reveals that Burke had returned to his office at 119 Wellington Street West in Toronto by the third week in October.[20]

Did Father Burke personally present his "Memorial on the Ruthenian Catholics of Western Canada" to the Catholic hierarchy at the Council? That is difficult but not necessary to determine. Rather, it is important to recognize that his "Memorial," dated 1 October 1909, after the Council had commenced, is a seminal document in the early history of Church Extension *and* Ukrainian Catholics. In it, Father Burke strongly asserted Church Extension's eagerness and organizational ability to assist the bishops and priests of the West in their Herculean struggle to provide leadership and much-needed relief to Ukrainian Catholic immigrants. Central to Burke's line of reasoning was the way in which he positioned Church Extension between the Latin Rite bishops and priests, on the one hand, and Ukrainian Catholics, the recipients of their Christian charity, on the other, in order to make Church Extension appear indispensable both to the Catholic clergy and to the ongoing spiritual and material welfare of Ukrainian Catholics. (Following the Council, Archbishop McEvay indirectly endorsed Burke in this matter in a circular of 24 January 1910 to the people of the Archdiocese of Toronto.[21])

Father Burke's "Memorial" informed the Council that the Society was ready to take action. He promised to finance the immediate construction of up to ten chapels for the exclusive use of Ukrainian Catholics, to provide the necessary funds for those Canadian seminarians willing to continue their studies and training in Galicia and adopt the Byzantine Rite, and to invest $1,000 for the set-up costs of a Ukrainian Catholic newspaper. Missing from the "Memorial" was any mention of a Society-sponsored missionary college. Burke closed his presentation by proposing the appointment of a Ukrainian bishop for Canada, which, while hardly novel or radical, was a bold proposition to put forth to the Council.[22]

In this delicate and controversial matter, Father Burke was not alone. Father Achiel Delaere, a Redemptorist who was the first Latin Rite priest to adopt the Byzantine Rite, published a memorandum on the Ukrainians in the West, in French, in 1908.[23] An English version of the memorandum appeared in print in 1909, and a condensed Latin version was ready for distribution to the bishops at the Council.[24] In the Latin version, Delaere made his case for a Ukrainian bishop with full territorial and spiritual independence from the Latin Rite bishops and answerable only to the apostolic delegate. This was exactly the position of Father Platonidas Filas, OSBM, superior general of the Basilian Fathers of Galicia and Canada, as stated in a letter of 12 May 1909 to Father Delaere.[25]

Father Hendrik Boels, another Byzantine Rite Redemptorist missionary among the Ukrainians, told Burke in a private letter of 13 October 1909 that Ukrainian Catholics had been abandoned by the Church and that nothing really serious or effective has been done yet for the Ruthenians and it is high time that the movement started by your Reverence should come to put an end to a deplorable situation. Moreover, we must avow it to our shame that the Protestants have worked a hundred times harder to corrupt the faith of these people than we have to preserve their faith.[26]

Boels's unvarnished criticism of the Church for its neglect of Ukrainian Catholics, and his hope that Church Extension would put things right, were like manna from heaven for Father Burke. Boels continued, "We may say that the most crying need is of priests and the most necessary thing is a Ruthenian bishop."[27] Burke sent a copy of Boels's letter to Monsignor Sinnott, secretary to Archbishop Sbarretti, the apostolic delegate, hoping that it might jolt Sbarretti "into a proper frame of mind to grasp the situation which is crucial and fame-making."[28]

Perhaps Boels's letter to Burke had a decisive influence on the speech that Sbarretti did give to the Council. But that is impossible to determine. More certain is the fact that Sbarretti, who had the pope's ear, did speak at length on the deplorable conditions of Ukrainian Catholics in the West and that his words were crucial in prompting the Council to take action.[29] The bishops appointed a committee composed of three Oblates – Archbishop Langevin, OMI, of St. Boniface, Manitoba, Bishop Albert Pascal, OMI, of Prince Albert, Saskatchewan, and Bishop Émile Grouard, OMI, vicar apostolic of Athabasca in Alberta – and Father Sozont Dydyk, OSBM, the provincial of the Basilian Fathers in Canada.[30] They recommended the training of more Latin Rite priests in Galicia, the establishment of a minor seminary, the publication of a Ukrainian-language newspaper and a national collection in support of the needs of Ukrainian Catholics. The committee did not recommend that the bishops petition Rome to appoint a Ukrainian bishop for Canada – the matter was referred to Rome, and Rome remained silent – and it said nothing about the go-between role of Church Extension as envisioned by Father Burke and Archbishop McEvay.[31]

On 30 October 1909, the Council decreed that the bishops would raise $10,000 a year for ten years in support of Ukrainian Catholics.[32] The amount expected of each diocese was calculated according to its Catholic population. The Archdiocese of Toronto, for example, was assessed at $300 per year.[33] All monies were to be directed to the Archdiocese of St. Boniface for distribution. The manner in which the money was to be raised in each diocese was left to the discretion of the local bishop. For the first year, McEvay ordered that a "Ruthenian Collection" be taken up in every parish and mission during Lent of 1910. But it is unclear from McEvay's rendering of the Council's decision in his "Circular" of 24 January 1910 what influence, if any, Church Extension would have in the overall distribution of these episcopal funds, and if the Society's own mission and fundraising in aid of Ukrainian Catholics might be adversely affected by the bishops' campaign.

Father Burke must have found himself in a quandary. The episcopal promise of money for Ukrainian Catholics was obviously a good and noble thing, but it was in direct competition with the Society's immediate ambitions. Burke firmly believed that only Church Extension could save the situation. Individual diocesan efforts, piecemeal in nature and organizationally isolated from each other, were completely useless, according to him.[34] To lead Church Extension's Ukrainian Catholic crusade in an effective manner, Burke recognized two needs: undivided episcopal support for the Society's leadership on the Ukrainian Catholic question, and at the very least a prominent voice in the disbursal of the money that the bishops pledged to raise.

Unfortunately for both Burke and the Society, neither need would be fulfilled. Church Extension's involvement with Ukrainian Catholics during Burke's seven-year presidency, while constant, genuine and generous, was not as productive as Burke imagined it would be in 1909. However, before any assessment can be made of Burke's handling of the "Ukrainian crusade," an assessment that will form a large part of any judgment on his presidency of the Society, it is necessary to have at hand an accurate understanding of the opening decades of Ukrainian Catholic life on the Canadian prairies.

CHAPTER 5

UKRAINIAN CATHOLICS: THE FIRST WAVE, 1891–1914

A lthough Father Burke believed in all sincerity that there were 150,000 Ruthenians in Canada in 1908, this claim was a wild exaggeration. It may sound like something that Burke the enthusiast would conjure up to suit his purposes, yet the truth is that this fantastic number originated not with the president of Church Extension but with the *Winnipeg Free Press*. In its Protestant zeal to keep Canada British, the *Free Press* spoke to the fears and ignorance of its readership with its estimation of 120,000 to 150,000 Ruthenians living within their midst. They were strangers, aliens, who needed to be assimilated.[1] For very different reasons, the Redemptorist missionary Father Achiel Delaere adopted almost the same range of figures. Father Delaere wanted to invoke the sympathy of his fellow Catholics. "Just think of these 100,000 and perhaps 150,000 Ruthenians, being deserted, as a flock of sheep to the fury of wolves, ravaging the fold," he wrote. "And these are Christian souls, these are our Catholic brethren, our brethren in Christ."[2] While the *Free Press* was not to be trusted, Delaere was.

For his part, Burke was only too willing to seize upon the higher and more dramatic number for the benefit of his untutored Catholic audience in the East. Possessing shock value, it was a powerful rhetorical weapon in the conduct of his emerging crusade. But the actual number of Ruthenians in the West at the time of the founding of Church Extension was not 150,000. No Church official at the time knew how many Ruthenians had settled in Manitoba, Saskatchewan and Alberta or how many more might follow to join those already living in rural settlements and towns.[3] Not until 1911 did Western dioceses compile their own census records of the different national groups (including Ruthenians) that belonged to the local church. Beginning in 1891, and from 1896, arriving en masse, the Ruthenians were a sociological and cultural mystery to Catholics in Canada and an unprecedented challenge to the administrative abilities of Ukrainian Church officials in Galicia and the United States and the Latin Rite hierarchy in Western Canada. But any attempt to arrive at a more realistic figure for the number of Ruthenians must begin with an examination of the meaning of the word "Ruthenian."

Herein lies the historical conundrum when attempting to define the immigrant community of Eastern Rite Catholics that Father Burke and Church Extension set out to save from proselytizers in 1908. There is no doubt that such a community already existed in recognizable numbers throughout Western Canada, and was growing ever larger year by year, as long as the gateway to immigration to Canada remained open, which it did until the commencement of the First World War. Questions abound. What are we to make of the name "Ruthenian"? What is its relationship to the name "Ukrainian"? Who were the Ruthenians, as they were commonly known, who immigrated to Canada? Where was their place of origin? How many Ruthenian/Ukrainian settlers actually arrived in Canada between 1891 and 1914, and what proportion were Catholic and in communion with Rome and thus the spiritual wards of the local Church until the arrival of their own bishop?

Religious affiliation, geographical origins and the emergence of national identification, in the absence of a nation-state, are inextricably linked in the answers to these questions. The operative word is Ukrainian, which refers to a distinctly recognizable people. Ukraine as an independent political entity is not part of the picture, because Ukraine did not exist until 1918, and even then it disappeared into

Poland after only a brief period of existence. Historical words include Ruthenians and Bukovynians, two sub-groupings of Ukrainians whose respective identities were rooted in religion and geography, and Galicia and Bukovyna, two autonomous provinces in the Austro-Hungarian Empire. A third sub-grouping of Ukrainians was located in Transcarpathia, a province under the more direct control of that part of the Austro-Hungarian Empire called the Kingdom of Hungary. These Ukrainians were not a noticeable part of the history of Ukrainian emigration to Canada. Nor for that matter were the overwhelming majority of Ukrainians, the estimated seventeen to twenty-five million that lived in Tsarist Russia. Only a negligible number of these Ukrainians left for North America, preferring instead to migrate to the virgin agricultural lands of Siberia, on the encouragement of Tsarist officials.

Our focus, then, is on Galicia and Bukovyna, for these two provinces supplied the bulk of the first wave of Ukrainian immigrants to Canada. At the turn of the twentieth century, there were approximately three million Ukrainians in Galicia, forming forty percent of the population. In Galicia, they were known as Greek Catholics (because of their use of the Eastern Rite or Byzantine liturgy conducted in Old Church Slavonic and their adherence to certain traditions and practices, such as married priests and the Julian calendar), and also as Uniates (because as a church they were in union with Rome according to the terms of the Treaty of Brest-Litovsk of 1596).

Ukrainians from Galicia were also known as Ruthenians. This was a Latinized version of the word "Rusyn," invented by officials from the Austro-Hungarian Empire, and adopted by the Vatican, giving it a public life outside of Galicia and the Empire. "Ruthenian" first appeared in Canadian immigration records in 1905. It was employed by hostile Protestant forces in their xenophobic attacks on all Ukrainians regardless of religious affiliation or province of origin in the Empire, and, ironically, by Roman Catholics because Church officials also used it. Regardless, Ruthenians were Ukrainian Catholics.

Ukrainians in Bukovyna, meanwhile, belonged to the Orthodox Church. There were some 300,000 of them, or forty percent of the population. Their liturgy and traditions, and the place of leadership that they accorded to their clergy, were strikingly similar to those of the Ruthenians in Galicia, but they did not recognize the pope as head of the Universal Church. Rather, they claimed allegiance to the Russian Orthodox Church. In the fluid New World setting of the Canadian West, the grip of the Old World began to loosen for Ukrainian Catholics in the absence of priests, and, of course, Orthodox autonomy lured many Ukrainian Catholics to abandon their ties to Rome.[4]

At the turn of the twentieth century, almost ninety-five percent of Ukrainians in Galicia and Bukovyna were peasants, working as subsistence farmers on small plots of land. This made them ideal candidates for the colonization of the Canadian West, where they could expect to receive 160 acres of farmland for the nominal fee of ten dollars. What was economic servitude with little hope of change or advancement in their native land was easily turned into a marketable advantage for them in the Prairie provinces.

It is highly doubtful if Canadian Catholics, including the hierarchy and prominent clergymen such as Father Burke of Church Extension, appreciated the very real distinction in religious affiliation between Ruthenians from Galicia and Orthodox from Bukovyna, both of whom were Ukrainian. Nor would Canadian Catholics realize that such a distinction, no matter how fundamental in the Austro-Hungarian Empire, could easily disintegrate in Western Canada due to conflict over the Vatican ban on married priests and the ecclesiastical veto of parochial trusteeship of Church property. These became serious flashpoints of dissension. Ukrainian immigrants to Canada were not a religiously homogenous group of people, but this simple fact seems to have eluded the host Catholic population and blinded them to the possibility that Orthodoxy in its various manifestations, both legitimate and fraudulent, might pose a greater threat than Protestantism to the ecclesiastical integrity and survival of Ukrainian Catholics.[5]

The most reliable immigration statistics for the years 1891 to 1908 show 79,607 Ukrainian immigrants from overseas and another 1,076 from the United States, for a total of 80,683. If Ukrainian Catholics from Galicia – Ruthenians – comprised two-thirds of this total and Ukrainian Orthodox from Bukovyna the remaining one-third, a ratio suggested by historians O.W. Gerus and J.E. Rea, there were 53,734 Ukrainian Catholics and 26,949 Ukrainian Orthodox immigrants in Canada in 1908. That was the year that Father Burke and Church Extension raised the alarm with cries of 150,000 abandoned Ruthenians. Even a statistical picture expanded to 1914 would still not produce that number. From 1891 to 1914, there were 170,132 Ukrainian immigrants from overseas and another 1,404 from the United States, for a total of 171,536. On the eve of the First World War, then, there were 114,242 Ukrainian Catholics and 66,890 Ukrainian Orthodox immigrants in Canada, if we assume the two-thirds to one-third ratio, with the vast majority of Ukrainians having settled in the West.[6]

The point is not that the *Winnipeg Free Press*, Father Delaere and Father Burke and, one supposes, others, too, had inflated the number of Ukrainian Catholics for their own motivations. Rather, there was something sizeable to inflate. Ukrainians seemed to be everywhere on the prairies, an exaggeration in itself, but public perceptions of the *other*, the foreigner, no matter how biased for or against, often is the fuel of public debate and conflict. Father Burke and Church Extension rushed into that developing debate in 1908, taking up the cause of Ukrainian Catholics.

Moreover, Ukrainians tended not to disperse among the host population but to build close-knit communities known as bloc settlements where they attempted to re-create Old World village life, succeeding to a remarkable degree during the first few decades of life in Canada. Ukrainians settled in "a wide arc along the southern edge of the Canadian shield," according to Gerus and Rea, "from the rock-strewn Stuartburn area of south-eastern Manitoba through the scrub lands of the Interlake to the Yorkton-Saskatoon district and along the valley of the North Saskatchewan to Vegreville, east of Edmonton."[7] This was generally the line of the Canadian National Railway, the primary means by which large numbers of people and goods were moved across the prairies. By 1905, the largest and most successful settlements were Edna-Star (Vegreville) in Alberta, which was the first and, for many years, the largest Ukrainian colony in Canada; Prince Albert,

Fish Creek and Yorkton and environs in Saskatchewan; and Dauphin, Shoal Lake, Interlake, Stuartburn and Whitemouth in Manitoba.[8]

The Ukrainian people came, but their priests did not. This was absolutely true for Ukrainian Orthodox clergy from Bukovyna and almost to the same extent for Ukrainian Catholic priests from Galicia prior to 1902. Before that, if there were any Ukrainian Catholic priests in Canada, they had come from the United States and were independent from the local Latin Rite hierarchy in their activities and movements. Regardless, the absence of homeland clergy, be they Orthodox or Catholic, would have a profound effect on the evolving religious alignment of Ukrainian settlers in Canada. The dearth of Ukrainian Catholic priests, however, would prove to be far more deleterious to the establishment of a Ukrainian Catholic Church than the complete absence of Ukrainian Orthodox priests would be to the preservation of Ukrainian Orthodoxy. Although Bukovynian Orthodoxy abandoned its flock, its flock was not abandoned by Orthodoxy.

According to an unwritten rule of Orthodox missionary practice, the Ukrainian Orthodox Church in Bukovyna had no ecclesiastical jurisdiction over missionary work in North America. That right belonged solely to the Russian Orthodox Church, because it had been the first Orthodox communion to establish itself on the continent. As a result, various Russian Orthodox bishops of the diocese of the Aleutians and Alaska, who were stationed in San Francisco, and later Archbishop Tikhon (1898–1907)[9] and Archbishop Platon (1907–1914), both of whom worked from New York City, were aggressive in their missionary endeavours. Recipients of generous and steady financial support from the Holy Synod in St. Petersburg and the Missionary Society of Russia, these Russian Orthodox prelates had measurable success not only in securing the allegiance of Ukrainian Orthodox settlers, but also in persuading a significant number of Ukrainian Catholic parishes to jettison Rome and join the Russian Orthodox Church.

Especially appealing to Ukrainians in Canada was the fact that the Russian Orthodox liturgy used Old Church Slavonic and was structurally much the same as the Byzantine liturgies of the Bukovynian Orthodox and Ukrainian Catholic churches. Also, the Russian

Orthodox Church permitted married secular clergy, made few financial demands on the people, and did not require incorporation of Church property.[10] The Russians were fond of pointing out that celibacy and payment for services were for Roman Catholics. Why submit to them? was a question they often posed. When it came to ownership, what the people bought and built, they owned. This was the essence of trustee-ship. It mattered little that it was unknown in the Old World. In the New World, trusteeship was a newfound freedom for many Ukrainians, who used it as a means to protect their religious faith and customs from the perceived threat of Latinization at the hands of Western Canada's French-speaking Oblate bishops. Until the appointment of a Ukrainian Catholic bishop in 1912, trusteeship as a bulwark of independence was just as popular with Ukrainian Catholics as it was with Ukrainian Orthodox.[11] Early Ukrainian Catholic priests visiting from the United States constantly urged their fellow Ukrainian Catholics not to sign their property over to the local Roman Catholic bishop, usually referred to in the pejorative as the "French bishop."

As if such inducements were not enough, many Ukrainians on the prairies were familiar with the startling story of Father Alexis Toth (Tovt). Father Toth, a widowed Eastern Rite priest, came to the United States in 1889 to minister to Ukrainian Catholics. At the time, there were nine Ukrainian Catholic parishes in the country. Most of them were in Pennsylvania, but there was one – St. Mary's – in Minneapolis. When Father Toth presented himself to Archbishop John Ireland of St. Paul, Minnesota, and asked his permission to conduct religious services at the parish, Ireland refused, claiming that Toth was not a priest and that the bishop who ordained him was not a bishop.[12] Ireland was not alone in the American hierarchy in his open hostility towards Ukrainian Catholic priests. This ardent champion of Americanism was simply more blunt and rude in his opinions of the Eastern Church and apparently more ignorant of the ecclesiastical reality of Ukrainian Catholicism than most of his episcopal colleagues. The American bish-ops, of Irish pedigree almost to a man, were horrified by the prospect of a married Catholic clergy in their midst, reacting to it as if it were an approaching plague on the priesthood, and they were quite willing to sacrifice the spiritual care of Ukrainian Catholics for the sake of maintaining clerical celibacy.[13] It was an attitude that ushered in disastrous results for the Ukrainian Catholic Church in the United States.

The Canadian bishops were also steadfast in their opposition to married clergy, but they avoided instigating a similar revolt by recognizing, albeit only eventually, that it would be better for the Church to find Ukrainian Catholic priests and to establish Ukrainian Catholic parishes and missions. But all this would take time to unfold, for minds to be changed, especially on the matter of a Ukrainian Catholic bishop for Canada. Missing from the episcopal plan of action, however, was an even rudimentary appreciation of the persuasive power of Russian Orthodoxy.

Insulted and humiliated, Father Toth decided to join the Russian Orthodox Church, and he persuaded 360 of St. Mary's parishioners to come with him. Bishop Vladimir, the Russian Orthodox bishop in San Francisco, officially received them on 25 March 1891. During his eighteen years as a Russian Orthodox priest, Father Toth convinced fifty Ukrainian Catholic parishes to follow his lead, and he established approximately 200 Orthodox parishes for the 200,000 to 250,000 Ukrainian Catholics who converted to Russian Orthodoxy.[14] He also founded a seminary. Father Toth died in 1909 and is generally regarded as one of the founders of Russian Orthodoxy in America.[15] His revolt against Rome was an inspiration to Russian Orthodox missionaries in Canada.

As early as July 1897, there were two Russian Orthodox missionaries in Wostok, Alberta, which was five to six miles from Edna-Star, at that time the largest Ukrainian Catholic settlement in Canada. Both settlements were in the Roman Catholic Diocese of St. Albert. Father Dimitri Kameneff and Deacon Vladimir Alexandroff came to Alberta in response to a petition from local Ukrainian Orthodox settlers and also to the appearance of Father Nestor Dmytriw, an American-based Ukrainian Catholic priest who was at Edna-Star for Easter 1897. Kamaneff and Alexandroff, who could speak Ukrainian and acted as translator, worked effectively as a team to maintain a functioning and thriving Orthodox congregation.

They were succeeded in Wostok by Father Jacob Korchinski. His charismatic preaching enticed numerous Ukrainian Catholics from Edna-Star to attend Divine Liturgy in Wostok.[16] Father Kameneff, Deacon Alexandroff and Father Korchinski were cited in the final judgment of a controversial and incredibly convoluted court case over the ownership of the Ukrainian church and property in Edna-Star. The case wound its way up to the Judicial Committee of the Privy Council in London, England, which resolved this dispute in favour of the Orthodox trustees, in a decision of 3 December 1907. On the losing side were Bishop Émil Legal of St. Albert and four Ukrainian Catholic priests.[17] The Catholic appellants spent $18,000 in a losing attempt to retain property worth only $1,000. The Russian Orthodox won similar cases in at least three other communities in Alberta: Chapman, Rabbit Hill and Buford.[18]

Perhaps the most successful Russian Orthodox missionary during this period was Archimandrite Arseniy Chekkovstev. Working in Canada from 1905 to 1911, he established a newspaper in Winnipeg, *Kanadiyskaya Niva (Canadian Field)*, founded a school with a residence (a bursa) in Edmonton, and converted an impressive number of Ukrainian Catholic parishes to Orthodoxy. He may have assisted Archbishop Tikhon when the latter consecrated what became Holy Trinity Russian Orthodox Cathedral in Winnipeg, in 1905. Dissenting members of the Ukrainian Catholic parish of St. Nicholas, which was overseen by the Archdiocese of St. Boniface, founded this parish.[19] Disappointed at his failure to be selected as the first Russian Orthodox bishop for Canada, Chekkovstev left for Russia, never to return to Canada. One can readily imagine how radically differently the Ukrainian religious landscape might have evolved had he become a bishop in Canada and continued his missionary endeavours among the Ukrainians.

According to one historian, "By 1917, the Russian Church had sixty-two priests, sixty-two churches, three monasteries, and thirty to forty missions in Canada."[20] Because of the Bolshevik Revolution, financial support for the Russian Orthodox mission in Canada evaporated. Consequently, the mission's ability to hold on to its impressive gains among Ukrainians in Canada soon deteriorated. As Russian Orthodoxy fulfilled its mission to Ukrainian Orthodox adherents, it gathered within its fold thousands of members from among the Ukrainian Catholics in Canada. Many Ukrainians would remain Russian Orthodox, but many more would form the Ukrainian Orthodox Church in Canada in 1918.

The early history of the Ukrainian Catholic clergy in Canada, although naturally intertwined with that of Ukrainian Orthodoxy, was different and more complicated, and certainly is more central to our examination of Father Alfred E. Burke's decision to have Catholic Church Extension Society champion the cause of Ukrainian Catholics. As he and many others saw it, the people simply would perish without priests. This was a pervasive, almost monomaniacal, mantra within the Roman Catholic camp. But not understood by many in that same camp, including Father Burke, was the lack of incentive for Ukrainian Catholic priests in Galicia to emigrate to Canada and just how injurious Rome's negative response to the immigration of married priests from the Austro-Hungarian Empire to North America would be to the establishment of a viable Ukrainian Catholic Church in Canada.

Priests in Galicia (and, for that matter, in Bukovyna) were members of a social and economic elite. The state paid their modest salaries, allowed them to collect donations for burials, weddings, baptisms and other religiously related services, such as catechism teaching, and provided them with substantial farms and access to local forests. In effect, priests were minor nobility. They belonged to a separate and privileged class that was educated and affluent, with autocratic powers on all matters of the faith and religious practice. Moreover, the families of these priests enjoyed their prosperity and power and often made sure that sons and grandsons "inherited" the priestly tradition. Also, in the social and political stratification of Galicia as a province of the Austro-Hungarian Empire, Ukrainian Catholic priests were useful bulwarks against the hegemony of the Roman Catholic Polish landlords.[21]

But even if Ukrainian Catholic priests and their families were willing to leave their relatively comfortable existence in Galicia for the uncertainties and hardships of life in Western Canada, as described in letters and newspaper articles from Ukrainian immigrants, Rome pre-empted any such ambition or inclination on their part. Pressured by the American bishops, the Congregation of Propaganda Fide, Oriental Affairs, issued a decree of 12 April 1894 that effectively barred Ukrainian Catholic priests in the Austro-Hungarian Empire from exercising their ministry in North America. They were forbidden jurisdiction. Since only three percent of the Ukrainian Catholic clergy in Galicia were celibate, this prohibition all but closed the door to secular priests from serving their co-religionists in the United States and Canada. Any real hope for recruiting missionary workers, then, fell to the priests and brothers of the Order of Saint Basil the Great (OSBM, commonly called Basilians). However, the Basilians, who were celibates, were not well known by many Ukrainian settlers. When they did begin to arrive on the prairies as resident missionaries, they were initially viewed as stooges for Roman Catholic bishops intent on Latinizing Ukrainian Catholics.

Three years later, on 1 May 1897, Rome issued a second decree in which the Roman Catholic hierarchy in North America was given jurisdiction over Ukrainian Catholic priests. This prompted all sorts of loud and angry protests on the part of émigré Ukrainian Catholic priests of "The Society of Ruthenian Church Congregations in the United States and Canada." In resolutions drawn up at a convention in Harrisburg, Pennsylvania, and dated 26 March 1902, this society demanded an independent Ukrainian Catholic hierarchy in the United States free of interference from Roman Catholic bishops. Later in 1902, Metropolitan Andrey (Andrew) Sheptytsky, Archbishop of Lviv, Galicia, the pre-eminent Ukrainian Catholic prelate, vigorously denounced their protests and demanded that the priests cease their agitation and pledge their loyalty to the pope.

Five years later, Rome finally acted. It took one step forward and one step sideways. By virtue of the papal bull *Ea semper*, dated 3 June 1907, Soter Ortynsky, a Basilian monk from Galicia, was appointed the first Ukrainian Catholic bishop in the United States. That was the step forward. The step sideways was that Ortynsky was not given full Ordinary jurisdiction over his own independent diocese until 28 May

1913. Until then, he was only an auxiliary (suffragan) bishop to each Roman Catholic Ordinary in the United States, meaning that before he could minister to Ukrainian Catholics in any particular diocese, he had to seek permission from the local bishop. Such an arrangement left Bishop Ortynsky severely hobbled, even humiliated, and his priests and people very disgruntled.[22] Moreover, he had no access to Canadian dioceses.

During the 1890s, Ukrainian Catholics in Canada were desperate for priests so they could celebrate with them the time-honoured Byzantine liturgy and live according to religious customs and traditions they had known in their native Galicia. Joseph Oleskiw, a pioneering advocate of Ukrainian immigration, witnessed first hand the spiritual destitution of his co-religionists during his three-month tour of Canada and the United States in the summer of 1895. He was a man of authority and persuasion and appeared at the right time in the nascent history of Ukrainian immigration. The son of a Ukrainian Catholic priest, Oleskiw was educated at the University of Lemburg (Lviv) and the University of Erfurt, Germany, where he earned a doctorate, and he taught agronomy at the teacher's college in Lemburg. Oleskiw was the author of two highly influential Ukrainian pamphlets: *Pro vilni zemli* (*About Free Lands*) and *O emigratsii* (*About Emigration*). Both works appeared in 1895. He also wrote a lengthy memorandum to the Canadian government, detailing his observations and conclusions concerning Ukrainians in Canada and the best methods to bring more of them over to the country. In 1898, the government appointed Oleskiw as its official immigration agent in Galicia.[23]

Oleskiw realized that if Ukrainian Catholics were to retain their identity and thrive in Canada, regardless of where they settled in the country, the retention of their Catholic faith was paramount. Success, however, was tied to the presence of Catholic priests, because of the sacramental nature of their religion and the social construct that supported and nurtured it. Oleskiw tried but failed in 1896 to convince the Canadian government to sponsor Father Ostap Nyzankiwsky, a priest and renowned composer from Galicia, for the Ukrainian Catholic settlers at Edna-Star, Alberta. The government passed Oleskiw's request to Archbishop Langevin of St. Boniface. As soon as Langevin realized that Father Nyzankiwsky was a married priest, he vetoed any idea of bringing him into his archdiocese.[24]

Disappointed but undeterred, Oleskiw took a different approach.[25] He looked to the United States and decided to assist Father Nestor Dmytriw, who had been selected by the Ruthenian National Association for missionary work in Canada. Stationed in Pennsylvania, Father Dmytriw was already well known as a contributor to *Svoboda* (*Liberty*), a Ukrainian-language newspaper published in Jersey City, New Jersey, since 1893. Father Dmytriw arrived in April 1897 and departed in August 1898, making him the first Ukrainian Catholic priest to serve in Canada. During that brief time, he organized parishes and commenced the construction of churches in Terebowla and Stuartburn in Manitoba, and he visited Ukrainian communities in Winnipeg, Edmonton, Fort Saskatchewan, Rabbit Hill and Edna-Star, where he spent most of his time. In Edna-Star, he was involved from the very beginning in what evolved into the protracted dispute between the Diocese of St. Albert and Ukrainian Catholics loyal to Rome, on the one side, and Russian Orthodox trustees, on the other, over the ownership of the church building and property. Dmytriw also enjoyed a part-time position in the Winnipeg immigration office as an assistant to Cyril Genyk, who was the first Ukrainian immigration agent in the country.[26]

Dmytriw's good and honest work was undercut by his outspoken and impolitic support of an independent Ukrainian Catholic Church in Canada, one led by its own bishop. That put him in bad odour with Archbishop Langevin, who was not sorry to see him leave.[27]

Father Dmytriw was followed by at least three other itinerant Ukrainian Catholic missionaries: Father Paul Tymkewicz, Father Damascene Polivka and Father Ivan Zaklinski. Tymkewicz was from Galicia and had the support of Propaganda Fide. He arrived at Edna-Star on 8 April 1898 and sided with those Ukrainian Catholics who did not want to vest the church property in the name of the bishop of St. Albert, thereby undercutting the bishop's authority in his struggle with the Russian Orthodox trustees.[28] Polivka was a non-Ukrainian

Basilian priest, also recommended by Propaganda Fide. He arrived in Winnipeg on 21 October 1899. In the absence of Archbishop Langevin, who had given him jurisdiction before leaving for an extended stay in Montréal, Polivka on his own decided to stay in Winnipeg instead of moving on to the Diocese of Prince Albert, as originally planned. He founded the Ukrainian Catholic parish of St. Nicholas (now Sts. Vladimir and Olga) but was unable to convince Langevin of the need to build a church. He then left Winnipeg in early 1900. From various cities in the United States and from Montréal, Polivka pleaded with Winnipeg's Ukrainian Catholics to have him as their pastor. But his plea came with two conditions. they had to support him financially, and they had to promise not to sign over church property to Archbishop Langevin. Polivka never did return.[29] Zaklinski arrived on the scene in July 1900. He, too, was involved in the tussle over trusteeship in Edna-Star and publicly opposed Roman Catholic jurisdiction over himself in particular and Ukrainian Catholics in general. Bishop Vital-Justin Grandin of St. Albert found Zaklinski's behaviour deeply disturbing.[30]

What Ukrainian Catholics needed were resident priests, not independent-minded wanderers who came and left seemingly of their own accord. What the Roman Catholic bishops in the West needed were celibate Ukrainian Catholic priests who would accept the bishops' jurisdiction over them and would work to convince the people that they need not fear the Roman Catholic hierarchy.

From 1891, when the first two Ukrainians appeared in Canada – Wasyl Eleniak and Ivan Pillipiw – to 1912, when Canada's first Ukrainian Catholic prelate – Bishop Nykyta Budka – arrived, the members of the Canadian hierarchy who played major roles in the spiritual and administrative care of Ukrainian Catholics were Adélard Langevin, Émile-Joseph Legal and Albert Pascal. Other episcopal players were Vital-Justin Grandin, bishop of St. Albert from 1871 to 1902; Gabriel Breynat, vicar apostolic of Mackenzie from 1901 to 1943; Pierre Grouard, vicar apostolic of Athabasca, from 1891 to 1929; and Olivier-Elzéar Mathieu, bishop and later archbishop of Regina, from 1911 to 1929. All seven bishops were French-speaking Oblates, but only Langevin and Mathieu were born in Québec. The other five were natives of France.

Archbishop Langevin's approach to the welfare of Ukrainian Catholics had been shaped by his battles with the Protestant establishment over the preservation of the French language and with the English-speaking Catholic establishment in Eastern Canada over the status of the West as an outpost of Québec Catholicism. Ukrainian Catholics, then, were a distinctly foreign and unexpected element. They were treated as if they were a problem, for which assimilation into the Latin Rite Church was the only long-lasting answer, and not, regrettably, as a fortuitous opportunity for the Catholic Church as a whole to expand and solidify its presence in Protestant Canada. Langevin would never completely relinquish his attachment to a policy of assimilation. It was founded on the assumption, one that was actively shared by Archbishop Diomede Falconio, apostolic delegate to Canada from 1899 to 1902, that as soon as Ukrainian Catholics lost interest in preserving their native language, over time and in the face of cultural attrition, they would lose interest in clinging to their Byzantine Rite and Ukrainian traditions.

The assumption proved to be false, and the fact that Langevin believed it proved to be harmful to Ukrainian Catholics. They held on to their language, their Rite and their customs, with a stubbornness that not only annoyed but also astonished Langevin and his brother bishops. Langevin's initial response, then, to the so-called Ukrainian Catholic dilemma was almost entirely negative and defensive. Of course, he vigorously opposed the presence of married Ukrainian clergy. In this matter, he was merely following Rome's injunction. But in other matters that required a more nuanced approach, he could not see things clearly for many years. He refused to establish Ukrainian Catholic parishes where Latin Rite parishes already existed; he thought that Ukrainian-speaking Polish priests were perfectly acceptable as pastors for Ukrainian Catholics; he did not think much of Latin Rite priests becoming Eastern Rite priests; he was adamant in his opposition to the erection of a Ukrainian Catholic eparchy (diocese) for Canada, with a bishop headquartered in Winnipeg, arguing that two masters in the same house would be a disaster; and he was suspicious of the intentions of Father Burke and Catholic Church Extension Society to take a prominent role in the "rescue" of Ukrainian Catholics.

Over time and prodded by experience, Langevin did change his opinions on most of these issues. At the annual meeting of the archbishops of Canada in 1911, Langevin, along with the bishops of St. Albert and Regina and the vicars apostolic of Athabaska and Keewatin, demonstrated a more open attitude to the prospect of a Ukrainian Catholic bishop within their midst.[31] At the same time, Langevin continued to take strong exception to any mention of a married clergy, which he could never countenance, and to Church Extension, which he managed to keep at arm's length while accepting its money for the Ukrainian cause. As soon as Rome announced the appointment of Bishop Budka as Canada's first Ukrainian Catholic bishop, Langevin accepted it as a fact of Church life. Leading up to Budka's selection, Langevin welcomed the first Basilian monks and Sisters Servants of Mary Immaculate, in 1902; he financed Ukrainian parishes and missions in both rural and urban areas, and defended bilingual Ukrainian Catholic schools;[32] he organized the distribution of monies collected from Latin Rite dioceses throughout Canada for the relief of Ukrainian Catholics;[33] and, in conjunction with Church Extension, he founded and financially assisted the publication of a Catholic Ukrainian-language newspaper, *Kanadyiskyi Rusyn* (*Canadian Ruthenian*), in 1911, to act as a defence against at least three other Ukrainian-language newspapers that were hostile to the Catholic Church.[34] They were *Kanadiyskaya Farmer* (*Canadian Farmer*), funded by the fervently anti-clerical Liberal Party in 1903; *Ranok* (*The Dawn*), set up by the Presbyterian Church in 1905, in support of the Independent Greek Church; and *Kanadiyskaya Nyva*, established by the Russian Orthodox Archimandrite Arseniy Chekkovstev to promote the interests of the Russian Orthodox Church in Canada.

The recruitment of celibate Ukrainian Catholic priests proved to be the biggest challenge facing Langevin and his two suffragans, Legal and Pascal, in their attempt to provide proper spiritual leadership for Ukrainian Catholics, as was their Rome-mandated jurisdictional duty.

The three prelates, working in tandem, actively sought viable solutions to this vexatious problem that grew ever closer to a full-blown crisis as the population of Ukrainian Catholics continued to increase. By 1911, there were 32,000 Ukrainian Catholics in the Archdiocese of St. Boniface and 14,000 in the Diocese of Prince Albert. In the recently erected Diocese of Regina, there were 13,000 Ukrainian Catholics.[35] Unhappy with the independent-mindedness of the Ukrainian Catholic priests from the United States, Langevin, Legal and Pascal travelled to Europe, where they sought the advice and co-operation of the Congregation of Propaganda Fide, Oriental Affairs, Emperor Franz Joseph and his ambassador to the Holy See and, most crucially, Metropolitan Andrey Sheptytsky of Lviv. They also composed various memoranda on the urgent necessity of a Ukrainian Catholic bishop.[36] On top of all this episcopal activity, Father Albert Lacombe, vicar general of the Diocese of St. Albert, had interviews in 1900 with Leo XIII, the superior general of the Oblates, the Emperor and Sheptytksy when he was bishop of Stanyslaviv.[37]

A Basilian monk, a reformer and an intellectual, Metropolitan Sheptytsky was an ardent and able defender of the spiritual and cultural interests of the Ukrainian Catholic Church, in Galicia and abroad.[38] He was an ecclesiastical lifeline to Ukrainian Catholics in Canada. Sheptytsky issued two pastoral letters: "To the Ruthenians Settled in Canada," in 1901, and "Truths of Faith," in 1902. He dispatched his personal secretary, Father Basil Zholdak, to Canada in September 1901; Zholdak remained until June 1902, returning to Galicia in the company of Father Alphonsus Jan, OMI. Father Zholdak submitted a detailed report on the state of Ukrainian Catholics on the prairies. In response to this report, Sheptytsky sent four Basilian monks (three priests and one brother) and four Sisters Servants of Mary Immaculate to Canada, also in 1902. Rome vetoed Sheptytsky's request in 1901 and 1902 to visit Canada, claiming in each instance that the time was not propitious, but Sheptytsky did attend the Eucharistic Congress in Montréal in 1910, and afterwards conducted an extensive tour of Ukrainian settlements. Of all the people and organizations, including Catholic Church Extension Society, that lobbied Rome to send a Ukrainian Catholic bishop for Canada, Metropolitan Sheptytsky exercised the most authoritative influence on the Congregation of Propaganda Fide, Oriental Affairs, which was directly responsible for such an appointment. Lastly, it was on Sheptytsky's recommendation that Rome chose his seminary rector, Nykyta Budka, as bishop of the Ukrainian Catholic Eparchy of Canada.

The visits, the lobbying and the negotiations produced some tangible results. Langevin convinced the Belgian Redemptorists to send missionaries to Western Canada. Father Achiel Delaere arrived in September 1899 and adopted the Byzantine Rite in 1906. Other Redemptorists to follow him were Hendrik Boels, Noel Decamps and Charles Têcheur. They became the nucleus of an Eastern Rite Redemptorist Congregation stationed at Yorkton, Saskatchewan. As we have already mentioned, Metropolitan Sheptytsky sent four Basilians and four Sisters Servants in 1902. They were Father Platonid Filias, Father Sozont Dydyk and Father Anton Strotsky; Brother Jeremiah Yanishevsky; and Sister Ambrosia Lenkevich, Sister Isidora Shipovsky, Sister Emilia Kalpoushok and Sister Taida Wrublevsky.[39]

The three Basilian monks constituted the first permanent group of Ukrainian Catholic priests in Canada. Their ranks were replenished and expanded over time, but still remained totally insufficient for the number of Ukrainian Catholics who needed priests. By 1909, there were only five priests. Their ministry among the people was nothing short of heroic. They celebrated the liturgy, brought the sacraments to remote communities, built chapels and conducted retreats.[40] Assisting them were the small band of Byzantine Rite Redemptorists and a homegrown religious community of French-Canadian priests who, also having adopted the Byzantine Rite, became known as the Congregation of St. Josaphat. Archbishop Langevin actively encouraged the establishment of this community. The first to join was Father Adonis Sabourin of the Archdiocese of St. Boniface. Other members included Dérisé Claveloux, Joseph Gagnon, Arthur Desmarais and Joseph Jean.

When Bishop Nykyta Budka arrived in Winnipeg in December 1912, there were eighteen Ukrainian Catholic priests in his diocese, but only nine of them were Ukrainian, the rest being either Flemish or

French.[41] This was a foundation, a beginning, won at great price, but hardly an ideal situation. Tens of thousands of Ukrainian Catholics scattered throughout the prairies were still without the spiritual benefits of a regular liturgical life conducted by Ukrainian Catholic clergy within an organized ecclesiastical structure. When Father Alfred E. Burke and Catholic Church Extension Society commenced their crusade on behalf of Ukrainian Catholics in 1908, the prospect of episcopal leadership was hardly secure. In his "Memorial" to the hierarchy at the First Plenary Council of Québec in 1909, Father Burke made promises about the willingness and readiness of Church Extension to finance chapels, the education of seminarians and a Ukrainian Catholic newspaper, and he openly lobbied for a Ukrainian Catholic bishop. But these were only promises and lobbying. What, then, did Father Burke and the Society actually accomplish on behalf of Ukrainian Catholics?

CHAPTER 6

CHURCH EXTENSION'S UKRAINIAN CRUSADE, 1908–1915

As president of Church Extension and editor-in-chief of the *Catholic Register*, Father Burke publicized the plight and championed the religious and cultural cause of Ukrainian Catholics. In numerous editorials, articles, stories and letters, issue after issue, the *Register* shed light on their history as an immigrant community, the beauty of their distinctive liturgical Rite, their ancient and rightful membership in the Catholic Church, and their needs and wants if they were to survive intact as a people in their adopted country. Father Burke stood by Ukrainian Catholics in unflinching solidarity. He told their stories; he rang the alarm bells; he rushed to their defense on numerous occasions; he gave them a voice; and he provided a platform for their missionary priests and, beginning in 1912, for Bishop Nykyta Budka, their first eparch.[1] No other organization in the Canadian Church could match the zeal, the righteousness and the actions of Church Extension in its solicitude and unwavering support for Ukrainian Catholics. With Father Burke directing the crusade and leading the charge, Church Extension's small army of supporters and volunteers, although hardly rich in the goods of this world, provided desperately needed practical assistance to Ukrainian Catholics, their priests and their religious communities, successfully setting in motion what became a fruitful association with the Ukrainian Catholic Church that continues to this day.

But the provision of the practical, the doing of good works as a means to preserve the faith of Ukrainian Catholic immigrants, however necessary and laudable, did not satisfy the more pugilistic side of Father Burke's character. From the very beginning of the crusade, he went on the warpath against what he saw as Protestant proselytizers – soul stealers and soul snatchers, as he was fond of labelling them – who were preying on Ukrainian Catholics. He relished a fight and soon had one with the Presbyterian Home Mission Society and the Independent Greek Church, described by Burke in one of his editorials as "a new mongrel sect, a cross between Presbyterianism and the grand old Rite of Cyril and Methodius."[2] In Burke's eyes, the Presbyterian Home Mission Society was the most egregious Protestant organization of its kind in Western Canada. Since it was better funded and more ambitious than similar societies sponsored by the Methodists or Baptists, it posed the greatest threat to the ability of Ukrainian Catholics – dispersed, disorganized and without priests – to maintain not only their Ukrainian Catholic faith but also their loyalty to the Ukrainian Catholic Church and their connection to Rome and the local Latin Rite Church.

Father Burke felt compelled to confront the Presbyterians and knock down their illegitimate ecclesiastical creation, the Independent Greek Church. He did this by accusing the Presbyterian Home Mission Society of a litany of sordid wrongdoing: conducting systematic proselytism in Ukrainian Catholic communities under the guise of Canadianization, what Burke called the good citizen scheme; educating and financially supporting Independent ministers, who were nothing but bogus priests celebrating bogus Masses and dispensing bogus sacraments, including confession; refusing to be open and honest in its desire to teach Presbyterian doctrine and practices to Independent ministers; keeping Presbyterians in Eastern Canada, who funded its work, in the dark about the Home Mission Society's establishment of a new church, which was not part of its mandate, and its tolerance of a liturgy that was supposed to be Protestant, but was not, and that looked Catholic, but was not; indirectly aiding and abetting the Independents in their underhanded confiscation of Catholic churches that were "built by Catholics and for Catholic worship";[3] and, since 1905, funding *Ranok*, denounced by Burke as "that vile publication."[4] This was quite a collection of accusations. The more often they were repeated, the more explosive they were.

The Presbyterian Home Mission Society could not hope to convert a large number of Ukrainian Catholics to the Presbyterian faith in an aboveboard manner because Presbyterianism, as a Reformation religion, was shorn of ritual and liturgically centred on the proclamation of Sacred Scripture and preaching. As a Christianity of the pulpit, it was too foreign, too full of talk, too dull and too drab a version of the Christian faith for the religious imagination of Ukrainians, whether Catholic or Orthodox. That is why the Presbyterians in Western Canada welcomed with open arms a sham ecclesiastical entity by the name of the Independent Greek Church. In matters of public worship, at least for the first while, before the trimmers started to prune the Byzantine liturgy until it was a rump of its former self, the ritual, sacramentals and church decorations looked and felt Greek Catholic enough. The long-term future of the Church, however, was another matter. The intention of the Presbyterians, although revealed only when Father Burke began to attack the Presbyterian-Independent alliance, was to make these Independents members in good standing of the Presbyterian community *and by extension good Canadian citizens attached to the British way of life*. That was the real agenda. In the meantime, the outright imposition of Presbyterian faith and practice onto the Independent Greek Church would have to wait for more propitious circumstances.

Regardless, this was proselytism, pure and simple, in the judgment of Father Burke and Church Extension. At this time, there was an unwritten but generally understood rule within the broad Christian community in Canada that forbade churches from openly poaching members from rival churches. "To each his own" was the governing principle of religious peace.[5] Conversion from one Christian denomination to another (although Catholics never considered their Church a denomination) was initiated by the individual and considered a private matter. When it came to the spiritual care of Catholic immigrants in Western Canada, this rule, as understood by the Catholic community, meant that the Catholic Church took care of its own, including, for the first time, Ukrainian Catholics.

But the Canadian Protestant elite did not appreciate that Ukrainian Catholics were just as Catholic as Roman Catholics although they were *not* Roman Catholics, and along with Roman Catholics they were in union with the pope. This perplexing bit of history escaped the comprehension of Protestant missionary societies. How could it not? And their ignorance allowed them to consider Ukrainian Catholics (always referred to as Galicians or Ruthenians, names that did not conjure up Ukrainian or Catholic) as either Roman Catholics desiring to flee the clutches of Rome or, even more advantageous to their way of thinking, as Old World religious orphans not subject to the jurisdiction or blandishments of Roman Catholic bishops. Thus, the Presbyterians never saw themselves as proselytizers and were always astonished and grieved to have the charge hurled against them.

To complicate the picture even further – from the Catholic perspective – the Church's repeated failure to provide meaningful and consistent spiritual care for Ukrainian Catholics, in the absence of Ukrainian Catholic priests, prompted many Ukrainian Catholics to abandon what little hope they had that the Church they once knew in Galicia would take root in their adopted country of Canada. Vulnerable and bereft, a not inconsiderable number of them sought spiritual solace and clerical leadership in a hybrid Church that seemed, on the surface at least, to be tailor-made to minister to their liturgical needs and cultural expectations concerning independence and solidarity. The Independent Greek Church would not have materialized, and would not have functioned even for the short time that it did, without the Catholic hierarchy's indifferent success in taking care of its own.

In a headline-screaming *Catholic Register* article – "Ten Churches Save 35,000 Souls" – Father Burke admitted as much, but with a self-serving twist. The Church in Canada, he wrote,

has made the costly mistake of having no missionary organization to cope with this situation [the luring of Ukrainian
Catholics] before the Extension Society was founded to prevent
wolves from ravaging the sheep-fold. The other denominations
were in the field early and waxed strong. Young and weak as is
the Church Extension Society, it has no right to hesitate or to
permit anything coming between it and its duty.[6]

This was Burke's battle cry, his *cri de coeur*, but it was not one
that would find a place in the thoroughly French heart of Archbishop
Langevin. In any event, the "wolves" had been hard at work.

The alliance of the Presbyterians and the Independents was formal-
ized in 1904. It was as unlikely as it was unorthodox, defying religious
logic for nearly a decade. There were two reasons why this marriage
of convenience flourished during its early years. Chief among them
was the fact that neither partner had any serious or sustained Catholic
criticism to deflect or diminish until Father Burke ascended his bully
pulpit at the *Catholic Register* and commenced to hector them from
on high, with all the righteous indignation of a Catholic priest turned
Old Testament prophet. Until then, the Presbyterians in union with
their allies the Independents had a free hand in the conduct of their
ecclesiastical business.

For starters, the Presbyterians had plenty of money and an experienced and dedicated band of missionaries. They had established
missions among the Ukrainians in Manitoba as early as 1900. In June
of that year, the Reverend J.T. Reid opened a medical practice in Sifton,
staying two years. In October, the Reverend J.A. Cormie, superintendent of the missions in the province, built three schools in Ukrainian
settlements. Other missionaries to follow included the Reverend R.G.
Scott, a Sunday school teacher in Sifton who learned Ukrainian and
gave lessons in the New Testament and theology; the Reverend C.H.
Munro, a medical doctor in Ethelbert who organized Sunday school
and conducted English-language services; and the Reverend George
Arthur, a medical doctor whose practice was located at the Lake Geneva
Mission in Wakaw, Saskatchewan. He was also a teacher.[7] In 1902, the
Reverend A.J. Hunter arrived in Teulon, Manitoba, where he would

work as a doctor and hospital administrator for many years. A keen observer of the Ukrainian people, Hunter wrote a memoir, *A Friendly Adventure*, in which he went to extraordinary lengths to explain and defend Presbyterian support of the Independent Greek Church and to deny that he – or, for that matter, any other Presbyterian missionary – was involved in proselytism.[8] Three years after Hunter's arrival in Teulon, the Reverend S. Blumberger, yet another medical doctor, established a practice among the Ukrainians of Northern Alberta.[9]

By 1905, the Presbyterians claimed that there were sixteen ministers of the Independent Greek Church working for their home mission society as colporteurs (distributors of religious tracts and Bibles) among the Ukrainians in Staurtburn, Brokenhead, Gonor, Teulon, Gimli, Winnipeg, Shoal Lake, Sifton, Ethelbert, Riding Mountain and Pleasant Home in Manitoba; Saltcoats and Yorkton in Saskatchewan; and Edna-Star, Alberta, northeast of Edmonton. They also claimed that 25,000 Ukrainians had identified themselves with the Independent Greek Church and that another 30,000 were "studying it, attending its services, and are friendly toward it."[10] The latter two figures were probably too liberal an estimate. But that is not the point. The Presbyterians were enjoying success in the missionary field well in advance of Father Burke's 1909 "Memorial" to the Catholic bishops. Any attempt by Church Extension, then, to deal a death blow to the Independent Greek Church would command a great deal of its time, energy and financial resources, not to mention the editorial bellowing of Father Burke bolstered by a constant stream of reports and pleas for help from Catholic missionaries. As soon as Burke had lined up his target – the Reverend Dr. E.D. (Ebenezer Duncan) McLaren, general secretary of the Presbyterian Board of Home Missions for Western Canada since 1902 – the war of words commenced.

The first official mention of Presbyterian work among the Ukrainians concerns missionary activity in 1903:

Four missionaries among the Galicians are making considerable progress in learning the language, in the hope of soon being able to use it in services for the people. Seven Galician colporteurs have been employed. They report monthly, and are doing good work. Copies of the New Testament in Ruthenian have been secured, and are being distributed. Mr. [Michael] Sherbinin has, since February, been teaching a class of about sixteen young Galicians in Winnipeg. The majority of these will likely be permitted by the Government to teach Galician schools during the winter. They maintain themselves by doing such work as offers. There was great difficulty experienced in finding them work for the winter. Those who get schools in the winter will be easily able to support themselves next summer if the class is continued.[11]

Elsewhere in the same report, it was noted that the Home Mission Fund for 1903–04 – which supported Presbyterian missionary activity throughout the country – had at its disposal $120,697.69.[12] This was an impressive sum. The following year, the Fund grew to $137,744.99.[13] Such outsized generosity was proof of Presbyterian resolve to deal with what the General Assembly called "our *alien population*."

Many of these people are not only aliens in speech and in all their conceptions and modes of life, but are also ignorant of the first principles of responsible government, and incapable of sympathizing with our traditions and aspirations. What effect their presence is to have upon the spirit of our national life will depend upon the way they are dealt with and the influences that are brought to bear upon them, during the earlier years of their residence in Canada.[14]

Such a condescending and mistrustful view of Ukrainian immigrants, who were seen essentially as outsiders, did little to impede the energetic work of the Presbyterian Home Mission Society. Indeed, its attitude of cultural and political superiority seemed to energize and clarify its mission: to provide economic, social and religious opportunities for Ukrainians to become good citizens *and* good Protestants, too. Citizenship and religion went hand in hand. Catholic bishops and priests also held this maxim to be true, but they insisted at the same time that Catholic immigrants did not need to sacrifice their Catholic faith to become good citizens of their adopted country. Citizenship was not tied to Protestantism. Which explains the following exchange between the Reverend McLaren and Archbishop Langevin. McLaren insisted that "The Presbyterian Church is not proselytizing the Ruthenians; it is Canadianizing them."[15] In response, Langevin readily agreed with him that it was necessary to Canadianize newcomers to Canada, but his agreement came with a caveat the size of a sinkhole. Langevin told McLaren that he had "grave doubts … as to the Canadianizing influence of any band of men whose main effort appears to be the stirring up of an immense feeling of distrust against the Catholic Church."[16]

The two religious camps, then, shared a common goal but had different and competing concepts of Canadianization (a rather clunky and political word for assimilation).[17] Which concept would prevail? From the outset, the Catholic camp was at a disadvantage in the public debate over the Canadianization of Ukrainian Catholics, because it appeared that Catholic authorities had defaulted in their obligations to Ukrainian Catholics or did not have any real obligations to them in the first place. In either instance, according to the Presbyterian view – which abhorred the prospect of a Roman Catholic majority ruling the roost in Canada – the preferred way to authentic Canadian citizenship was through Protestant doors held open by Protestant teachers and shepherds.

In its understanding of the inception of the Independent Greek Church, the Presbyterian Home Mission Society eagerly highlighted the failure of the Catholic bishops to take care of people that they insisted belonged to them:

> When the Galicians moved to the Canadian West an effort was made to bring the new settlements into fuller harmony with the Roman Church. The people were not sent Greek Uniat[e] priests who would conduct the church services in their own language, using the Greek ritual, but were sent French priests who conducted the services in Latin. The people refused to acknowledge these priests or accept their services. In the meantime, Bishop Seraphim undertook the organization of an Orthodox Greek Church in the West. Before he had completed its organization the priests he had ordained formed themselves into the Independent Greek Church of Canada.[18]

The story of Seraphim and his priests is much more complicated than the rather disingenuous one presented in the official records of the General Assembly of the Presbyterian Church in Canada. Seraphim's real name was Stefan Ustvolsky. He was an excommunicated Russian Orthodox priest who drifted into Western Canada in 1903. He was an imposter, a fraud, who styled himself Bishop and Metropolitan of the Orthodox Russian Church of North America. His assistant was one Makary Marchenko. Both men displayed signs of mental instability, but that did not stop them from "ordaining" up to fifty priests and several deacons by means of a simple sprinkling ceremony and attracting thousands of followers within a matter of months. Before too long, however, Seraphim's bizarre behaviour became too much of an embarrassment for the more educated and ambitious of his priests. After convincing Seraphim to return to Russia in the autumn of 1903, to obtain the support of the Holy Synod, the Reverend Ivan (John) Bodrug and the Reverend Ivan (John) Negrych, with the assistance of Cyril Genyk, the Ukrainian immigration agent who had facilitated Seraphim's entry into Canada, staged a coup against Seraphim. They founded the Independent Greek Church (its official name in Ukrainian translates into English as the Ruthenian Orthodox Independent Church) and entered into a secret agreement with the Presbyterian Home Mission Society for financial and administrative assistance. Upwards of sixteen other Seraphimic priests joined Bodrug and Negrych.

The first synod of the Independent Greek Church was held in Winnipeg starting on 28 January 1904. After four days of intense debate among the thirty-five or so delegates, it passed a series of resolutions on needs as diverse as its own newspaper, a residence school for Ukrainian boys in Winnipeg, theology courses for Seraphim's priests at the Presbyterian-run Manitoba College, a cautious approach to Church reform, and the dissemination of the Bible, which was a distinctly Protestant undertaking and one that was probably insisted upon by the Presbyterians. Elected to executive office were the Reverend Alexander Bacynski, president; the Reverend John Danylchuk, secretary; Wasyl Novak, treasurer; and the Reverend John Bodrug, superintendent (bishop). These men were able to fend off Seraphim on his return to Canada in 1904 and effectively ignore him and his antics until he departed for a second time to Russia in 1908, never to reappear in Canada.[19]

The Presbyterian trump card against Catholic charges of proselytism had been the claim, never disputed even by the fiercest Catholic critic, that it had been Bodrug, Negrych and others busy establishing their own Church who had approached the Presbyterian Home Mission Society for guidance and support in 1904.

> The Galicians, dissatisfied with the teaching of the Church of Rome, sent a deputation to interview the leaders in our home Mission and College work in Winnipeg. On their advice and with their help an Independent Greek Church was formed, governed by a Consistory which is constituted on the principle of a Presbytery. The Consistory is composed of all the ministers and an equal number of laymen, and meets annually or oftener if necessary. The Consistory takes no important step without the knowledge and approval of the Executive of the Synodical Home Mission Committee in Winnipeg.[20]

And that was not all. Ministers of the Independent Greek Church agreed to become more evangelical, and new candidates for ministry were to be ordained not by a prelate but by the Consistory. This was all very Presbyterian and a radical departure from Ukrainian Catholic practice.

The grand experiment began to unravel as early as December 1907 and came to an inglorious end in 1912. The Presbyterian Home Mission Society decided that it could no longer support the Independent Greek Church if it continued to balk at becoming Presbyterian in heart and in practice. "These modern 'Protestants,'" chided the *Presbyterian*,

> sought help from the Presbyterian Church, and received it. But they did not become Presbyterians … upon the whole their preaching seems to have been pretty soundly evangelical. But most of them thought it necessary to retain a good deal of the Greek ritual, to which the people were accustomed in their worship.[21]

Moreover, the Presbyterian Synod no longer wanted to invest in church property not legally vested in the Presbyterian Church of Canada or in Independent ministers who resisted the direct control of the Synod.[22]

Ukrainians, then, were just as obstinate with the Presbyterians as they were with Roman Catholic bishops and priests about trusteeship of Church property and Church authority. Only a Ukrainian Catholic bishop, autonomous in jurisdiction, and answerable to no one but the apostolic delegate, could begin to chip away at such opposition to proper ecclesiastical governance. But all this was in the future. When Father Burke set his sights upon E.B. McLaren of the Presbyterian Home Mission Society in September 1909, neither side in the ensuing debate could have predicted the short lifespan of the Independent Greek Church. While there is no doubt that it imploded from within, because its leaders could no longer play both sides of the religious divide – the Catholic off the Presbyterian and vice versa – there is room to believe that Father Burke's relentless and shrill assault on McLaren and his Presbyterian colleagues helped to hasten the day of the implosion.

Father Burke would have been apprised of the history of Seraphim, the Independent Greek Church and Presbyterian Home Mission Society through Father Achiel Delaere's 1908 pamphlet on Ukrainian Catholics, *Mémoire sur les tentatives de schisme et d'hérésie au milieu des Ruthènes de l'Ouest canadien*. It appeared in English in 1909 as *Memorandum on the Attempts of Schism and Heresy Among the Ruthenians (commonly called 'Galicians') in the Canadian Northwest*. Page after page, in a rising fury of righteous indignation, this Redemptorist missionary railed against the imposter Seraphim, Ivan Bodrug and his fellow Independent ministers, Cyril Genyk, the *Kanadiyskiy Farmer* and *Ranok*, and indubitably the Presbyterians, whom he treated as the *bête noire* of a well-orchestrated campaign to seduce Ukrainian Catholics away from their true religious faith and home.[23] Father Delaere's pamphlet, in either language, was at times hysterical and at others inflammatory and almost libelous. For all of that, it was compelling reading for the Catholic mainstream and was the kind of punchy polemic that would have appealed instantly to

Father Burke, who was no stranger to the nineteenth-century art and mechanics of acidic writing.

But Father Delaere's pamphlet, while much welcomed, was not enough for Father Burke and Church Extension. Delaere was an excellent witness to the calamity facing Ukrainian Catholics, but his audience was too small. For his planned *Catholic Register* crusade, which was intended to be a national campaign, Father Burke needed his own eyewitness accounts reporting directly to him. To Bishop Legal of St. Albert, one of his steadiest episcopal cheerleaders, Burke wrote on 15 May 1909, "I am particularly interested in having an account of the Ruthenian or Russian position with all the difficulties which lead up to the demoralization of that people there so that we may make use of them in the interest of this work."[24] There is no record of Bishop Legal's reply to Burke's request, but by August 1909, Church Extension had two priests on a grand tour of the West.[25] Their main directive was to issue a report on the conditions of Ukrainian Catholics on the Prairies.

Father Hugh J. Canning and Father Joseph T. Roche were the two emissaries of Church Extension. Father Canning was pastor of Our Lady of Lourdes in Toronto and director of Church Extension for the Archdiocese of Toronto. He would later become the "Question Box" columnist in the *Catholic Register*. Father Roche was an assistant editor of the *Register*, and for a brief period, before he headed off to Europe (he never returned), he was a close and trusted collaborator of Father Burke in the work of the Church Extension. The two priests did exactly what Burke expected them to do: provide ammunition with which to attack the Presbyterian Home Mission Society.

Canning and Roche spent approximately three weeks gathering the facts and filing stories for the *Register*. Since Roche had experience as a journalist, most likely he was responsible for the articles published by Burke. They visited Sifton and the surrounding region in Manitoba, headed to Prince Albert, Saskatoon and Battleford in Saskatchewan, and from there went to Edmonton and Calgary in Alberta, ending their trip at a Knights of Columbus rally in Winnipeg attended by 500 of Winnipeg's leading Catholic laymen.[26]

They spent a good deal of time with Father Sabourin of Sifton, who took them for a forty-mile journey throughout his vast mission territory, at one point stopping for dinner at the home of a Ukrainian family. Roche described Sabourin's missionary work as a lonely war of one impoverished priest against an odd combination of "schismatics, apostate priests, Orthodox missionaries and Presbyterian money."[27] After reading Sabourin's translation of several passages from the Presbyterian-financed *Ranok*, in which the editor asserted in one story without proof that Pius IX had a harem of 150 women in Bologna and a "garaglia" [seraglia] of 200 nuns close to the Vatican palace in Rome, Roche angrily reacted by calling the newspaper "the vilest missionary literature with which I have ever come in contact,"[28] and promised to ask the Presbyterians for an explanation on his return to Toronto. In the interim, Burke commissioned Canning and Roche to reveal Church Extension's promise of $1,000 for a Ukrainian Catholic paper.

Roche, however, reserved his harshest words for the Brandon Normal School, which was in the business of training teachers. If Ukrainian Catholics were ever to lift themselves from the bottom rung of the social and economic ladder, they needed schools – and those schools needed teachers of their own faith and language. But the Brandon Normal School, he charged, was displaying scant interest in the pedagogical welfare of Ukrainian Catholics. He called the school "a nasty, lowdown, proselytizing Orange institution … an eyesore to the whole Catholic population of the province."[29]

What to do? Not one to let slip away a fundraising opportunity, Roche performed a Catholic guilt trip on his readers. Referring to Father Sabourin's church and rectory in Sifton, he wrote:

> I wish some of our well-fed and well-clothed Catholics sitting in the pews of our Ontario churches could step into the poor little hall which serves as a chapel and see the primitive altar with its cheap white cotton to take the place of paint and gilt, the little rough tabernacle in which our Lord dwells and the bare interior without furniture or pews in which the people stand during Mass, said according to the Ruthenian Rite. I wish they could see the bare interior of the place which he calls

home, the few poor, hard chairs, the table with its oil-cloth covering, the dishes, the cutlery, the humble fare served up by the Ruthenian boy who serves as his cook, his servant-man, his server and man-of-all trades.[30]

Soon the contributions poured in. While most were modest, a dollar or two, sometimes as much as five or ten, from priests but mostly from lay people who lived in small-town Ontario, a few donations were substantial, such as the $1,000 pledged by George Lynch Stanton, and the $500 promised by an E.M. Behan.[31] Burke regularly published the names of donors and the amounts they gave, no matter how seemingly insignificant. Also, he could not resist adding his own voice to what he hoped would be a rising Catholic chorus of the most strident opprobrium directed against the Presbyterians. In the same issue of the *Register* that featured Roche's stories – 16 September 1909 – Burke published an article titled "Manitoba's Recent Immigrants." He presented a dire portrait of the vulnerability faced by the 35,000 Ukrainian Catholics in the Archdiocese of Manitoba:

In Western Canada ... they find themselves in new and strange conditions. They are no longer in a purely Catholic country. There is no such thing as state support of churches and priests. Schools are conducted in the English language, and they have to build their own schools and pay the teachers. They find too that they must build their churches or go without the services of religion. Agitators, disturbers, schismatics and Protestant missionaries have added to their confusion. Catholic peoples who speak a foreign language are always fair game of these misguided sects. Experience has always shown them [agitators, etc.] time and again that their efforts merely serve to make agnostics and haters of all religion, but they still keep on, happy in the thought that they are winning a few away from Rome. Today Presbyterian mission societies are paying salaries to schismatic priests who are saying Mass and teaching their people to kiss the Crucifix and pictures of the saints and to pray to the Blessed Virgin, but what do these mission societies care provided they can make them [Ukrainian Catholics] independent.

The Ruthenians are exceedingly jealous of their language and their rite, and the agitators have worked upon this jealousy. When they build their little churches here and there they preferred to keep the titles to the property in the name of their church communities. This has led to endless difficulty. Every apostate priest, every designing missionary knave, has thus been enabled to go about amongst them in order to close the church doors to regularly commissioned priests. As Bishop Legal recently said, "It is now the acute stage in this people's religious career," and much patience is being exercised in order that they may slowly be brought to a realization of the fact that the clergy and hierarchy have no designs … against their language or their rite.[32]

Thumping about dastardly Protestant missionaries was all well and good, but Father Burke needed to do something dramatic for Ukrainian Catholics to show everyone, especially the Western hierarchy, that Church Extension meant business. Otherwise it was all sectarian bluster signifying nothing but useless Catholic impotence in the face of Protestant advances. Burke took action on 8 September 1909 when he sent a telegram to Father Canning, in the middle of his and Father Roche's tour of the West. The telegram, which Burke published in the following week's issue of the *Register*, read: "Tell Father Sabourin Extension pledges Ten Churches necessary preserve faith Ruthenian people. Construct immediately. Draw on us for money."[33] These churches would never fall into the hands of the Independent Greek Church.

The *Catholic Register* of 16 September 1909, which was one of the most high-strung and denunciatory issues published by Burke, caught the eye of the Reverend E.B. McLaren. He must have read an advance copy, because his reply to the *Register* appeared in the 16 September issue of the Toronto *Star*. McLaren openly acknowledged the work of the Presbyterian Home Mission Society among Ukrainian Catholics and the society's financial support of *Ranok*. The primary aim of the mission, in McLaren's opinion, was simple and above suspicion. He wrote, "We have been seeking to elevate them to Canadian citizenship."[34]

Burke chose to respond in the Toronto *Telegram*. He lampooned *Ranok* and the Presbyterian assertion that its efforts were all about turning Ukrainian Catholics into good citizens, as if they could not be Catholic and good citizens at the same time; attacked the Brandon Normal School, while acknowledging that McLaren knew nothing about it; asserted that the majority of Ukrainians were Catholic and not Orthodox, as McLaren insisted; and wondered long and loud why the Presbyterians denied that they were trying to turn Ukrainian Catholics into Presbyterians. For Burke, who was in high dungeon every time he thought about the Presbyterian Home Mission Society, this was the essence of the Presbyterians' ham-handed deception of Ukrainian Catholic settlers and their lame attempt to fool the public. Proselytism was a real long-term program, regardless of all the denials to the contrary:

> If Presbyterians in general will kindly remember that the cler-gymen in these Independent Ruthenian churches, supported by their funds, go through the motions of saying mass, hearing confessions, administering the seven sacraments according to the Catholic rite and practice, they will understand the occa-sion for our protest .... It is this deception of a simple people, this trickery, this fraud, against which we protest. We know its objects. We know the ultimate purpose is to win them away from their allegiance to the Catholic Church. Is this necessary for a higher Canadian citizenship?[35]

Burke warned McLaren and the Presbyterian Home Mission Society that the "Ruthenians are Catholics. The Church is bent on keeping them as such."[36]

The Toronto-based *Orange Sentinel* did not pass up the chance to weigh in on the debate. It came to the defense of McLaren and all Protestant mission societies working in the West:

> The right of the Protestant denominations to evangelize the pol-yglot horde of Roman Catholics who are pouring into Canada should not be waived by Rev. Dr. McLaren, the Presbyterian home mission superintendent, or any other authority. Dr. McLaren stated in his able defense of Presbyterian activity

among the Ruthenians that no attempt was being made to pros-
elytize the Greek Catholics, even those owning the supremacy
of the Pope, but these people were being encouraged to build
up an independent church of their own, along very much the
same lines as they were accustomed to in the old world. The
principal work of his church, he said, was to establish schools,
provide medical skill, and generally do things which would en-
able these poor foreigners to become good Canadians .... The
tide of immigration is rapidly being diverted into Canada, and
the evangelical churches must awake to their opportunities or
this country will ultimately be ruled from Rome.[37]

There was a curious logic to this argument, and it was the same
kind of logic exhibited by the Reverend E.D. McLaren. Evangelization
of Ukrainians was not proselytism as long as it was channelled
through the ministers of the Ukrainian-created, Presbyterian-financed
Independent Greek Church. Of course, such a synthetic church was
only superficially modelled on the one in Galicia and was not con-
nected to it in any way, and its priests were not real priests and had no
sacramental right to celebrate Mass or administer the sacraments. No
matter. Evangelization of Ukrainian Catholics, who were not Roman
Catholics, must proceed to save the country from Roman Catholic
majority rule. Such fear mongering had been a traditional staple of
Orange propaganda and opinion, and was trotted out by the usual
suspects in the Burke-versus-McLaren dispute.

Except for reprinting the *Orange Sentinel* article, Burke wisely
stayed clear of the Orange Order, choosing instead to take his fight
directly and openly to the people who mattered the most – the executive
of the board of the Presbyterian Home Mission Society. He presented
translated passages from *Ranok*, the same ones that Roche and Canning
had found so offensive, and then proceeded to ask in a cover letter

as to your purpose in attempting to start a new religion
amongst the Ruthenians, this religion being identical in belief
and practice with that taught by the Catholic Church, and I
and many amongst us are anxious to learn if you approve of

the Independent clergymen, supported by your funds, passing themselves off as genuine Ruthenian Catholic priests?[38]

It was a question that Burke would ask repeatedly.

McLaren and the Reverend J.A. Carmichael answered in a letter in the Toronto *Globe*, which was reproduced in the *Catholic Register*. The Presbyterians were involved at

> the request of the Ruthenians themselves, who represented that practically no provision was being made for their religious needs either by the Roman Catholic or by the Greek Church. Investigation showed that they were not only being neglected spiritually, but also that little, if anything, was being done for their physical well-being or their intellectual improvement. In this destitution is to be found the explanation of the efforts put forth on their behalf by the Presbyterian Church.[39]

Those efforts included involvement in the Independent Greek Church, the education of young Ukrainian boys at Manitoba College, the maintenance and equipage of three hospitals and two nursing homes in Ukrainian communities, and the funding of a Ukrainian-language newspaper, *Ranok*. Concerning the paper, McLaren and Carmichael contended that the executive board had no control over its content, but on reflection they thought that more oversight was needed. Having made this concession, they ended on a defiant note:

> Let it be remembered, too, that according to the statement made a few years ago by an official of the Immigration Department, one-half of the Ruthenians [Ukrainians] in the Northwest are connected with the Orthodox Greek Church, and that in its arrogant demand that the Protestant Churches should cease their efforts on behalf of these foreigners and leave them all to be ministered to by the Roman Catholic Church, that Church is exhibiting the very spirit of proselytizing zeal with which it has unjustly charged the Presbyterian Home Mission Committee. One can hardly conceive of a more urgent appeal to the human sympathies, patriotic fervor and religious instinct of any body of Christians, than that made by the necessitous condition of the ignorant and neglected Ruthenians in the early days of their

settlement in Canada. Whenever such an appeal is made to the Presbyterian Church it does not propose to ask the consent of any individual or any organization before undertaking the work to which, in the Providence of God, it believes itself to be called. And when its work in any field of Christian activity is so abundantly fruitful as this work amongst the Ruthenians has been, it does not propose to relax its efforts because of the criticisms of the Catholic Register.[40]

Burke's reply to these two leading Presbyterians dripped with sarcastic scorn. He wondered, "It strikes us as rather strange that 'humanitarian motives' do not inspire them to go to work amongst the degraded poor of England or of some other distinctly Protestant country."[41] He had nothing but the utmost contempt for Manitoba College, Seraphim's priests of the Independent Greek Church, and McLaren's and Cartwright's artless concessions about *Ranok*. "It establishes a new principle in business as well as in religion," Burke wrote. "These good people put up their money to aid a journal whilst remaining in total ignorance as to its character and the nature of its contents."[42] He also accused McLaren of being confused in his use of the word "Ruthenian," although in almost the same breath Burke revealed his own ignorance about the language of the Ruthenian Rite. It was not Bulgarian. Burke ended his counterthrust by claiming that he had nothing against ordinary Presbyterians, an oft-repeated disclaimer of his. Rather, the problem was the sleight-of-hand practices of the Presbyterian Home Mission Society. "Once again, we take the liberty of inquiring if the Home Mission Board believe in Presbyterianism, why do they not try to teach it to the Ruthenians of Western Canada?"[43]

The Burke–McLaren duel of words was loud enough to catch the attention of the Jesuit journal *America*. Its contributor wrote in 1910 that Burke and Church Extension's "crusade in favor of the Ruthenians in the west, and the exposure of the shameless methods of certain proselytizers, excited interest throughout the Catholic Canada, which is daily waking up more and more to its duties and responsibilities in that direction."[44] The writer for *The Canadian Annual Review*, while more objective in his reporting, took a parting shot at what for him was nothing more than nasty sectarian squabbling over foreigners and their strange religion:

> Meantime, in the far West, a dispute of some violence had arisen regarding the 150,000 Ruthenians scattered amongst the three Provinces, professing a curious faith which was said on the one side to be of the Russian Greek Church [Independent Greek Church?] and approximating toward Protestantism and on the other to be emphatically Catholic. Into this field came the Presbyterian Church missionaries by, it was claimed, the request of the people or a portion of them. A proselytizing newspaper called *The Ranok* was published and helped largely by Presbyterian funds and from this sheet the *Catholic Register* of Toronto quoted many offensive and untrue statements as to the Roman Catholic Church. Hence the strong words used in return by this latter paper, the denunciations of the Brandon Normal School as an institution doing Orange work amongst the teachers of Manitoba, and finally, the pledge of the Catholic Church Extension Society to send ten priests into this Western field. So much for two antagonistic schools of thought and ideal and policy in Canadian life – each of which has been here allowed to speak for itself.[45]

There the matter between Burke and Church Extension and McLaren and the Presbyterian Home Mission Society rested until June 1910, when the *Register* published a lengthy extract from the Reverend Carmichael's optimistic report on home missions and the Independent Greek Church to the General Assembly of the Presbyterian Church in Halifax on 2 June 1910. Very cheekily, Father Burke inserted in the middle of Carmichael's report a black-bordered call to his readers – "Wanted at Once" – asking them to consider donating to the construction of five Ruthenian chapels, at $500 each, to the education of twenty Ruthenian students for the priesthood, at $125 per student per year, and to the purchase of twelve Ruthenian liturgical vestments, in black, red and white. He also invited his readers to make an offering for a Ruthenian boarding school at Edmonton or a Ruthenian hospital at Vegreville, Alberta.[46] The message from the president of

Church Extension to the Presbyterian Assembly was very clear – the Ruthenians were Catholics and the Catholic Church was not about to abandon them to the Reverend Carmichael and company. The Burke–McLaren imbroglio did not explode on the pages of the *Register* again until 1 December 1910.

But there was to be no outright ceasefire in the crusade. That would have been too generous a gesture from Father Burke when Ukrainian Catholics needed all the firepower that he and the Society could muster on their behalf. So, Burke turned to his clerical comrades in the missionary field and published their first-hand accounts of their ministry among Ukrainian Catholics. He did this not only for the ongoing edification of *Register* readers, whom he hoped would rise to the occasion, donate to the cause and take out a subscription to the paper, but also as a means to keep the pressure on the Presbyterian Home Mission Society – that is, if its members ever bothered to read the *Register* and felt inclined to put up with Burke's bombastic bullying. Enlisted by Father Burke were Father August Bernier, the pastor of Vegreville; Bishop Émile Legal of St. Albert; Father Sabourin of Sifton, Manitoba; Father Alphonse Jan, OMI, of Calgary, Alberta, who spent six months in Galicia; Father Hendrik Boels, C.Ss.R., and Father Noel Decamps, C.Ss.R., of Yorkton, Saskatchewan; Father Miron Hura, who tended to 15,000 Ukrainian Catholics in a territory that stretched 150 miles south and 100 miles north of Edmonton;[47] and Father Leo I. Sembratowicz (Sembratowich).

Father Sembratowicz was a rare example in 1909 of a Galician-born and -educated Ukrainian Catholic priest, with excellent connections to the hierarchy in his homeland, who was very willing to be conscripted by Father Burke in his Ukrainian crusade. A nephew of the late Cardinal Sylvester Sembratowicz and the late Metropolitan Joseph Sembratowicz, and for two years the secretary to Metropolitan Andrey Sheptytsky, Father Sembratowicz was educated in Rome and spoke five languages. In 1906 he was made an honorary canon of the arch-cathedral in Lviv, Galicia, and in 1907, he was requested by Bishop Soter Ortynsky, the first Ukrainian Catholic bishop in the United States, to compile a report on the conditions of Ukrainian Catholics in his country-wide diocese.

At the time that he came in contact with Burke, Sembratowicz was living at St. John the Baptist parish in Buffalo, New York. He looked after Ukrainians at two parishes in the city and at parishes in Rochester, Brantford and Toronto.[48] Sembratowicz had introduced himself to Archbishop McEvay in a letter dated 23 April 1910 and written in German on the letterhead of the cathedral in Stanislau, Galicia.[49] In September 1911, Father John T. Kidd, administrator of the Archdiocese of Toronto, instructed Father Sembratowicz to announce to Ukrainian Catholics at St. Helen's Church in Toronto, on Sunday, 24 September 1911, that he had been "appointed to be in charge of their spiritual welfare in this Archdiocese."[50] Two months later, Kidd wrote a testimonial letter in support of Sembratowicz:

> Rev. Leo Sembratowicz who is of the Ruthenian Rite has attended to the spiritual welfare of the Ruthenians of Toronto for some time and has proved himself to be an energetic, capable and zealous priest. He has done very much good work for the Ruthenians here and elsewhere.[51]

By January 1912, however, Father Kidd was writing to Bishop Soter Ortynsky in Philadelphia for a resident priest for the Ruthenians of Toronto. At one point in his letter, Kidd wrote, "Father Sembratowicz understands the difficulties there are here and can explain them better to Your Lordship."[52] This may have been an elliptical remark about the fact that Sembratowicz was a married priest who was separated from his wife. For his part, Father Burke chose to ignore this double impediment and the gossip about Sembratowicz's wife having an affair with an Austrian officer.[53] Burke needed Sembratowicz and Sembratowicz needed Burke.

After reading one of Father Burke's articles in the *Catholic Register* on the plight of Ukrainians in Western Canada, Sembratowicz sent him a letter dated 4 October 1909. "I never thought," he wrote, "that the Canadian Catholics would have been too much interested in the matter [of Ukrainian Catholics] and on the other side I thought, that the Basilian Fathers were sufficient for the spiritual needs of the Ruthenians. From your paper I see the bad conditions of my people."[54] In reply, Burke asked Sembratowicz for his opinion on the situation of Ukrainian Catholics in Canada.

Sembratowicz complied in a letter of 18 October 1909, in which he argued forcefully for the recruitment of secular Ukrainian priests, celibates or widowers, the appointment of a Ukrainian Catholic bishop, and the need for a Ukrainian Catholic newspaper. Although Sembratowicz danced around the topic of married priests, knowing Rome's firm opposition to their emigration to North America, he was adamant that limiting priestly recruitment to monks was a failure. In all of Galicia, the Order of St. Basil the Martyr was the only community of monks, there were only ninety of them, and their level of education was not as high as that of secular priests. Moreover, there would never be enough French Roman Catholic priests willing to adopt the "Ruthenian Rite" to supply the spiritual and liturgical needs of the tens of thousands of Ukrainian Catholics already living in Canada. Sembratowicz did not question their zeal or commitment, but he did question their ability to learn the language and traditions of the people to an extent befitting their priestly ministry. He charged that

> They [the French priests] misrepresent the real character and manners of the people and lead the public to believe that they were brought here as Protestants whilst the truth is that these people have always been proud of their religion, devoted to the Holy See and never inscribed as anything but Catholics.[55]

Impressed, Burke asked Sembratowicz to write an in-depth article on the history, language and rite of Ukrainian Catholics, their loyalty to Rome and the problems they encountered as settlers in a new and sometimes inhospitable and even incomprehensible land. His submission, published on the front page of the *Register* of 28 October 1909, was a first for the newspaper.[56] Burke's Ukrainian Catholic crusade finally had given a platform to a Ukrainian writing about Ukrainians. Sembratowicz's article imparted considerable legitimacy to Church Extension's self-given mandate to save Ukrainian Catholics. Also, it prompted Burke, in a burst of naïve enthusiasm, to write two letters on the same day – 23 October 1909 – to Archbishop Fergus McEvay. He asked the chancellor of Church Extension to support the idea of the Society sponsoring Sembratowicz on a trip to Galicia, where he would recruit priests for the Canadian missions, lobby Metropolitan Sheptytsky to pay a visit to Canada [the Eucharistic Congress in Montréal in 1910], and then work on Sheptytsky to convince Rome to appoint a Ukrainian bishop for Canada.[57] In the second letter, Burke revealed the degree to which extravagant daydreaming had led him to believe that Sembratowicz was their man.

> If they [the apostolic delegate and the Canadian bishops] leave this matter to us, we will settle it wonderfully, in one year, and we will undertake the financial exactions of the whole case. You may think I am losing my head, and imagining we have money to burn, but I have thought out the whole situation and see many opportunities of recouping every cent we shall expend as well as doing a good which nothing else could do. Now then, take the matter up earnestly and prayerfully and see what you can do down there.[58]

The "down there" referred to Quebec City, where the First Plenary Council was meeting. Burke hoped that McEvay would take his plan directly to his brother bishops.

Burke wrote one more letter to McEvay on the same subject, bearing the date of 28 October 1909. He was in something of a panic. Burke needed to tell Sembratowicz by no later than 30 October if he had the financial backing of Church Extension, because Sembratowicz had booked passage for Galicia for 7 November.[59] In the absence of a reply to any of Burke's three letters, there is no evidence to suggest that McEvay gave his blessing to the project. The explanation for his inaction is simple: he could hardly act on any aspect of the so-called Ruthenian Question without the agreement of the rest of the hierarchy.

In the end, Church Extension did not fund Sembratowicz's journey, but Burke continued his relationship with the peripatetic Ukrainian Catholic priest. Sembratowicz is mentioned in a *Register* article on a French translation of the Ruthenian liturgy,[60] and he made at least two more contributions to the paper, one concerning his return to the

West in 1912, and the other a lengthy article on the Russo-Ruthenian Question published in 1913.[61] Interestingly, despite his marital status and problems, it was Father Sembratowicz who accompanied Bishop Nikyta Budka to Winnipeg in December 1912.[62]

It appears from Burke's three letters to McEvay regarding Sembratowicz that he saw his proposed priest-gathering mission in Galicia as a convenient and legitimate way to take the pastoral care of Ukrainian Catholics out of the hands of the French bishops in Western Canada. He closed his first letter of 23 October with these words: "The French can't do the job: they shouldn't be allowed to do it."[63] In the second letter of the same date, he told McEvay that the "whole solu tion of this [Ruthenian] question is contained in getting the matter out of the hands of the French Bishops and into our own."[64] In the letter of 28 October, he repeated his assertion that Sembratowicz was the right man:

> He can get the men [the priests]. He can help save those souls to the church, I believe, as nobody else can. They should not bar the way. The Extension Society is ready to do something – everything – to win the esteem of the 'most reverent, high and mighty seigneurs' of the plains.[65]

There was only one seigneur on the plains – Archbishop Langevin. His suffragans were natives of France. McEvay would have agreed at least with the overall sentiment and tone of Burke's opinions on the larger matter of French domination of the Church in the West, but, again, as archbishop of Toronto he was not ready to intrude in the diocesan affairs of another bishop, especially Langevin.

In addition to the testimonials and stories submitted by (or about) missionary priests, the *Register* provided extensive coverage of Metropolitan Andrey Sheptytsky's pastoral visit to the West during October and November 1910.[66] His Canadian visit, a first for a Ukrainian Catholic Archbishop of Lviv, was a huge morale booster to Ukrainian Catholics wherever he ministered to them. It was a long time in coming, and was a truly historic occasion for the Canadian Church, one that was trumpeted by the *Register* in numerous stories and photographs as living proof that the Church, in this case in the person of Metropolitan Sheptytsky, was actively involved in giving spiritual comfort and leadership to Ukrainian Catholics in Canada. And as if the Ukrainian agitation was not enough to keep Burke sufficiently occupied, he championed the cause of Father Jules Pirot, a secular priest from Belgium who was missionary to the Hungarian Catholics at Kaposvar, Saskatchewan.[67] He also took big swings at James S. Woodsworth, the author of *Strangers Within Our Gates*, the Methodist Conference of 1910 and the Baptist Home Missions.[68]

Father Burke was in his element during what was the high point of his career as a Catholic journalist, apologist and agitator. But, surprisingly, it was not Burke but his second-in-command at the *Register*, Father Joseph Roche, who rekindled the controversy over the Presbyterian Home Mission Society. During a November 1910 tour of the Maritimes with the Church Extension chapel car, Father Roche goaded the Reverend McLaren until he admitted that the Mass as celebrated by the ministers of the Independent Greek Church was, in Roche's own words, "'a bogus one; it was not the genuine Mass of the Roman Catholic Church, or even of the Greek Church.'"[69] This was no big deal for McLaren. Since the Independent ministers had never professed to their congregations that they were celebrating Mass as understood by either Roman Catholics or Greek Catholics, there was no fraud committed on their part and by inference on the part of the Presbyterian Home Mission Society that supported these ministers. Indeed, from the very beginning of the Independent movement, there had been a conscious effort on the part of the ministers "'as rapidly as the enlightened consciences of their people would permit of its being done, to omit those portions of the service that converted the sacrament into a sacrifice, and were inconsistent with the Protestant interpretation of New Testament teaching.'"[70] And, because it was a success, Father Roche had decided to attack him.

As if to prove his point, McLaren laid out a statistical profile of the Independent Greek Church. It had seventy-two congregations, ten churches and nineteen ministers. There were Ukrainians in twenty other settlements asking for ministers to come and preach. There was more:

> During the past summer sixty young Ruthenians who had been prepared for this work in Manitoba College were employed by the Governments of the three provinces as public school teachers. This winter three young men are enrolled as students of theology in the first year; six are taking the minister evangelist course of study for the ministry, and fifteen others are preparing to matriculate, and intend to take the course in arts and theology.[71]

This was enough to send Burke into a paroxysm of rage. Under a front-page banner headline that read "Ruthenian Situation Acute: The Proselytizers Admit Nefarious Work," he went on the offensive and kept up his attacks for the first eight months of 1911. His editorials minced no words: "Proselytizers of the Ruthenians as They Are"; "Proselytizers and Proselytized"; "The Latest From the Ruthenian Field"; "The Wolves in Sheep's Clothing"; "Now the Enemy Comes out in the Open"; "Bogus Priests They Must Condemn"; "Proselytizers Working in Our Midst"; "The Ruthenian Situation Reviewed."[72] Metropolitan Sheptytsky, Father Delaere and Father Decamps joined the fray with comments and letters.[73] Burke even published a Ukrainian student's denunciation of McLaren.[74] On 4 March 1911, one thousand Ukrainian Catholics in Winnipeg protested against McLaren and the Presbyterian Home Mission Society. They were upset by McLaren's article entitled "Our Work Among the Ruthenians in Western Canada," published in the February issue of *The Presbyterian Record*.[75]

Of course, there were critics of Father Burke who thought that his long-running invective against the Presbyterians was too harsh in its tone and language, too divisive in its methods, and too alarmist in its diagnosis of the situation. Burke was having none of it:

> At the commencement of our campaign against the Presbyterian proselytizing agencies busily engaged in the nefarious work of perverting these strangers to our shores, we placed before our readers full and concise information regarding the exact location and urgent needs of these Catholic colonists; and our

articles on the matter were, of necessity, vigorous; and, should occasion arise in the future – and there is no knowing whether or not it will, for the forces of evil are ever rampant – we shall not hesitate to pursue the proselytizers with as much vigor as we have in the past. It is true that our methods and means of attack have been severely criticized by our opponents, and even some who would call themselves our friends have ventured to enter feeble protests against our denunciatory articles. But where the salvation of Catholic souls is at stake, there is no time to be wasted in mealy-mouthed objections to the tactics adopted by unscrupulous proselytizers. The burglar within the home is not to be handled with kid gloves. We must show them that the Catholic press is a force in the land. We must give them to understand that every Catholic, no matter what his nationality, rite or record, when his faith is attacked by deceitful adversaries, is supported by the Catholic pen, and we must not hesitate to let them feel the weight and influence of that pen.[76]

Although the Presbyterian Home Mission Society cut off funding for the Independent Greek Church by the end of 1912, it took Father Burke until February 1914 to acknowledge its demise in an editorial. "The Presbyterian experiment with the Ruthenians," he wrote, "has then ended in ignominy. We do not know what it has taught the Presbyterians, but it has cost them a mint of money and a tremendous descent in self and public respect."[77]

So much for the anti-Presbyterian pugilism. Was the crusade more than just fighting words directed against a convenient Protestant enemy? Was it just bluster and bombast? What did Church Extension accomplish on a practical level for Ukrainian Catholics?

In essence, Father Burke successfully laid the foundation for long-term assistance for the Ukrainian Catholic Church in Canada. Recognition of the importance of that assistance came early in the history of Church Extension. In *Allata nuper ad nos*, the Apostolic Brief of 9 June 1910 that constituted Church Extension, Pius X commended the Society for its great success "in protecting the poor Catholic Ruthenians, dispersed throughout the North-West, against the wiles of non-Catholic sects which, with every machination, sought to subtract them from the bosom of the Catholic Church."[78] In his "Address on the Ruthenian Question," dated 18 March 1911, Metropolitan Andrey Sheptytsky paid generous tribute to Church Extension for having contributed "a great deal to the works designed to assist the Ruthenians"[79] and to the *Catholic Register* for considering the spiritual plight of Ruthenians as "one of the most serious questions of the Catholic Church in Canada."[80] When Burke met Pius X in a private audience in December 1911, the pope promised him "categorically to give the Ruthenians of Canada a Bishop of their own."[81] This was all Father Burke's doing. To him must be given the lion's share of the credit for creating a new communal experience for Canadian Catholics as he called upon them to step out of their particular historical enclaves (Irish, French, English, Scottish), regardless of their origin or location, and to recognize, welcome and assist their Ukrainian Catholic brethren.

It is difficult to imagine how the Ukrainian Eparchy led by Bishop Nykyta Budka from 1912 to 1927 would have survived without Church Extension's constant solicitude and generosity, a program initiated and sustained during Father Burke's presidency of the Society and his editorship of the *Register* and which continued uninterrupted long after his departure from the scene. This, too, was the result of Burke's genuine concern and organizational genius. His was an early voice, and perhaps one of the loudest and most insistent, to alert the Catholic community of the terribly straitened circumstances of Ukrainian Catholic immigrants, making their cause Church Extension's primary mission at the commencement of its corporate existence, and he was one of the first Catholic churchmen in Canada to call openly for a Ukrainian Catholic bishop.

Father Burke was a solid supporter of Bishop Budka, in his positive opinions of his ministry and in the disbursement of funds for his eparchy. One of the nine means adopted by Church Extension to carry out its principal objects was the "Organization of Ruthenian Catholics of Canada and the exposure of the proselytizing methods amongst them."[82] Hard on the heels of the collapse of the Independent Greek Church, Burke changed the fourth object of the Society to read: "To aid the Bishop of the Ruthenians in his missionary work."[83] Burke published details of Budka's biography and his episcopal ordination; he announced the news of the ordination to Toronto's Ukrainian Catholics from the pulpit of St. Helen's church, at one point asking that each Ukrainian family donate one dollar to the new bishop (his pleas fell on deaf ears);[84] he arranged payment for Budka's and his secretary's passage from Galicia to Winnipeg;[85] he wrote extensively about Budka's arrival in Canada and the beginning of his episcopal ministry in his vast diocesan territory;[86] he highlighted the 1914 ordination of the first class of Ukrainian Catholic seminarians at St. Augustine's Seminary in Toronto;[87] he vigorously defended Budka in August 1914 after the latter in a pastoral letter had initially called upon Ukrainian Catholics to return home and take up arms on behalf of the Austro-Hungarian Empire, a position that he reversed in a second pastoral letter as soon as Great Britain declared war on Germany and its main ally, the Empire.[88] And Father Burke never ceased to raise the alarm about the needs and sufferings of Ukrainian Catholics and to issue appeals on their behalf.[89] One such appeal carried this ominous headline: "The Fate of the Ruthenian Catholic Church in Canada at the Present Time is in Your Hands."[90]

Unfortunately, not until 1918 do records exist that reveal the generosity of Church Extension in its funding of Bishop Budka's episcopal work as he sought to establish order and regularity into the corporate life of his eparchy. For the fiscal year ending on 28 February 1918, Church Extension had donated $8,293 to the Ukrainian eparchy, the second-largest donation to any diocese among the seventeen dioceses and vicariates that were recipients of that year's expenditures.[91] From 1919 to 1927, the Ukrainian eparchy received a total of $264,947.78 from Church Extension, making it by far the largest beneficiary of the nineteen dioceses and vicariates that received funding from the Society.[92] The point is that this tradition of remarkable generosity had its genesis in the work and personality of Father Burke. It was Burke the crusader, the in-your-face firebrand, who enabled Church Extension to throw a financial lifeline to the nascent Ukrainian Catholic Church.

Within the overall context of Church Extension's aid to the missions in Western Canada, Ukrainian Catholics received their share of memorial chapels, Mass intentions, loans at reasonable rates and Church goods, such as Mass vestments, altar linens, chalices, ciboria and censers, although, as in the matter of the exact amount of money donated to Ukrainian Catholics prior to 1919, it is difficult to say with any precision what percentage of the chapels and such went to them. But the *Register* did carry stories about Ukrainian Catholic chapels. From its pages can be detected the emergence of these chapels on the landscape of Western Canada.[93] Archbishop McEvay was the first to respond to the *Register's* call for chapel donations with a gift of $500, which in 1909 and for decades thereafter was the basic cost of erecting one of these simple yet efficient and distinctive houses of worship.[94] Anthony A. Hirst of Philadelphia, a lawyer and supporter of Church Extension in the United States, is credited with actually building the first $500 chapel for Ukrainian Catholics in Canada. Dedicated to St. Anthony, it was erected in the Diocese of St. Albert, in 1909, in memory of his son who had died two years earlier.[95] In 1910, a Ukrainian Catholic chapel was built in Vegreville, a large Ukrainian settlement in the Diocese of St. Albert, to counter the presence of the Independent Greek Church.[96] Of course, there were the ten chapels for the Archdiocese of St. Boniface promised by Father Burke when Father Canning and Father Roche were touring the West in 1909. These took time to build because of the shortage of priests. In June 1911, one was completed in Sifton, Manitoba, under the direction of Father Sabourin.[97]

The *Register* also carried stories about Church Extension's support of St. Josephat Ukrainian Catholic School in Edmonton, which was run by Ukrainian nuns. Father Burke enjoyed publishing a sampling of student thank-you letters. Luvonka Gill, Pawlo Karpec, Krenia Chomtak, Hania Simituk, Mary Chomlak, Ksenia Chomliak and John Tymoczko are the names of some of the students whose letters appeared in the paper.[98] They are touching in their simplicity and genuine in their gratitude.

Lastly, the *Register* published small stories about the Sisters of St. Joseph and the Loretto Sisters in Toronto producing Ukrainian Catholic vestments.[99] It must have been quite a novelty for them. Ukrainian Catholic priests and their congregations gratefully acknowledged receipt of these vestments,[100] but Father Burke early on realized that only a more organized effort under the auspices of Church Extension would be able to produce the quantity of Church goods and literature so desperately needed not only by Ukrainian Catholic missionaries in the West, but also by Catholic missionaries throughout Canada. Thus was born the Women's Auxiliary of the Catholic Church Extension Society of Canada, in 1910. The women made sure that the work went on.

CHAPTER 7

THE WOMEN'S AUXILIARY OF TORONTO, 1910–1915

N ear the end of what would be his final year-end report to the board of governors of the Catholic Church Extension Society, on 26 April 1915, Father Alfred E. Burke rhapsodized about the work of the Women's Auxiliary of Church Extension. He wrote:

> If the Catholic Church Extension Society of Canada had done nothing else outside of the establishment of the Women's Auxiliary, it would have justified its existence. What has been accomplished through the heroic self sacrifice of a few Catholic ladies in Toronto is shown in the report presented by the President of the Auxiliary, Miss M. Hoskin. The financial report is splendid but when we add to that the labour and energy expended by these good ladies on behalf of the poor missions we have a result, than which there is none grander in the field of Catholic endeavour in Canada.[1]

These were not words of empty praise. On the verge of having to forfeit his position as founding president of Church Extension and editor-in-chief of the *Catholic Register*, his two greatest achievements, Father Burke was genuinely grateful for the missionary work of the

Women's Auxiliary. The world that he had so carefully constructed and nourished by the force of his personality and the power of his pen was quickly crumbling. But, as he was about to depart, he could look with fondness upon the Auxiliary and give thanks to this small band of dedicated and dependable women who quickly became indispensable to the fulfillment of Extension's mandate in providing spiritual and material support to the missions in Canada and, more specifically, to Catholic immigrants. The Auxiliary proved that with very little money, many good and lasting works were possible. They also proved that given a modicum of freedom within priest-centred Church structures, they could fashion their own distinct identity and dynamic as a community of parish-based Catholic women working in union with that rarest of creatures in the Canadian Church: a national Catholic organization. "The Catholic women of Canada," wrote the Women's Auxiliary columnist for the *Register* in 1911, "have put their hands to the plough; this is the first instance in the history of this country that they have banded together for missionary purposes."[2]

This is what made the Auxiliary unique. It was not just another version of an altar society, a lend-a-hand society, a sodality, a pious association or a confraternity, as valuable as these were to Catholic life in countless parishes across the country. It was hoped that the branches of the Women's Auxiliary would collectively invigorate the charitable life of the Canadian Church to a degree not imagined prior to the establishment of Church Extension in 1908. It was also hoped that the Women's Auxiliary would become a powerhouse of mission work in the Canadian Church as its parent organization, Church Extension, was gaining support in the number of bishops willing to champion its mandate and broadened its rank-and-file membership (and readership of the *Register*) to include Catholics in every part of the country.

Although Father Burke referred to "a few ladies in Toronto," and was correct to use the word "few" to describe their number, the Women's Auxiliary did not originate in the Archdiocese of Toronto, as one might suspect. Rather, it first came to life in the Diocese of St. Albert in Alberta. Bishop Émile-Joseph Legal, OMI, a governor of Church Extension and a regular contributor to the *Register*, informed

Father Burke in a letter that he had given a free hand to a Mrs. Robert Kneil and her two sisters, Katherine and Cornelia Hughes, to organize a Women's Auxiliary Society in Edmonton.[3] (This was the same Katherine Hughes who founded the first branch of the Catholic Women's League in Canada, in 1912, also at the behest of Bishop Legal.[4]) The inaugural meeting was held at a convent on 25 April 1910, and within a few days, the Edmonton Auxiliary was operating a night school for Ukrainian Catholic girls.[5]

A second branch was formed in Calgary on 9 May 1910 (Calgary belonged to the Diocese of St. Albert until 1913). On the advice of Mrs. Kneil, who was invited to attend, the women elected a slate of officers – president, vice-president, treasurer and secretary – and appointed members to four standing committees: to conduct a night school for Catholic girls, especially foreigners; to watch out for and "render service to needy and unprotected Catholic girls, to visit hotels, hospitals, and keep in touch with friendless girls"; to make altar linens for missionary priests; and to collect clothes and pack them for shipment to needy missions.[6] Calgary's administrative and committee structure became the basic model for all subsequent Auxiliary branches. A record of Calgary's monthly meetings from 1910 to 1916 reveal the modest ambitions and plain hard work of a group of like-minded Catholic women selflessly devoted to Church Extension.[7] The Calgary and Edmonton branches occasionally submitted reports for publication in the *Register*,[8] and Mrs. Kneil even spoke to the Women's Auxiliary in Toronto, on 7 June 1911, as part of an Ontario tour. She tried but failed to establish Auxiliary branches in Ottawa and Montréal (in each case, the archbishop was absent from the city), but she found an attentive audience of committed women in Toronto.[9] Later that same summer, she was in Vancouver trying to persuade the lend-a-hand societies to join the Women's Auxiliary of Church Extension.[10]

Father Burke understood the practical genius of having a Women's Auxiliary as an arm of Church Extension, to counter the well-funded and very active women's auxiliaries of the various Protestant missionary societies. At the same time, he wanted Church Extension to have oversight, if not outright control, of the auxiliary's work. There were to be no autocephalous auxiliaries. Clerical authority administered through Church Extension was, for him, of paramount importance. In the same editorial in which Burke enthusiastically reported the founding of the Edmonton Women's Auxiliary, he wrote:

> We shall welcome the establishment of Extension Auxiliaries everywhere among the ladies – nowhere more gladly than in Winnipeg – but we want to keep the run of this work and we want those who engage in it to earn the spiritual favors which the Holy See has attached to any act done for the forwarding of the works and interests of Canadian Catholic Extension.
>
> Besides, we cannot hope that any great movement of permanency will eventuate from local organizations working under their own charter, even with local Episcopal approval and the favor of pastors immediately concerned. The elements of permanency are not there. We need the great Society with its charter and privileges from Rome, with its act of incorporation from Ottawa, with its favors spiritual and business facilities, to do the great work of caring for the missions of Canada generally, and we have that Society in Catholic Church Extension. We will be glad to show the ladies at any time how they may make this particular branch a success. We will forward them the necessary literature and they can all be workers in the blessed cause with the surest prospects of doing something which is worthy and lasting and with the Holy Father's completest approbation.[11]

To modern ears, this all sounds very condescending and more than a bit ham-handed on Father Burke's part. He saw a good and wonderful thing, an enormous potential, and he wanted the Society to control it. He even wanted members to wear special badges. It is very doubtful, however, that the president of Church Extension, or, for that matter, any member of the board of governors or of the board's executive committee, could teach Catholic women a thing about the women's work that the Women's Auxiliary was expected to do – mainly sewing and repairing altar linens and vestments for poor missionary priests.[12] To his credit, Father Burke regularly attended the Toronto Auxiliary's

Supreme Council monthly meetings, and occasionally those of its parish sub-councils. Sometimes he brought with him guest speakers, such as Father Joseph Roche, who regaled the women with stories of his world travels, and Father James B. Dollard, who recited his poetry and spoke about Irish songs. Despite all his initial bluster about the need for clerical control, however, Father Burke was essentially an outsider to the corporate life and charitable endeavours of the Toronto Auxiliary. And that was fine with him. He sincerely appreciated the Auxiliary's substantial work and their rock-solid loyalty to Church Extension. He wisely left them to their business and gave them a weekly column in the *Register*, where they could report on the fruits of their labours and air their opinions and criticisms.

It was Father Burke's second editorial on the Women's Auxiliary that set the tone and direction for the subsequent formation of a Women's Auxiliary in Toronto. He may have thought that Winnipeg would follow Edmonton and Calgary, but it was Toronto that became not only the next Auxiliary but also the Auxiliary standard-bearer. He wrote:

> It is the women themselves who have gone ahead and have conquered our own timidity. We feel sure, too, that the other members of the Hierarchy in Western Canada [in addition to Bishop Legal] will bless and approve this new undertaking. These women will set the West aflame with zeal for mission undertakings of every kind. The priests of Canada know what the women of their parishes are capable of doing. They have before them the striking examples of what has been accomplished by non-Catholic women in the missionary field, and they realize that our women as a whole have been waiting and longing for an opportunity of this kind. His Grace Archbishop McEvay, the Chairman of the Society's Board of Governors, has looked forward from the beginning to the hour when the Women's Auxiliary should have a part in the work of Extension, and no one is more rejoiced than he is to see at last, that it is not only a possibility but a reality.[13]

The Women's Auxiliary in Toronto was established sometime in April 1910, according to the recollections of its members.[14] Perhaps this was an official date to coincide with the founding of the Edmonton Auxiliary. More likely, the Toronto Auxiliary was not up and running until May or June at the earliest. (In any event, it preceded the establishment of the Women's Auxiliary of the Catholic Church Extension Society in the United States by at least nineteen months.)[15] The *Register* reported on a meeting of the Auxiliary on 21 July 1910, in St. Peter's Hall (St. Peter's parish), on Bathurst Street.[16] Father Burke attended and read a letter from Father Noel Decamps, C.Ss.R., in which the Redemptorist thanked the Society (but, curiously, not the Auxiliary) for the set of Ukrainian vestments that had recently arrived. Also mentioned in the same story were the Watch-Out Committee and the Vestment Committee. Mrs. J.E. (Amy) Day headed the Watch-Out Committee.[17] It was commissioned to raise funds for a boarding house for Catholic girls and young women working in Toronto whose wages were insufficient for them to afford decent rooms and a safe place to live. The Vestment Committee assigned itself the task of sewing vestments for Ukrainian missions.

The inaugural president was Margaret "Grettie" Mallon. The daughter of John Mallon and Ellen Woods Mallon, Margaret was born on 2 April 1869 in Toronto, where she lived her entire life. She was the aunt of the four Mallon brothers – Hugh, Paul, Gregory and Francis – who became Basilian priests, and in December 1911 she hosted an entertainment in support of the Auxiliary at their parents' home on Spadina Heights.[18] She remained president of the Auxiliary until March 1912, when ill health forced her to resign. She later rejoined the Supreme Council as vice-president. Margaret Mallon died on 27 January 1930 and was buried with her many relatives in the Mallon plot in St. Michael's Cemetery.[19]

The second president was Mary Hoskin. She remained in that office for sixteen years. If the Women's Auxiliary needed a forceful and imaginative personality, a woman who was not too shy to beg for money, time and time again, and not too reserved to demand loyalty, constancy and hard work from its members, it was this English immigrant and convert to Catholicism. Of the hundreds of women involved in the Auxiliary during its first five years, no one did more than Mary

Hoskin to carry it past its initial enthusiasm and to set it on a firm foundation and a course of diligent and effective missionary work in conjunction with Church Extension. Along with being president from 1912 to 1928, she was president of the St. Basil's sub-council and the "Dorothy" who wrote and edited the weekly Women's Auxiliary column in the *Register*.

In her role as "Dorothy," Hoskin revealed a capacity for independence, assertiveness and shrewdness that was unique for the head of a women's group in the Church at the time. She took full advantage of the opportunity given her to comment on a wide variety of issues and topics: from the 1910 Apostolic Brief, *Allata nuper ad nos*, by which Pius X constituted the Catholic Church Extension Society[20] to the "woman movement";[21] from the need for more money and members[22] to detailed sewing instruction for altar linens, albs and surplices;[23] from the plight of immigrant women in the city[24] to letters from Ukrainian children;[25] from bearding Bishop Pascal, who thanked Father Burke instead of the Auxiliary for the Christmas toys that the children in his diocese had received,[26] to blasting an anonymous critic who thought that sending toys was a waste of time and effort.[27] Hoskin was constantly rallying her troops and exhorting them to carry on their work. In an editorial titled "Let Us Not Grow Weary,"[28] she quoted St. Paul's Letter to the Galatians, 6:9-10: "And in doing good, let us not weary, for in due time we shall reap, if we faint not. Therefore, whilst we have time, let us work good to all men but especially to those who are of the household of faith." Mary Hoskin was one member of the Women's Auxiliary who never grew weary.

Born in 1849 in Devon, England, Mary Hoskin came to Canada with her parents and brothers when she was seven years old. After four years in Bowmanville, Ontario, the family moved to Toronto. While still a Protestant, she was sent to finish her schooling at an Ursuline convent in Québec. She entered the Church on 13 July 1867, when she was eighteen years old.[29] The following year, having joined her family in Toronto, she thought that she had a vocation to join the Sisters of the Precious Blood, a cloistered community then living in a small house at the corner of St. Joseph Street and Bay Street, a stone's throw from St. Basil's Church. Father Charles Vincent, a Basilian priest, dissuaded her. The French-speaking Father Vincent wore many hats. He was superior of St. Michael's College, pastor of St. Basil's church and confessor for the Sisters of the Precious Blood. In this latter capacity, his opinion concerning Hoskin's vocation would have had great weight in the Precious Blood community.

At the same time, though, the Sisters did not want to lose Hoskin, and so persuaded her to live with them and be their ally and advocate in the outside world, so to speak. She accepted the Sisters' invitation and moved into two small rooms, effectively becoming an honorary member of the cloister. It was a relationship that was to last for forty years. During that time, she enjoyed the privilege of going in and out of the cloister as she saw fit and never lived anywhere else for the rest of her life. A woman of astute business sense, and perhaps blessed with a private income, for she never seems to have worked for a living, Hoskin was able to raise enough money to purchase the building at 113 St. Joseph Street for a newer and larger monastery for the Sisters and to dispose of the old one for a profit.

At the time of her death on 17 July 1928, at the age of seventy-eight years, Hoskin was a scion of St. Basil's parish[30] and only the second woman in Canada to have been awarded the cross Pro Ecclesia et Pontifice.[31] She was buried in the company of her good friends the Precious Blood Sisters at Mount Hope Cemetery.[32] In 1930, the Women's Auxiliary sponsored the "Mary Hoskin Memorial Chapel."

Mary Hoskin took up the reins of the presidency on 10 April 1912. In her acceptance speech, which was published in the *Register*, she put forth her patriotic and theological understanding of the work of the Women's Auxiliary:

> You have chosen me for your President, whether wisely or not remains to be seen. I have accepted the office with many misgivings, but I promise to try to do my duty, and I am sure you will all help me. Alone, I can accomplish nothing, a head without hands and feet; is useless, as also are hands and feet without a head. Together, I hope we shall do great things for

the Church in Canada. I trust that we shall always work in perfect harmony.

As true Canadians, and loyal subjects of Great Britain, our endeavors should be to do what will be for the greatest good of our country. We have faith in Canada, we know she is destined to become, one day, the finest country in the world, who ever may live to see it. Our care, then, should be to see that the true faith be planted in those new parts now being opened to civilization, our hope should be that future generations may find Canada a Catholic country, as she ought to be, having been first discovered and civilized by true sons of the Church. My message is this: I want you to let this thought sink deep into your hearts. All our work is for the salvation of souls. Whether we are making or repairing vestments or linens for the altar, or teaching poor foreigners the language of the country; whether we are saving our mites to build mission chapels, or visiting the sick in the hospitals, whether we are dressing dolls, making toys or flowers, or helping some poor girl to help herself, or even gathering in second-hand clothing, we are doing God's work, we are exercising an Apostolate, and we should thank God Who has done us the favor to allow us to be associated, in however remote a degree, in the salvation of souls. It is an honor, my friends, to be chosen to work for God. Let this thought encourage us when we are tempted to grow tired, when disappointments come, as come they will. Let us brace ourselves up, and say, the salvation of some poor soul depends on my work today.[33]

For Mary Hoskin there was also a scriptural model for the Women's Auxiliary. That model was Tabitha, more commonly known by the Greek equivalent of her name, Dorcas, which means "gazelle." She appears in the Acts of the Apostles 9:36-45. A convert, Dorcas was known for her "constant good deeds and acts of charity." Shortly after her death in Joppa, the local Christian community called for Peter, who was in nearby Lydda, and he came immediately. "All the widows came to him in tears and showed him the various garments Dorcas had made when she was still with them." Moved by their love for her,

Peter raised her from the dead. It was a miracle that persuaded many people in Joppa to join the Church. The reader of this passage is left to assume that Dorcas continued her life of good works.

In her first "Dorothy" column, Hoskin expounded on the virtues of Dorcas, tying them to the current challenge facing Canadian Catholic women. She wrote that ever since Dorcas and the Christian community of Apostolic times, "women have done their share of the material work so necessary to the proper and orderly execution of the spiritual work of the Church."[34] It was now the second decade of the twentieth century. The call remained the same. "Catholic women of Canada, let us not neglect this call, a duty rests upon us to do our share of missionary work, to provide those things which are necessary to the missionary in the sacred office, also for his maintenance while he is engaged in God's work."[35] Hoskin repeated her message in a spirited address to the delegates at the Second American Catholic Missionary Congress in Boston, in October 1913.[36]

During the first five years of the Women's Auxiliary in Toronto, its membership under the presidencies of Margaret Mallon and Mary Hoskin achieved six major things: a written Constitution and By-Laws, which were revised in 1912; the purchase and management of Rosary Hall; the construction of four mission chapels; the purchase and management of St. Philip Neri Hostel; the production and collection of a wide range of church goods; and the collection and timely distribution of thousands of Christmas toys and books. In Toronto, the Auxiliary was also involved in hospital visitations, the Mercer Reformatory for Women, and night schools for immigrants at St. Mary's and St. Helen's separate schools. They conducted the night schools with the assistance of the St. Vincent de Paul Society and the co-operation of the Toronto Separate School Board.[37] Given that only five of the forty-five parishes then comprising the Archdiocese of Toronto sponsored parish sub-councils – St. Peter, St. Helen, St. Anthony and St. Mary (1910) and St. Basil (1912) – and that consequently the number of members at any given time likely did not exceed 450, substantial credit is due to these Catholic women, the loyal foot soldiers of Church Extension, for accomplishing so much of value in such a brief period of time, and in a way that ensured that their work would carry on long after the first generation of volunteers had finished their work.[38]

••••

A very detailed Constitution and By-Laws were published in two installments in the *Register* in November 1910. Significant revisions were made in April 1912.[39] Since the original Constitution and By-Laws resembled, to a degree, the general structure of those of Church Extension itself, Father Burke probably authored them. The 1910 Constitution was divided into six articles:

Article 1: Name
Article 2: Object, Aims and Purposes
Article 3: Membership
Article 4: Administration
Article 5: Officers
Article 6: Change of the Constitution

Article 1: Name. The name was the Women's Auxiliary of the Catholic Church Extension Society of Canada. The absence of any mention of the Archdiocese of Toronto implied that this was a national society or council to which all other councils or branches of the Women's Auxiliary, regardless of their location or date of formation, were subordinate. Toronto was certainly the national headquarters of the Women's Auxiliary. It was the location of the General (later Supreme) Council and was duly acknowledged as such by other councils. But during the Auxiliary's first five years, the Edmonton and Calgary councils conducted their business outside the direct administrative control of the Supreme Council in Toronto, and moreover were later absorbed into the Catholic Women's League (CWL) and functioned as committees of the CWL. It took until November 1915 for the Supreme Council to establish on its own initiative a branch of the Auxiliary outside of Toronto. This was St. Patrick's Council in Montréal. In the meantime, the Supreme Council's jurisdiction was effectively limited to the five subordinate councils in Toronto.

Article 2: Object, Aims and Purposes. The Women's Auxiliary was organized to co-operate with the work of Church Extension in Canada. Its primary objects were five in number:

(a) To aid in the work of erecting little Mission Chapels.

(b) To help priests laboring in poor places.

(c) To establish and support wherever necessary Catholic schools, particularly for newly arrived immigrants.

(d) To organize agencies having for their purpose the education and instruction of neglected children and adults, and the safeguarding of their Faith along lines approved by the proper Ecclesiastical authorities.

(e) To foster and extend in every possible way a more widespread interest in Home Mission activity of every kind, not only through the distribution of literature, but through every other legitimate means whereby the Catholic people can be brought to the realization of their duty to their neglected brethren of the faith.[40]

The 1912 changes to Article 2 included an additional clause to (b): "To make and repair vestments, linens for the altar, albs and surplices."[41] This reflected the fact that the women were spending a great deal of their time, energy and money in this particular work. Added was a sixth article, (f): "To encourage the circulation of Register-Extension [*Catholic Register*], the official organ of the Catholic Church Extension Society of Canada." This may have been done at the behest of Father Burke, who was always anxious to increase the circulation of the *Register* as a means to justify the Society's ownership of the paper. Of the six Objects, the Women's Auxiliary fulfilled (a) the erection of Mission Chapels, although not to the degree one might suspect due to the relative poverty of its members, and the revised (b), in particular, the production of vestments, altar linens, albs and surplices. The women excelled at this work. The Auxiliary never established any schools or agencies, as described in (c) and (d). It struggled against rather formidable odds to maintain night schools in Toronto, but several of its members, on their own initiative, sponsored the education of young boys in the Ukrainian convent in Edmonton.[42] The collection and distribution of toys, children's literature and used clothing were the main means by which they met the goals of (e).

Article 3: Membership. There were four classes of membership: Founders ($500), Life ($100), Fifteen Year ($10) and Annual (one dollar per year). Those who donated an additional twenty-five cents a year received a year's subscription to the *Catholic Register*. The 1912 revisions substantially lowered the cost of membership for Founders ($100) and Life Members ($25), maintained the rates for Fifteen Year Members and Annual Members, and eliminated the twenty-five cent subscription.

Article 4: Administration. This called for a Board of Governors to be comprised of fifteen women. They were Lady Fitzpatrick (wife of Sir Charles Fitzpatrick), Mrs. Robert Kneil, Miss Katherine Hughes, Mrs. P.J. Nolan, Mrs. Costigan, Mrs. C. Rochereau de la Sablière, Mrs. Morin, Mrs. Rouleau, Mrs. D.T. Lynn, Mrs. Patrick Shea, Miss M. Foy, Miss M. Hoskin, Miss Mary O'Brien, Mrs. Jno. Maloney and Miss Margaret Mallon.[43] This reads like a who's who of prominent Catholic women from Ottawa, Edmonton, Toronto and perhaps other cities. The list even included the names of several French Canadians. But the board may have been nothing more than fancy window dressing. There is no record that it ever met. The 1912 revisions eliminated Article 4 and any other mention of the board, placing the daily governance of the Auxiliary in the hands of its Officers.

Article 5: Officers. The Officers were the chairman of the board, the president, vice-president, general secretary and treasurer. The members of the Auxiliary would elect, on an annual basis, the chairman of the board, the vice-president and the treasurer; the board of governors would elect a president for a two-year term; and the president would appoint the general secretary and any assistant secretaries. The 1912 revisions streamlined the election of officers, added the president of Church Extension to the roster of officers, and inserted a section on committee conveners.

> The officers of this Society shall consist of the President of the Catholic Church Extension Society, a President, a Vice-President, a General Secretary, and a Treasurer.

These officers, excepting the President of the Catholic Church Extension Society, shall be elected by the vote of the majority at the annual meeting, and shall hold office for the term of two years.

Assistant Secretaries may be appointed when necessary.

Conveners – Committees shall be formed to carry on the various works as stated in Article 2. Each Committee shall have a Convener, whose duty it shall be to regulate the work of the Committee.[44]

Article 6: Change of the Constitution. Any changes had to be approved by a two-thirds vote of the board of governors and the president of Church Extension. Having dropped the board of governors, the revision also made changes to the Constitution (and, one assumes, also to the By-Laws) subject to a two-thirds vote of the members and the approval of the president of Church Extension.

The By-Laws provided detailed descriptions of the functions and responsibilities of chairman of the board, president, vice-president, treasurer, auditors, temporary chairman of the board, subordinate councils and delegates to the annual meeting. It also gave instructions on the appropriate disbursal of funds and designated gifts collected by the Auxiliary, including *this* directive – fifty percent of the membership dues were to be forwarded to the president of Church Extension.[45] The revised By-Laws of 1912 made no reference to a board of governors or auditors and substantially changed the section on Funds in order to give the Auxiliary more autonomy in its work. All dues collected by the Auxiliary were to remain in its hands:

> The funds of the Society are to be employed in purchasing the material for vestments, altar linens, etc., for the erection of Mission Chapels, and any home missionary work that may be voted upon by a majority at a monthly meeting. The annual fees paid in by members of Subordinate Councils are to be given to the Treasurer of the Supreme Council, unless in particular cases the Supreme Council decide otherwise.[46]

Father Alfred E. Burke
a founder and first president of the Catholic Church Extension Society (CCES)
(Catholic Missions in Canada)

Father Francis C. Kelley
as a young priest; a founder of CCES
(Archives of the Archdiocese of Oklahoma City)

Archbishop Fergus Patrick McEvay of Toronto
a founder and first chancellor of CCES
(ARCAT Ph07-04P)

Rt. Hon. Sir Charles Fitzpatrick, KCMG
Chief Justice of the Supreme Court of Canada and a founder of CCES
(LAC C-030726)

HIS HOLINESS POPE PIUS X.
Confers the Apostolic Benediction, and sends his Delegate
Apostolic to the United States as a Special Representative to the
First American Catholic Missionary Congress.

Pope Pius X
(Francis C. Kelley, *First American
Catholic Missionary Congress* [Chicago:1909])

Archbishop Donato Sbarretti, OFM
Apostolic Delegate to Canada; a founder of CCES
(Francis C. Kelley, *The First American
Catholic Missionary Congress* [Chicago:1909])

Archbishop Alfred Arthur Sinnott of Winnipeg
secretary to the Apostolic Delegate and a founder of CCES
(Archives of the Archdiocese of Winnipeg)

Left to Right: Bishop Thomas J. Dowling of Hamilton;
Archbishop Donato Sbarretti, OFM, Apostolic Delegate;
and Archbishop Fergus Patrick McEvay of Toronto
(Catholic Missions in Canada)

Bishop John Thomas Kidd of Calgary
a founder of CCES
(ARCAT PH26 rectors 3-2)

Bishop Albert Pascal, OMI, of Prince Albert, Saskatchewan
(Archives of the Diocese of Prince Albert)

Bishop Émile-Joseph Legal, OMI, of St. Alberta, Alberta
(Missionary Oblates, Grandin Collection
at the Provincial Archives of Alberta OB 3272)

Father Joseph T. Roche
(Father Francis C. Kelley, *The First American
Catholic Missionary Congress* [Chicago: 1909])

Bishop Nykyta Budka
First Ukrainian Catholic Bishop in Canada;
CCES sponsored his passage from Europe to Canada.
(Ukrainian Catholic Archeparchy of Winnipeg Archives NB2151)

Metropolitan Andrey Sheptytsky of Lviv, Galicia (Ukraine)
His first visit to Canada, in 1910, was widely reported in the *Catholic Register*.
(Ukrainian Catholic Archeparchy of Winnipeg Archives 12.14.12)

Archbishop Adélard Langevin, OMI, of St. Boniface, Manitoba
(Collection générale de la Société historique de Saint-Boniface SHSB 336)

Archbishop Adélard Langevin, OMI, with four members of the
Ukrainian Sisters Servants of Mary Immaculate (SSMI).
Seated left to right: Sister Taida Wrublevsky, Archbishop Langevin
and Sister Ambrosia Lenkevich. *Standing left to right*:
Sister Emilia Kalpoushok and Sister Isidora Shipovsky
(Basilian Fathers Museum, Mundane, Alberta)

Judge Nicholas Beck
member of the CCES board of governors
(Provincial Archives of Alberta J. 312/2)

George C.H. Lang
member of the CCES board of governors
(Courtesy of the Waterloo Historical Society)

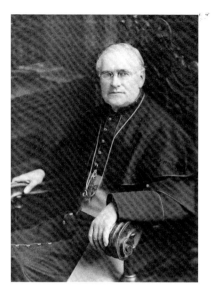

Archbishop Neil McNeil of Toronto
second chancellor of CCES
(ARCAT PH08-03P)

HIS EMINENCE RAPHAEL CARDINAL MERRY DEL VAL.
Secretary of State to His Holiness Pope Pius X.

Cardinal Raphael Merry del Val
secretary of state, the Holy See
(Francis C. Kelley, *The First American
Catholic Missionary Congress* [Chicago:1909])

Father Sozont Dydyk, OSBM
(*Pioneer Bishop: The Story of Nicetas Budka's
Fifteen Years in Canada* [Sask:1990])

Father Achiel Delaere, C.S.s.R.
(Archives of the Edmonton-Toronto Redemptorist Province)

Father Platonidas Filia, OSBM
(*Pioneer Bishop: The Story of Nicetas Budka's
Fifteen Years in Canada* [Sask:1990])

Father Alphonsus Jan, OMI
(Francis C. Kelley, *The First American
Catholic Missionary Congress* [Chicago:1909])

PHONE MAIN 489

CATHOLIC REGISTER AND CANADIAN EXTENSION

PUBLISHED BY

THE CATHOLIC CHURCH EXTENSION SOCIETY
OF CANADA

EXECUTIVE BOARD
MOST REV. F. P. McEVAY, Archbishop of Toronto.
RT. HON. SIR CHARLES FITZPATRICK, Chief Justice of Canada
REV. A. E. BURKE, D.D., LL.D., President of the Society.

119 WELLINGTON ST.W.

OFFICE OF THE PRESIDENT

TORONTO, CANADA

April 23rd. 10. 19

Rt.Rev.E.J.Legal D.D.
Bishop of St.Albert.
St.Albert. Alta.

My Dear Lord,

Before the other things which I wrote you
about have reached us,I feel that we must forward the sum
previously named to help out your necessities there,viz:-
$1500. A cheque for this amount is therefore enclosed. I
think,according to the list,that this amount would best be
distributed as follows,viz:-

Rev.C.Desmaris,Athabasca Landing,Alta........$50.00
Rev.Father Lecomte,Castor Alta...............$100.00
Rev.A.Claremont,Brosseau,Alta................$200.00
Ruthenian Church at Vegreville...............$500.00
Rev.A.L.Forner,Provost,Alta. (loan at 4%)....$500.00
Rev.F.Meyer,Warner Alta......................$150.00

However I leave this altogether to your
Lordships discretion,although I would like those parishes
which have been writing,and whose claims have been filed
here,if approved by you,to get this much assistance. The
parishes which may be likely to pay back,and which you know
better than I do,can do so at four per cent,interest,and half
of the grant,if you think well of it,need not bear interest.

With regard to the Ruthenian School at
Edmonton,a plan was forwarded to me by one of the Fathers,
whereby,if we were to give $1000.,they would be able to
finance the other $6000.,necessary to put up the school with.
Our Board thought that we could not very well go into Convent
building,especially with so many poor churches all over Canada,
and if we did,we could not give more than $500.00,to any one
building,this amount being also the limit of the United States
Society. Of course I know the circumstances in Edmonton
are exceptional,and I would be glad to work out some plan
with your Lordship,if you think it judicious to go on with it.

As you will see,some of the smaller
amounts enumerated above,will necessarily have to be gifts,
but I expect a detailed list from your Lordship,when I will
forward the forms to be filled out,to the satisfaction of the
Society.

Hoping that your Lordship,is very well,
and that all this will be satisfactory to you, I remain,

Faithfully yours in Christ,

A.E.Burke

President.

THE CATHOLIC CHURCH EXTENSION SOCIETY OF CANADA.

Father A.E. Burke to Bishop Émile-Joseph Legal, OMI, 23 April 1910,
outlining donations from CCES to the Diocese of St. Albert.
(Archdiocese of Edmonton Archives 1.6.19B)

CCES-sponsored chapel at Brooksby, Diocese of Prince Albert.
(Archives of the Diocese of Prince Albert)

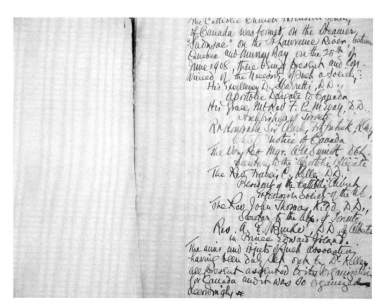

Opening Page of the *Minute Book of the Catholic Church
Extension Society of Canada*, dated 25 June 1908.
In Father Burke's handwriting.
(Church Extension Archives)

PIVS PP. X

Venerabilis Frater, salutem et aplicam benedictionem. Allata nuper ad Nos nuncia de constitutione et gestis frugiferae illius Associationis, quae duobus abhinc annis erecta fuit in hac civitate tua Torontina sub eodem titulo atque illa quae extat Chicagi in Foederatis Civitatibus Americae Septentrionalis, nempe: "The Catholic Church extension Society,, eundemque contendens ad finem tutandae ac provehendae fidei Catholicae in Canadensis Dominii territoriis, jucunda sane Nobis et gratissima extiterunt. Nec sine magna laetitia novimus explicita et gravia suffragia, quibus Venerabiles Antistites Dioecesium Dominii eiusdem, non minus quam amplissimi viri tum ecclesiastici, tum laici, unanimi consensione institutionem hanc vestram luculento laudis praeconio prosequuntur, praestantissima comme

First page of the Apostolic Brief "Allata nuper ad nos,"
9 June 1910, recognizing CCES as a Pontifical Society.
Signed by Cardinal Merry del Val.
(ARCAT ME RC9307)

Ad Sanctitatem Suam

PIUM X.,

Pontificem Maximum, Universalis Ecclesiae Pastorem.

Beatissime Pater:

Societatis diffundendae rei Catholicae in foederatis provinciis Canadensibus orta, cum brevi robustis viribus adolevisset, a Vestra Sanctitate per litteras die 3 Decembris anno 1908 ad admodum reverendum virum Patritium Fergum McEvay Archiepiscopum Torontinum datas benigne approbata est. Cuius Societatis Collegium Rectorum sese ad pedes Vestrae Sanctitatis proiiciunt rogantes atque orantes ut Societas "canonicum" institutum fiat eiusque constitutiones Apostolica auctoritate approbentur. Quae quidem constitutiones, suo quaeque ordine et loco dispositae ut Vestris, quae sciamus, optatis quam maxime respondeant, proximis comitiis die 22 Iunii anno 1909 habitis, Collegium extra ordinem coegimus, quod plenam haberet potestatem hunc libellum componendi compositumque pro omnibus nostris sodalibus porrigendi et mutandi, quodcunque Vestra Sanctitas pro Vestra sapientia temperandum esse censuisset.

Ad pedes Sanctitatis Vestrae humillime provoluti.

[signature] Fergus Patritius M'Evay

[signature] Archiepis Torontinus

Cancellarius.

[signature] Alfredus E. Burke, S.T.D.,

Praeses.

[signature] Joannes T. Kidd

Librarius a Secretis.

[signature] Fergus Patritius M'Evay.

[signature] Charles Fitzpatrick

[signature] Alfredus E. Burke, S.T.D.,

Administratorum Collegium.

First page of the much-disputed Latin or Roman Constitution of the CCES. It was drawn up by Father Burke and approved by Church Extension's Board of Governors on 6 April 1910. It was signed by Archbishop Fergus McEvay, Chancellor; A.E. Burke, President; and John Thomas Kidd, Secretary. It was then signed by the Executive Committee: McEvay, Sir Charles Fitzpatrick and Burke.

(ARCAT OC07.HI02)

Following the second annual meeting of the Women's Auxiliary, on 10 April 1912, the Auxiliary published a complete organizational chart. Officers of the Supreme Council were Mary Hoskin, president; Miss Dwyer, vice-president; Miss Breen, secretary; and Miss J. Collins, treasurer. The Supreme Council was akin to an executive committee and met on the first Wednesday of each month. Their meetings were regularly covered in the Women's Auxiliary column in the *Register*. Committee conveners were Miss Dwyer, vestments; Mrs. Lamburn, altar linens; Mrs. Fulton, hospital visitation; Miss Soucie, teaching (night school); Mrs. Armstrong, toys; Mrs. Cassidy, clothing; Mrs. Ferry, flowers; and Mrs. Amy Day, Rosary Hall Association. The conveners were expected to attend the monthly meetings and report on the activities of their respective committees. Presidents of the subordinate councils were Mrs. W.J. Herod of St. Helen's; Miss Dwyer of St. Peter's; Mrs. Mackay of St. Anthony's; Mrs. D.J. Ryan of St. Mary's; and Mary Hoskin of St. Basil's. Each subordinate council had its own conveners and monthly meetings, which were also regularly covered by the *Register*. St. Peter's subordinate council was the most active, and Father Lancelot Minehan, the parish priest, was very supportive.[47]

•••

The establishment of Rosary Hall in Toronto is a peculiar chapter in the early history of the Women's Auxiliary. It was really Amy Day's project. She had the personality, the wealth and the connections to the city's Catholic business community and political elite that made the Hall a sure thing at a time when the majority of Catholics had yet to gain entrance into the middle class. Her aim was "to provide a permanent house where Catholic girls coming to Toronto from a distance to earn their livelihood may find a comfortable and safe home."[48] Since Amy Day was one of the original members of the Auxiliary, Margaret Mallon, in her capacity as president, sponsored Day's work, and Mary Hoskin, the editor of the Auxiliary column in the *Register*, reported on every aspect of the Watch-Out Committee's progress, publishing no fewer than thirteen stories, from a first mention in July 1910 to the Hall's grand opening in December 1911.

That Day and her committee had the Hall purchased, renovated and open for business within eighteen months was nothing short of amazing. By early January 1911, they had subscriptions for $10,000, ranging in size from one dollar to $100.[49] This was extraordinary. To maintain their momentum, the Watch-Out Committee hosted an information meeting at Margaret Eaton Hall on 17 January 1911. Two hundred people came and listened to speeches by Amy Day, Dr. Amyot and Thomas Long. An Advisory Board of well-heeled Catholic men was established. Its members were Thomas Long, L. Cosgrove, Mr. Rochereau de la Sablière, W.P. Murray, R.P. Gough, T.P. Phelan, F. Hayes, J.J. Walsh, John F. Brown, L.V. Dusseau and A.C. Macdonnell.[50] They were expected to bring in the money, and they would not disappoint Amy Day. Contributing also were J.J. Seitz and Sir John Eaton.[51]

In April 1911, the members of the committee formed the Rosary Hall Association and received the support of Archbishop McEvay, who donated $500 of his own money.[52] In November they succeeded in securing a charter of incorporation from the Ontario government.[53] The association drew up a set of by-laws and established a board of directors while retaining its advisory board. Amy Day was president and Mrs. Cornish was treasurer.[54] The original intention was to raise the princely sum of $50,000 and with it construct a new building. In the end, the Rosary Hall Association and the Catholic businessmen who supported it were able to generate $20,000 in subscriptions, still a sizeable amount of money. With that money, the association purchased the Heardmore Estate at the corner of John Street and Grange Road for $15,000. The remaining funds were spent to improve the plumbing, wire the building for electricity, purchase furniture and hire a matron, cook, maid, occasional charwoman and furnace man. All debts were paid, and boarding fees were set at $3.50 to $5.00 per week, depending on the location of the room.[55] An additional feature was a Rest Room, the gift of Bertha Mackenzie. The fee for its use was set at $4.00 per week:

A room will be set apart and furnished with all that is necessary to make it comfortable and convenient for semi-invalids. Here young women will be received for a time, who, on leaving a hospital, are not yet strong enough to resume work, or those who are not well but are not so ill as to require to go to a hospital, and who will recover if they can have a season of rest. Patients received here are not supposed to require nursing, but merely rest and quiet, however, they are to be indulged to the extent of having their breakfast carried up to their room.[56]

Rosary Hall was officially opened on 8 December 1911, the Feast of the Immaculate Conception. Amy Day and Lady Falconbridge received almost a thousand visitors, including Lady Mackenzie, who provided $1,000 to furnish the rooms. The Women's Auxiliary column in the *Register* closed its story on the opening with these words:

> Rosary Hall is now fairly started and we wish it Godspeed. In a short while the accommodation will be altogether inadequate, and it is to be hoped that benefactors will come forward and build an addition.

> Mrs. Day and her Committee have worked untiringly ever since this burden was laid upon them by the Women's Auxiliary of the Extension Society, and they deserve praise, and, what will please them better, encouragement and help. A boarding house for Catholic young women earning their own living is much needed in Toronto, and these brave ladies who have started the project should have every assistance to keep it going; they have done their part, let the Catholic public do theirs.[57]

Although founded by a committee of the Women's Auxiliary, Rosary Hall was a legal entity unto itself and took on a corporate life of its own that was completely separate from the Auxiliary's regular work. The hall was an outstanding achievement, the brainchild of Toronto's Catholic women, but it never was an integral part of the Auxiliary's missionary mandate. Moreover, never again would a committee of the Auxiliary raise that kind of money for any purpose. Its members were as poor as church mice, as shown by their struggles to build and furnish mission chapels.[58]

••••

The building and equipping of mission chapels may have been the first object of the Women's Auxiliary, keeping in sync with the missionary work of Church Extension itself, but the Auxiliary did not open a chapel subscription list until 3 May 1911, and it took a year to collect $533.73. Members lived in a world of small sums and self-denial weeks, and they resorted to the distribution of a thousand mite boxes, the enlistment of schoolchildren and weekly tallies of monies collected as a way to remind the membership that failure to build mission chapels was not acceptable. It was all about chasing nickels.[59] There were few women among the Auxiliary's rank and file who could afford to pay the entire cost of a chapel and altar. Two Auxiliary women, however, eventually did come forward with the kind of big money that Catholic donors usually gave directly to Church Extension. Mrs. Patrick Hughes donated $557 for a chapel and altar and Mrs. Hannah Collins $1,200 for two chapels and two altars.[60]

St. Philip Neri Ruthenian Chapel opened on 21 September 1912, the Eastern Rite Feast of the Nativity of the Blessed Virgin Mary, in the Diocese of Regina. Father Noel Decamps, C.Ss.R., of Yorkton, was placed in charge of the mission church. The members of the Auxiliary not only paid for and named the chapel, but also purchased the altar and contributed the vestments, altar linens, veils, chalice, ciborium and monstrance, missal book and stand, furnishings and decorations.[61] It was a collective triumph. By 1915, the Women's Auxiliary had sponsored four more mission chapels, St. Peter's, St. Helen's and St. Anthony, named after three sub-councils, and St. Patrick's, which was donated by Mrs. Patrick Hughes of St. Basil's sub-council.[62]

••••

St. Philip Neri Hostel in Toronto was opened in May 1913 as a shelter for immigrant servant girls. Church Extension purchased the building and the Women's Auxiliary managed the hostel's daily operations. Father Burke first suggested the idea of assisting immigrant women at a meeting of the Supreme Council on 6 March 1912. It came at the end of his report on his audience with Pius X.[63] Mary Hoskin took the hint and wrote a strong editorial in support of his proposal. It was time for Catholic women to look after immigrant Catholic women:

We have been too apt in the past to think this question is no concern of ours; immigrants are pouring into the country, among them many Catholic young women, yet our sympathies have been asleep; we would not trouble ourselves to give the matter a thought.

Young women, mere girls, many of them, separated from their families, strangers in a strange land, with no one of their own faith to give them a welcome or guide them in their new sur-roundings, is it to be wondered at that in many cases they have wandered from the Fold?

It will be necessary eventually to have a temporary home where these women may be received and kept for a few days before being sent on to those who have engaged their service ....[64]

By July 1912, the Women's Auxiliary had been in contact with the Catholic Women's League of Britain.[65] Founded in 1906 by Margaret Fletcher (1862–1943), a convert to Catholicism, the CWL organized various immigration schemes on behalf of Catholic women and was anxious that host countries, such as Canada, be prepared to accept these women by providing modern and safe living quarters for them on arrival.[66] A Catholic hostel specifically devoted to the needs of newly arrived immigrant women was deemed the best and most af-fordable solution. During a visit to England in September 1912, Father Burke met with the leaders of the CWL. Impressed by the wide range of charitable work conducted by its 4,000 members, Burke listened to Margaret Fletcher when she insisted that it was the duty not of Church Extension but of the Women's Auxiliary to establish a proper hostel. Burke told the Auxiliary at its monthly meeting, on 2 October 1912, that Rosary Hall, with only thirty rooms, was not equipped to absorb immigrant women. The Hall had taken in two successive bands of women, but would not be able to sustain the work. Moreover, the care of immigrant women was not part of the Hall's mandate. A house would have to be found.[67] Within a week, the Auxiliary had already collected a table, two chairs and an assortment of dishes, and requested not only its members but also the general readership of the *Register* to scour their homes for tables, chairs, a kitchen stove, quilts, blankets, sheets and cutlery.[68]

It was a struggle. But by March 1913, Church Extension had purchased the Lane property at 251 Sherbourne Street, just above Wilton Avenue and below Allan Park. It was near Union Station and was on the Belt Line streetcar. A substantial brick mansion with an annex, it measured 63 feet by 200 feet and was large enough for forty-two rooms. Renovations cost $25,000 and included a new hot water system, up-to-date plumbing and electric light. Agnes Horgan was appointed the superintendent.[69] During its first full year, it turned a profit of $1,000, a sure sign that the hostel was in constant use.[70] However, it only lasted until 1916, the First World War having put a halt to immigration.[71]

• • • •

In its five-year report, 1911 to 1915, the Women's Auxiliary published a thorough review of its missionary work. On receipts totalling a modest $9,076.13, which included designated gifts for three chapels and five altars, the Auxiliary was able to produce and ship the following church goods, flowers, toys, cards and books:

> *Vestments*: 279 Latin Rite and 39 Ukrainian Rite, 19 Copes and 84 other articles. *Altar Linens*: 5,757. *Albs, Surplices and Altar Drapes*: 72 Albs, 77 Surplices and 43 Altar Drapes. *Tabernacle and Other Veils*: 373. *Flowers*: 285 bunches. *Toys*: 16,000. *Cards and Books*: 3,100.[72]

(Not included in the report were the numbers of bundles of used clothing collected and sent to the missions.)

This information appeared not only in the *Register* (the Auxiliary published a yearly summary of its receipts, expenditures and productivity), but also once, in 1915, in the "Minutes" of the Annual General Meeting of Church Extension.[73] This was Father Burke's doing, an essential part of his swan song.

Upon examination of the tenth- (1920) and twentieth- (1930) anniversary reports published by the Women's Auxiliary, it is reasonable to conclude that the basic organizational structure of the Auxiliary, and the type of mission work that its members so faithfully conducted, did not change substantially over time.[74] Its objects and aims and its model of service remained the same. Its membership grew, at one point reaching 700, and the number of its sub-councils increased, allowing it to raise and spend more money on mission work. But despite its most valiant efforts to broaden its appeal among Catholic women in Canada, the Women's Auxiliary was fated to remain a society of few hands doing much good for a great many.

CHAPTER 8

McEVAY, BURKE
AND THE FRENCH

T he death of Archbishop Fergus Patrick McEvay from pernicious anaemia, on 10 May 1911, was a huge disaster for Father Alfred E. Burke, president of Church Extension in Canada and editor-in-chief of the *Catholic Register*.[1] At fifty-eight years of age, McEvay was relatively young and had been archbishop of Toronto for just over three years. Almost from the beginning of his episcopacy, he had been Burke's patron and protector, giving him the freedom and independence to pursue a very different kind of clerical career: Burke had been incardinated priest of the archdiocese for a special task. It was a career that put the Prince Edward Island priest firmly on the national stage at a critical time in the history of Catholic immigration to the Canadian West, but it also aroused a noticeable degree of hostility towards him from other archdiocesan priests who resented his status as an outsider and upstart. McEvay may have been only ten years older than Burke, but there was something of a father–son relationship that held them together. This might explain the remarkable degree to which McEvay tolerated Burke's pretentious personality and penchant for delivering polarizing opinions, and the extraordinary loyalty that Burke showed McEvay right to the end. He was at McEvay's bedside when he died,[2] and he honoured his mentor with a heartfelt and praise-filled editorial in the *Register*.[3]

But as McEvay lay dying, Burke must have realized how vulnerable not only he but also Church Extension would be when the archbishop was no longer in the picture. The prospect of no McEvay at his side defending him left Burke desolate and desperate, prompting him to write a self-pitying letter to Father Kelley on 3 May 1911, eight days before McEvay's passing. In his reply, Kelley was having none of it:

> I received your letter of the 3rd inst. It certainly was a sorrowful production. You cannot go on conducting a paper, if you do not cheer up. I know perfectly well that you have much to worry you, under the circumstance. You will lose the best friend you ever had in the world when the Archbishop dies; but the Society has gotten to the point now where the death of one man will not make so much difference. It is canonically established and you hold your position from the Holy See. You have a good friend in Sinnott, and I am confident that everything is coming out right.
>
> I do not know what is going on up there [Toronto], of course; but on general principles, I know that the Archbishop will take care of you. It is his work as much as yours. There is no use getting down-hearted when there is no reason.[4]

It is curious that Kelley mentioned the name of Monsignor Arthur A. Sinnott, secretary to the apostolic delegate, but not that of the new delegate, Archbishop Pellegrino Francesco Stagni, OSM, who had been appointed to the post on 3 November 1910. Stagni arrived in Ottawa in March 1911, in the midst of McEvay's final illness. The departure of Archbishop Sbarretti, a founder of Church Extension and another of Burke's staunchest allies, only intensified Burke's feelings of vulnerability. He had no idea where Stagni stood on Church Extension or whether he appreciated the Society's role in the life and ongoing struggles of the Church in the West. Following McEvay's death, however, Burke would need Stagni on his side in any board-level struggle that might erupt over the management and control of Church Extension and the *Catholic Register*.

Father Burke's greatest exposure lay in the minefield of English–French relations within the Canadian Church. As long as McEvay was archbishop of Toronto and chancellor of Church Extension, Burke was safe from attack from the French. McEvay's demise, then, stripped Burke of the kind of episcopal protection that he needed when launching his own bombshells in Canada's increasingly bitter language battles, in his capacity as president of the Society enunciating policy, or as editor-in-chief of the *Register*, editorializing on the issues of the day. Burke and McEvay had shared the same unbending Anglo-centred opinion about the Catholic Church in Canada: for the Church to survive and flourish, especially during this time of massive and unprecedented Catholic immigration from Eastern Europe, the English language would have to be paramount in the public life of the Church as it was destined to be in the public life of the nation. (The lone exception to this sweeping panoramic of Church and State view was Québec. As a matter of history and geography, it was the one province where the French language was constitutionally protected and French-speaking Catholics had exclusive jurisdiction over the Church.) In other words, outside the boundaries of French-speaking Québec, it would be English-speaking bishops and priests in charge of the Church's administration and development, in a cultural and language lockstep with the evolving and inevitable Anglicization of the country.[5]

That Church Extension was nothing more than a tool of Anglicization, in the eyes of many French Canadian prelates, did little to enhance the Society's reputation as a national Catholic organization or to further its missionary work among Catholics who had neither English nor French as their mother tongue. That McEvay the chancellor and Burke the president of Church Extension rarely pushed back against this French perception of Anglicization, no matter how exaggerated and self-serving it might have been, at times, on the part of the French clergy, says a great deal about the dogged determination of these two men to pursue a language agenda that was bound to be detrimental to the growth and acceptance of Church Extension and divide even further an already fractured and fractious Catholic community of faith. McEvay's and Burke's views on what they held to be the entwined destinies of the English language and the Church's proper place in twentieth-century Canada shed ample light on Burke's arrogant and roughshod attitude towards the French clergy and on McEvay's willingness to defend Burke (and Church Extension) against the criticisms of the French-Canadian clerical establishment.

There can be no doubt that Father Burke – another English-speaking priest with an Irish surname, another *irlandais* – was an unabashed Canadian nationalist and British Imperialist.[6] Also, there is no doubt that he harboured an almost irrational antipathy towards French Canadian nationalists and *their* language agenda for the West. In Burke's worldview, Québec nationalism and the French language did not represent the future of Canada or the Church, and it was the future on both counts that was at stake. In his memorandum of April 1909, to the Duke of Norfolk, Burke was blunt to the point of open hostility in his assessment of French Canadians. He was so categorical in his judgment of them that he introduced the memorandum to Norfolk with a covering letter to Sir Charles Fitzpatrick in which he wrote, "You will see that somethings [sic] which are said, are only intended for friendly eyes and might tend to arouse the national spirit in some people; however, we must state facts; let the results be what they will."[7] In his memorandum, number 8, Burke wrote:

> The dual language and the spirit behind it, makes anything like unanimous effort on the part of organization of this kind much more difficult than elsewhere. The French-Canadian Members of the Board [Bégin, Archambeault and Taschereau] co-operate only to a very nominal extent and the general feeling among them usually, is that they have everything they should have in Quebec and do everything they should do in seeing that the local needs there are satisfied. This dogged conviction cannot be removed in a day. It can only be overcome by persistent and unmistakable work. Then, the desire to make the Northwest, which was once French and which has expanded beyond all possibility of a return to the domain of that language, is somewise [sic] tributary to them, greatly embarrasses the

work. From all points of view the difficulties are great, from the point of view of collecting funds in a young country in which Catholics are so divided and generally without wealth, from the race divisions, which make a distinct cleavage in the National and religious computation.[8]

Burke accused the French of parochialism in their native Québec and of daydreaming about retaining the Northwest as a constituent part of the French-language universe. When he mentioned "race divisions" as a problem plaguing the Catholic community, he was referring to language divisions. His comment was unintentionally ironical, for it was Burke who would be characterized as having a race problem. But that did not surface until later. In 1909 and 1910, Burke had an attentive and agreeable audience for his anti-French pronouncements.

After Norfolk, it was McEvay. To the archbishop, then in attendance at the Plenary Council of Québec, Burke claimed that Church Extension was doing everything "to win the esteem of the 'most reverent, high and mighty seigneurs' of the plains."[9] This was an irreverent way to describe Archbishop Langevin, Bishop Legal and Bishop Pascal. It was also incorrect. If there were a seigneur on the Western plains, it was the Québec-born Langevin, who was archbishop and metropolitan. He was in charge of the Church on the Prairies. The French-born Pascal, although loyal to Langevin and a fellow Oblate, was quite happy to receive assistance from Church Extension, and the French-born Legal, another Langevin loyalist and Oblate, became a very active member of the board and a regular high-profile promoter of the Society's work when he was bishop of St. Albert and even more so after he became archbishop of Edmonton.

Fitzpatrick was another sounding board. In 1910, there was growing anxiety over the impending appointment of the first bishop of Regina. The wait had begun as early as 1907, the year that Father Kelley's opinion about the matter had leaked its way to Archbishop Langevin [see Chapter One]. Three years later, Burke wrote to Fitzpatrick, a man who shared his views:

There is much speculation about the See of Regina. I see that His Grace of St. B. [Archbishop Langevin of St. Boniface] is on his way back [from Europe]. Indeed, I think he occupies the same boat with Earl Grey [the governor general]. They will have a grand time of it coming over. The advance of religion and the whole Ruthenian question is largely tied up by the solution of that question there, and while much has been done otherwise it is but a mill-stone about the neck of the Church in Canada. We can only hope for the best.[10]

For Burke, of course, the best outcome would have been an English-speaking bishop. His appointment by Rome would have been a sure sign that the rising light of the English-speaking Church had eclipsed the power and influence of Langevin and the Québec clergy in the ecclesiastical affairs of the Western provinces. But Langevin and his allies won the day. Olivier-Elzéar Mathieu became the first bishop of Regina in 1911.

McEvay had been of like mind with Burke on the hoped-for outcome of all the backroom jockeying that went into the selection process for Regina. In a letter dated 18 April 1911, to Archbishop Gauthier of Ottawa, McEvay expressed his disappointment and negative assessment of the choice of a French Canadian from Québec:

I have no doubt but that you have received a letter from His Eminence Cardinal De Lai in reference to the new See of Regina. Before replying to Rome I am making use of the permission granted, in writing to you.

As to the Priest proposed for the See, I have nothing to say. Outside the ecclesiastical Province of St. Boniface his appointment may be satisfactory. However inside that Province I consider his appointment as a serious matter and against the best interests of religion.

We all know that His Grace of St. Boniface has been for years the head and exponent of the Prelates, Priests, Editors and Politicians who want to tie the Catholic Church in this country to one nationality viz. French-Canadianism. We know how much injury this absurd and dangerous agitation has brought to the Catholics in many parts of this country and especially in the ecclesiastical Province of St. Boniface. The question is, – would not this appointment be a victory for this national craze and a quasi-approval of the Holy See and a sign that would be construed to perpetuate this propaganda?

For these reasons, I would submit that I believe the appointment is not in the general interests of religion. I am however always satisfied with any decision reached by the Holy See.[11]

McEvay may have lost to Archbishop Langevin and company when it came to the politics of choosing a prelate for Regina. In any event, it was a matter not even indirectly in his power to control or influence. (What is more, he would be dead three weeks later.) McEvay had been on surer ground, however, when he stood up for Burke and Church Extension in the face of French criticism, in 1909 and 1910. The first occasion involved Langevin. He had been suspicious of Church Extension ever since Father Kelley had contacted him in November 1907. His suspicions deepened when he heard that the Canadian branch of the Society had been established in June 1908, and these suspicions were confirmed as fact, according to his logic, after he had read the official proceedings of the First American Catholic Missionary Congress that had taken place in November of the same year.

In general terms, Langevin was incensed – and rightly so – that an English-oriented Church Extension Society operating out of Toronto presumed that it could proceed with its program of chapel building and financial assistance to Ukrainian Catholics in his episcopal jurisdiction without prior consultation and his agreement and co-operation. No bishop, then or now, can or should countenance outside interference in the management of his diocese. More specifically, Langevin was insulted by Father Burke's speech at the Congress, on the "Need of a Missionary College," which was a direct challenge to Langevin's right and responsibility to recruit and train candidates for the priesthood in his jurisdiction. [12] And he was astonished by Father Kelley's boast in *his* speech at the Congress that *his* Church Extension Society "has established Canadian Church Extension, which in five months has secured over $30,000 in cash, owns its own weekly newspaper, and is about to build its missionary college ....."[13]

The final provocation came when Burke, in the course of publicizing the Society to the Canadian bishops, sent Langevin a copy of Cardinal Merry del Val's letter of 3 December 1908 announcing Pope Pius X's "approbation, blessing and encouragement" of Church Extension in Canada.[14] Langevin felt obliged to protest to Archbishop McEvay in a lengthy, rambling and exclamatory letter of 16 January 1909. Langevin's letter is worth quoting in full. It shows his basic objections to the prospect of Church Extension's meddling in his affairs, outlines some of his more pressing needs, and explains and justifies his care of Ukrainian Catholics and other immigrant Catholic groups. Langevin repeated many of these same criticisms and concerns in his correspondence during 1908, 1909 and 1910, and found ample justification of his fears about Church Extension, as expressed in letters from his many clerical correspondents scattered across the West.[15]

> I have received the text of the blessing of the Canadian Church Extension Society by His Holiness Pope Pius X and I thank your Lordship very sincerely for it.

> First of all, the idea of helping the missions is indeed excellent and when, last year, Rev. Father Kelley, President of the United States Church Extension Society, wrote to me about it, I answered favorably and I communicated his letter to my venerable suffragants [sic; Pascal and Legal], but we came to no definite action about it.

> In August 1908, when I arrived from Europe, I was quite surprised to hear, in Montreal, from His Grace Archbishop Bruchési that a branch of the Church Extension Society had been established in Canada and that the presidents, vice-presidents and directors were appointed, and what surprised me to the utmost, that in view of supplying our dioceses of the West with priests, the college of St Dunstan, in the maritime provinces, had been chosen to recruit priests! What a revelation it was for me! It will be easily admitted by any bishop that if an organization is willing to help him by sending him priests,

he should be notified of the fact! Since this time, no news of the thing has reached me. Naturally, we, the bishops of the ecclesiastical Province of Saint Boniface, should, it seems to me, know better than any one else, what are the spiritual needs of our people. The French and English and German speaking people of our dioceses are not in danger of losing their faith. (I do not speak of those who are scattered and hidden among Protestants and who do not care for the priests.) "Perditio tua ex te Israel." They lose the faith through their own fault.

It is not very difficult now to provide these Catholics with priests speaking French or English or both. But, we need priests for the Galician people, Polish and especially Ruthenian, and also for Hungarians, and we need means to counterbalance the efforts of the schismatics and heretics (Presbyterians and Methodists), and to build churches, and spread catholic literature among them. The pamphlet of Rev. Father Delaere, C.SS.R., shows clearly that the faith of these Galicians is in great danger.

Now, if the Canadian Church Extension Society wishes to help us, would it be too much to ask that we be first notified of this object and intention.

Secondly, we should be helped according to the needs of the moment. Surely, students in St. Dunstan's College or elsewhere in the East could not be of much use to us, and we see no other College (perhaps with the exception of the seminary of Saint Albert), appropriate for the clerical needs of the moment than the college of Saint Boniface, under the direction of the Reverend Jesuit Fathers, where boys and young men of all nationalities are admitted, and where there is a university course given with great success in competition with the Protestant colleges.

We need above all, priests for the Ruthenians and for other foreign nationalities; and the archiepiscopal Corporation spends about one thousand dollars, every year, to help the Ruthenians alone. We need also money given free or lent without interest or at a low interest, to build churches, to establish in Sifton or Dauphin a center in order to minister to over ten thousand (10,000) Galicians, without a residing priest until now. This year, Rev. Father Sabourin began to reside in their midst. These Galicians of the region of Dauphin are exposed to the proselytizing action of the Protestants and of the schismatics, and large sums of money are spent for this purpose.

We need $10,000 dollars for churches and priests' houses, and also to start a Ruthenian paper in Winnipeg, where the Methodists publish, for the last six or seven years, a paper in this language, "The Ranok", the slanderer of the Pope, the Cardinals, the priests and the nuns.

The Basilian Fathers of Saint Nicolas' Church, in Winnipeg, take care of over six thousand (6,000) Ruthenians. The archiepiscopal Corporation has built for them a church and a priest's house with money borrowed at 6 per cent from the bank, and this religious establishment is loaded yet with a heavy debt. Had we not built, the Presbyterians would have given, in 1904, $50,000 to build for the Ruthenians in Winnipeg. Their parochial school of Saint Nicolas, in Winnipeg, is taught by Ruthenian Nuns in the basement of the church, a most unfavorable place. This fact together with the poverty of the people who cannot contribute to the free school are the reasons why so many children go to the Public Schools, and on this point, the Ruthenians are an exception. Consequently, it would be urgent to build a parochial school for the Ruthenian children in Winnipeg.

My Dear Lord Archbishop, I hope that you will forgive me if I write at such a length; but you will understand that my solicitude for our Catholic people is my excuse; and, besides, I am fully convinced that your Lordship and all the officers of the Canadian Church Extension Society, as well as Rev. Father Kelley, are anxious to help us, and have nothing else in view.

I read in the speech of Rev. Father Kelley at the Catholic Miss. Congress of Chicago, Nov. 16th, 1908, these words: "It has established Canadian Church Extension which in five months has secured over $30,000 in cash, owns its own weekly paper, and is about to build its missionary college."

I take the liberty of remarking that the bishops interested should learn directly from the proper sources what good people intend to do for their dioceses.

Hoping, Dear Lord Archbishop, that you will take all this in good part, and that you will realize that something must be done at once for the Ruthenians, I remain yours very sincerely in Xto & M. Im.[16]

Responding as one archbishop to another, McEvay did take Langevin's letter "in good part," but he sidestepped or minimized each of his complaints and concerns. He kept his response of 19 January 1909 as gentle and general as possible, assuring Langevin of the Board's co-operation and leaving open the door to further communication on the pressing matter of Ukrainian Catholic priests:

I beg to acknowledge receipt of your letter of the 16th and am pleased to have the information which it contains. The missionary needs of the Northwest are certainly of a nature which it is difficult indeed to exaggerate. There is no difficulty in dispensing funds, the trouble is to get them together and that is what we are trying to do at present. No doubt when the proper time comes to make donations, gifts or loans the needs of Your Grace and the other Bishops of that immense region will be relieved in as far as our limited circumstances will permit. So much is wanted that Your Grace will see at a glance that thorough general organization is requisite to secure a sufficiency of donations and funds to make any considerable improvement.

As to the College, let me say that we are indifferent about the place students attend for the present. The great concern is to secure good priests. Your Grace says that there is a sufficiency of French and English speaking priests and in this you are certainly fortunate beyond most of us who require numbers of both in the worst way. With regard to the Ruthenians, might

I be permitted to advise that it would be well to secure some ecclesiastics ready for ordination who would be willing to go over [to] their Rite and thus save great delay in the instant work of their protection in the Faith. I am sure the Board would be willing to help in this all-important matter. Please write me in detail on this subject.[17]

There is no evidence that Langevin replied to McEvay, as the latter had politely requested. That is a pity. McEvay was doing his diplomatic best to assuage Langevin, who had legitimate grievances, and to ensure that Church Extension, which had yet to make any donations, let alone found a missionary college, would not perish in its infancy. The stakes were too high for failure to intrude.

Diplomacy, however, was not one of Burke's virtues. Unlike McEvay, who held the same core beliefs on language and religion as Burke did, but avoided confrontations with his co-religionists if possible, Burke, pompous and rash, found his bearings in a good brawl whenever an opportunity presented itself and he believed he had the upper hand. This was especially true in his dealings with Langevin. Surviving are two exchanges of letters between the two men that demonstrate just how abrasive Burke could be, leaving little wonder as to why Langevin could never work with him or trust Church Extension as long as Burke was president.

From his perch in the Chateau Frontenac in Quebec City, where he was staying during the first weeks of the Plenary Council, Burke wrote the following letter to Langevin, dated 3 October 1909:

The Catholic Church Extension Society of Canada, acting on reports and petitions from priests in the Archdiocese of St. Boniface, promised to build Ten Chapels at $500.00 each and upwards, to pay the expenses of a priest to Galicia, whilst assuming the Ruthenian Rite, and to contribute at least $1000.00 to the purchase of a press for the Ruthenian people, so necessary to counteract the poison of the "Ranok" and other pernicious organs.

We intended to do much more, as we are in a position to do much more. However, being now informed that Your Grace objects to our Modus Operandi of the Society, and as there are many other places whose Bishops are asking for aid, we hasten to inform Your Grace that we shall withdraw the offer made to St Boniface Diocese, and to assure you that we shall not offend again by attempting to impose our services upon you.

Craving pardon for any unintentional offence we may have given and assuring Your Grace of our sentiments of respect and veneration ....[18]

Langevin replied in a letter of 12 October 1909:

Your letter of third instant surprised and grieved me very much; but I cannot deny that I have objected to the modus operandi, as you say, of the Catholic Church Extension Society of Canada, because many things were published and done outside of the knowledge and the approval of all the bishops interested in the matter.

Nevertheless, I am perfectly satisfied that nothing was done to offend us and I accept willingly the expression of your regret.

I sincerely hope Rev. and Dear Father, that all clouds will be dispelled and that your society founded in an apostolic spirit to help our poor Ruthenians, will not refuse to assist them.[19]

Langevin accepted Church Extension money and Church Extension continued to assist Ukrainian Catholics. But the clouds of mutual suspicion and hostility were never dispelled. A second exchange of letters between Langevin and Burke, this time in April 1910, shows that matters had not improved. In response to a misunderstanding of Church Extension's intent to donate $1,000 towards a Ukrainian Catholic newspaper, as promised, Langevin told Burke that "if nothing had been said in the 'Catholic Register' to belittle the works of those who labour here for nearly a century there would have been no friction!"[20]

Langevin's charge, which was not without merit, points to Burke's misuse of the *Catholic Register* as a convenient and personal forum to air his anti-French sentiments. Burke's language polemics inevitably opened the door for him to commit an egregious error in editorial judgment, an error that resulted in the resignations of Archbishop Bégin and Bishop Archambeault from the board of governors in November 1910. Burke's blunder was to take sides in the bilingual schools crisis gripping Ontario in the autumn of 1910, by condemning the use of French as a language of instruction in Catholic separate schools,[21] and to offer space in the *Register* to Bishop Michael Francis Fallon of London, who, as the leading episcopal opponent of bilingual education, was at the centre of an increasingly shrill civil war of words among Catholics on the dicey and divisive topic of bilingual education.[22] Burke's open and partisan participation in this internecine strife harmed Church Extension's image and impeded its mission.

Once again, McEvay had to come to the rescue of the Society. Bégin's and Archambeault's resignations were duly noted in the "Minutes" of the meeting of the board of governors of 19 November 1910: "That such resignations be not now accepted, but that the Chancellor be authorized to write the venerable prelates, and ask them to reconsider their actions."[23]

McEvay sent two letters to Bégin. Both were dated 27 December 1910. Illness kept McEvay from writing earlier. McEvay's first letter was issued in his capacity as chancellor of Church Extension. Five and a half pages in length, it asked Bégin to reconsider his resignation for the sake of the Church, calling it inopportune, presented a capsulated history of the formation of the Society, defended the role of the laity in its administration, delineated the sole purpose of the Society – "to promote the cause of Catholic faith regardless of nationality, locality or class" – reaffirmed the necessity of the English language in missionary work among immigrants in the West, scoffed at the notion that the Society interfered in the distribution of Church patronage, attacked the French-language press in Québec for making such charges, and commented on the current national question regarding bilingual schools, strongly denying that the Society had played any role in the current controversy.[24]

McEvay's second letter was more personal. It was one of his archbishop-to-archbishop missives. He presented his record of good relations with French-speaking Catholics as bishop of London and now as archbishop of Toronto and asserted that he was not and never had been prejudiced against French-speaking Catholics. Then he went on the offensive. He laid the blame for the present fiasco on the shoulders of "certain politicians, editors and clergymen in the Province of Quebec, who week after week write the most unfair and prejudicial statements concerning the conduct and action of the English bishops, priests and their co-religionists generally in this Province."[25] And he excoriated what he called the French-Canadian Congress for Ontario (l'Association canadienne-française d'éducation d'Ontario), which at its inaugural meeting in Ottawa in January 1910 made a vigorous and highly political defense of bilingual education that provoked not only the Ontario bishops but also the provincial government. It was obvious that McEvay was worn out by the language controversy.

Burke's two letters left the archbishop of Québec unmoved. Bégin let his resignation stand and replied to the chauvinism of Church Extension by establishing the Oeuvre Protectrice des Immigrants Catholiques (Catholic Immigration Association of Canada) in 1911. He put Abbé Phillippe Casgrain, one of his ablest priests, in charge of the enterprise.[26] McEvay and the board of governors of Church Extension understood Bégin's decision to resign as a hostile act cleverly planned to undermine Church Extension's mission.

As for Archambeault, he asked McEvay that his letter of resignation not be submitted to the board, and he promised that he would come to Toronto to explain his decision in person.[27] In the end, he, too, left the board. The damage was done.

Burke gave his interpretation of the resignation affair in a letter of 29 December 1910 to Cardinal Sebastian Martinelli, the cardinal protector of the Society:

> In the national craze which is spreading over Canada, to the great detriment of religion to-day, and without giving any cause, both Mgr. Begin and Mgr. Archambeault offered their

resignations as Members of the Board of Governors. A copy of those resignations is herewith enclosed to you. The Board thought it a grave affair, and refused to accept them in the circumstances, until its Chancellor, Mgr. McEvay had put the matter before them and urged reconsideration. His Grace in writing for the Society thought it best also to discuss the gravity of this national situation with His Grace of Quebec who has a quasi-primatial character, and should be particularly anxious to remove all difficulties from the way of the Church. I need not assure Your Eminence that so far as the Society is concerned, it has never considered any man's nationality, only the good of God's Church.[28]

Burke kept the *Register* and Church Extension out of the "national craze" until September 1913, when he decided to reproduce on the front page of the *Register* an article from *Le Droit* of Ottawa that savaged Church Extension for its anti-French bias. Burke responded immediately, taking *Le Droit* to task in a caustic editorial reply that followed the article, and continuing with an onslaught against *L'Action sociale* of Quebec City.[29] The affair alarmed Archbishop Stagni, the apostolic delegate, who denounced both sides for behaviour that was injurious to the unity of the Catholic Church in Canada, in two letters of 18 September 1913 to Archbishop Neil McNeil of Toronto.[30] This time, Burke would have no McEvay standing in the wings ready to protect him.

CHAPTER 9

AN INTERLUDE, 1911–1912

N ineteen months would elapse before Archbishop Neil McNeil of Vancouver would be installed as archbishop of Toronto and assume his role as chancellor of Church Extension. How did Father Alfred E. Burke, president of the Society, spend his time during this prolonged interlude when it was obliged to function without a chancellor? Since the chancellor was the ultimate source of authority and direction for the Society, Burke (with the acquiescence of the board of governors) decided to maintain the status quo – to manage the daily operations of Church Extension, including its flagship publication, the *Catholic Register*, as it had done in previous years – and to leave any initiative for changes to the Society's missionary mandate and its manner of conducting business to the new chancellor. While Burke patiently waited for a new archbishop, and fretted about who it might be, he travelled overseas three times, chased after Church honours (with the connivance of Father Francis C. Kelley), and allowed the recently minted Church Extension to languish as a corporate body. Burke minimized his usefulness to the Society and lowered his profile across the country. In essence, he rendered himself largely ineffective in his capacity as president.

For someone who was so proud of his part in the founding of Church Extension, and who acted as if he were a kingpin in the Canadian Church, Burke should have known better. Between McEvay's death in May 1911 and McNeil's much-delayed installation in December 1912, Burke should have stayed close to home and made himself visible at Church Extension's headquarters in Toronto as the surest way to demonstrate leadership and impart a sense of stability for the sake of the Society's future. Instead, Burke chose to absent himself for prolonged periods of time, letting the Society drift on its own, and to be consumed by his pursuit of the Roman dignity of a Protonotary Apostolic, the highest rank of monsignor in the Catholic Church.

• • • •

In the wake of McEvay's death, Father Kelley invited Father Burke to accompany him to Europe. He extended his invitation in July 1911. Burke had turned down two previous opportunities, in 1909 and 1910. On this occasion, he did not hesitate, for he felt that there was nothing urgent to keep him at the helm of Church Extension in Canada. The two priests left from Montréal on the *Royal Edward* on 8 August 1911. Their itinerary included Rome, a journey through France and a final stop in England.[1] "My advice," wrote Kelley to Burke, "is to hurry on to Rome and get there, as it is getting late now, and if we postpone the Roman business we may have to chase all over Italy to find the Cardinals we have to see."[2] Kelley's elliptical reference to "Roman business" probably concerned the succession to the Archdiocese of Toronto. According to James P. Gaffey, Father Kelley's biographer, Kelley was so anxious to protect the Canadian Society that he lost his sense of good judgment when he proposed Burke for the vacant see of Toronto to Cardinal Martinelli, cardinal protector for both Extension Societies, and Cardinal Merry del Val, secretary of state.[3] It was an unsolicited recommendation made in a city where such hint dropping may have been a pastime for countless clergymen promoting themselves or their friends, but not an action necessarily bound to produce the desired result. Having made it, however, Kelley pressed on, as was his lobbying style.

While Kelley and Burke were in London, Kelley wrote Cardinal Merry del Val that Burke "is one of the strongest men in English-speaking Canada"[4] and that his friend deserved the distinction of protonotary apostolic as a means of bringing him to the attention of the right people in Rome when it came time to choose a new archbishop for Toronto. Kelley did not let up. Five months later, he wrote to Monsignor Sante Tampieri, one of his contacts in the Roman Curia who was on speaking terms with Cardinal Merry del Val, "Without a doubt, Burke is the ablest English-speaking ecclesiastic in Canada, and the only man, I know, who has all the qualifications necessary."[5]

It was all nonsense. It was as if Kelley believed that no one in Rome knew a thing about the Canadian Church or that the apostolic delegate did not have the measure of his man Burke. There is no evidence to suggest that Burke ever encouraged Kelley in his one-man campaign to get a mitre for him. Yet, at the same time, there is no hint in their voluminous correspondence that Burke ever discouraged him from indulging in what was a hopeless fantasy. The Holy See would not have chosen anyone as imprudent and pugilistic as Burke had been in his public dealings with the French-speaking clergy of Canada to lead the nation's most important English-speaking diocese. One wonders to what degree Kelley was serious in his promotion of Burke to Toronto. Or, was it something else? It may have been a simple matter of Kelley abandoning his well-honed political instincts to support a colleague whose future as president of Church Extension in Canada seemed to be hanging in the balance. In the name of priestly loyalty, Kelley let his own high art of flattery get the best of him.[6]

No sooner had Burke returned from his first European adventure, sometime during the second half of September, than he was preparing to embark on another one. But this transatlantic trip had nothing directly to do with the work of Church Extension. Writing from the New Russell Hotel in Ottawa on 16 October 1911, Burke informed Kelley that the "Church needs my influence with the govt."[7] In the next few lines, he refers to the prime minister and the viceroy (governor general) – but not by name – and to a Sir C., which must have been Sir Charles Fitzpatrick. That is all. No details. Burke had returned to

Toronto before the end of October.[8] On 23 November 1911, he was writing Kelley from the *Empress of Ireland*: "I am here on a very private and confidential mission clothed with fullest authority & all expenses paid."[9] Again, Burke gave no details.

The story, coming from the pen of Burke himself, in two letters to Cardinal Merry del Val, is this.[10] The Conservative government of Sir Robert Laird Borden sent Burke to Rome to confer with Pius X (the audience took place on 22 December 1911) about the controversy then raging across Canada on this question: Did Church law supercede Civil law in determining the validity of marriages contracted outside the Catholic Church, between two Catholics or between a Catholic and a Protestant? In 1908, Rome issued *Ne Temere*, a decree that, in the words of one Catholic historian, "made it clear to Catholics that a marriage between two Catholics, or between a Catholic and a Protestant, must be witnessed by a Catholic pastor and two lay persons."[11] The original intention of the decree was "to protect Christian women from private marriages of convenience that could afterward be repudiated."[12] But its public ramifications, at least in Canada, were far different.

In 1909, Archbishop Bruchési of Montréal, invoking the papal decree, annulled the marriage of one Eugène Hébert and E. Cloutre, which had been solemnized by a Methodist minister in Québec, and the Québec Superior Court upheld the annulment. The response of various Protestant bodies was fairly predictable, but the political and judicial establishment had not foreseen the force and intensity of the backlash. The status of *Ne Temere*, in terms of the civil law, and the perceived interference of the Catholic bishops in the purely civil matter of marriage, became a political and judicial hot potato.

After his audience with the pope, Burke travelled to London to assure the Duke of Norfolk, the premier Catholic peer in Great Britain, and Earl Grey, who had recently finished his term as governor general of Canada, that Cardinal Merry del Val and the Holy See "were disposed to do everything consistent with Catholic principles to promote peace and harmony among the different peoples of Canada."[13] He also assured the two men that the cardinal "had reciprocated the personal good wishes of the Prime Minister, and the other eminent men who had, in the spirit of patriotism, and good will, approached [him] and that all might expect the best results from the mission."[14]

The Québec Superior Court revisited its decision in February 1912 and upheld the validity of the Hébert-Cloutre marriage, declaring that *Ne Temere* had no application in the realm of civil law and that the archbishop's annulment of the marriage had none either. According to Burke, this information did little to tamp down agitation on the matter, which had evolved into another bitter battle between the Orange Lodge and Québec Nationalists.[15] Subsequently, the Supreme Court of Canada, led by Chief Justice Sir Charles Fitzpatrick, ruled in favour of the validity of mixed marriages.[16]

Father Burke's third trip to Europe took place in August and September 1912. Father Kelley was with him for the first part of the journey. They did a leisurely tour of Belgium, travelling through the countryside and spending time with the leading professors at the University of Louvain. Next they attended the Catholic Congress of Germany, where they met the president and executive of the Catholic Church Extension Society of Germany. After Germany, the two men parted, with Burke going to England to participate in the Catholic Conference in Norwich and to discuss, with the Catholic Women's League of Great Britain, Church Extension's plans to assist in the settlement of English Catholic girls immigrating to Canada under the auspices of the CWL.[17]

••••

The title of monsignor (monseigneur) originated in the Avignon papacy and was bestowed upon clerical members of the papal household. There were different titles designating different court functions. Over the centuries, and outside of Rome, the title of monsignor evolved into an honorary designation given to priests around the world, either on the pope's own initiative or, more commonly, on application from the local bishop. There were until the 1970s three levels of monsignor nominated and created from the ranks of the clergy. From lowest to highest, they were Papal Chamberlain (PC), Domestic Prelate (DP) and Protonotary Apostolic (PA).[18] All monsignors, regardless of rank, were entitled to wear a "crimson-lined and a crimson-buttoned cassock."[19] Although the honour is increasingly rare in the post-conciliar Church outside of Rome, during Father Burke and Father Kelley's day they were a fairly common and inexpensive means for a bishop to recognize and reward outstanding diocesan priests for their parochial accomplishments or administrative responsibilities.

It was not unusual, then, for Kelley and Burke to have believed that they deserved the rank of monsignor. Two reasons were uppermost in their desire for the so-called purple piping. One, as presidents of Pontifical Societies established by the Holy See to head Catholic home missions in their respective countries, the rank of monsignor would have been commensurate with their standing and responsibilities. Two, wearing the rank of monsignor while on Society business would open many more doors at the Vatican. This way of thinking was not unreasonable, but there were two problems with it. Both men founded Church Extension, Kelley in the United States in 1905 and Burke in Canada in 1908, without the assistance of personal rank in the Church. They were mere priests. And black cassocks did not impede either man from gaining regular access to the cardinal secretary of state or to a private audience with the pope. Kelley had a private audience in May 1910, and Burke had one in December 1911, in each case with Pius X.

These contradictions aside, the really egregious aspect of the two men's quest for rank and dignity within the Church was their presumption that they deserved the highest rank of monsignor – the Protonotary Apostolic. But the egregiousness did not stop there. A bigger prize was always on the horizon: a bishopric. When did a simple priest ever become a bishop or an archbishop? To rise, one needed to have rank, and the highest rank was the much-coveted and lofty-sounding Protonotary Apostolic. It was all about carefully climbing the ecclesiastical ladder. That is why, when writing to Cardinal Merry del Val on 22 September 1911, Kelley insisted to the secretary of state that Burke be given the PA as soon as possible. Without it, he would have no chance at becoming archbishop of Toronto.

But to climb upwards in the Church, Burke and Kelley needed a helping hand, and no hand could advance their cause better than that of their Ordinary. While Burke turned to Archbishop Fergus Patrick McEvay of Toronto, Kelley sought the support of Archbishop James E. Quigley of Chicago. A third player was Archbishop Sbarretti, the apostolic delegate to Canada. He insisted that the PA be bestowed on Burke and Kelley at the same time. To co-ordinate such a manoeuvre, Quigley had to contact McEvay, who was already on board. The delegate believed that it would take only "one line"[20] from Quigley to initiate the process whereby a petition requesting the bestowal of the PA would wind its way to Rome. That one line from Quigley never came.

Talk of a PA between Burke and Kelley began as early as August 1909 and did not end until October 1911. During that time, the two men exchanged at least eleven letters and one telegram that mentioned the subject whether in passing or at some length.[21] It is clear from their correspondence that Quigley was the problem. For reasons that the archbishop of Chicago never disclosed to Kelley, or, if he ever did, Kelley never shared with Burke, Quigley was not moved to promote the president of Church Extension in the United States to the rank of monsignor. And no promotion of Kelley meant no promotion for Burke. Kelley showed remarkable patience as he awaited word – any word, one way or the other – from Quigley. While he bided his time, he lobbied Cardinal Merry del Val in Rome and Monsignor Tampieri in Rome and in New York,[22] and suggested to Burke that either Monsignor Sinnott, secretary to Sbarretti, or McEvay write a letter to Quigley, informing him of Rome's inclination to give the honours.[23] Nothing worked. Quigley stayed silent on the subject.

By the beginning of February 1911, Kelley was at his wits' end. He wrote to Burke:

> I do not know anything about the P.A. business. I wrote to the Archbishop asking him to please notify the Archbishop of Toronto, what he intended doing, and said I thought that he was in honor bound, if he thought it best not to go ahead in the matter himself, to at least give such information to Canada and leave Archbishop McEvay free to proceed along his own lines. If he has not written to Archbishop McEvay, it looks as if he is going ahead with it, after all. I am very indifferent on the

matter now. Whatever good might have been gained, so far as this office is concerned, could not be gained now.[24]

Kelley had given up. It was a rare defeat for him. Quigley did not write McEvay and did not proceed with a petition to Rome. His reticence had defeated Kelley. Kelley's last word on the subject to Burke was this: "I do not know what JEQ [James Edward Quigley] is doing. He has not said a word since I sent him that last letter. He is one great, large sized mystery. We had a meeting of the Executive Committee Tuesday, and he was in a great humor; but that is about all."[25]

Perhaps Quigley hesitated to raise Kelley to the dignity of a PA because he was an outsider to the Archdiocese of Chicago and was seen by many as an overly ambitious and freewheeling priest who revelled in his freedom of action and influence over others. As for Burke, he had experienced Europe and liked what he had seen and had spoken to Pius X in a private audience. But the prize of the Protonotary Apostolic had eluded him. Quigley's silence had defeated him, too, even before the death of McEvay in May 1911 had ended all hope of a papal honour. Burke would have to forget about being anything else but the priest-president of Church Extension in Canada. To his credit, mention of the PA disappears from his correspondence with Kelley. But the close of this far from edifying chapter in his life, which had begun to take on the quality of a two-man *opéra bouffe*, unfortunately did not present itself for what it was – a chance for Burke to be an active and imaginative president during the interregnum when the Society had no chancellor. Instead, Burke chose to be careful and conservative, to do the minimum in terms of leadership, and to spend an exorbitant amount of time overseas. It was the biggest mistake of his career at Church Extension.

••••

What, then, did Church Extension accomplish from 1 March 1911 to 1 March 1913? The answer to that question can be found in the "Minutes" of two annual general meetings of the Society for the fiscal years ending on 28 February 1912 and 28 February 1913, respectively, and in the "Minutes" of an Executive Meeting that was held on 1 December 1912 and of an adjourned meeting on 16 April 1913.

At the Annual General Meeting of 17 April 1912, with Monsignor John T. Kidd in the chair, Father Burke delivered a fairly comprehensive review of the Society's work. His report was divided into seven sections:

1. Church Goods: 300 sets of vestments; 9,000 pieces of linen and an unspecified number of chalices, ciboriums, monstrances, statues and stations of the cross
2. Clothing for the Clergy: eight tons to twenty-five different missions
3. Mass Intentions: 20,000 Mass Intentions to 150 priests and all the bishops of Western Canada
4. Loans and Donations: $6,000 for memorial chapels in twelve different locations; $1,450 donated to missionaries and students
5. Distribution of Literature: 1 million pieces, including pamphlets to Ukrainians and Native people of the Northwest, without specifying what kinds of literature
6. Women's Auxiliary: much praise but no details of the auxiliary's accomplishments
7. *Catholic Register*: circulation had increased twenty-five percent but no exact figures.[26]

At a meeting on 1 December 1912, the executive committee decided to give grants to several churches, make two loans and purchase property for what became St. Philip Neri Hostel for immigrant women.

All in all, Church Extension had continued to carry out its missionary mandate in 1911/12, but failed to exert itself much beyond the level of past achievements or to make any innovative changes to its fundraising efforts. The board members were very pleased with the work of the Women's Auxiliary. Almost overnight they had become the Society's foot soldiers. But, inexplicably, the board also seemed satisfied with the Society's low profile within the Catholic community. No one on the board expressed on the record any anxiety about atrophy setting in if Church Extension did not enhance its public image among Catholics and raise more funds to be distributed to the home missions.

The "Minutes" of the Annual General Meeting of 2 April 1913 is a curious document for many reasons. A good deal of the meeting was given over to Father Burke's "President's Report." This was the first time he had delivered such a report, and he did so to impress Archbishop Neil McNeil, who was attending his first meeting of the board of governors. McNeil was now the chancellor of Church Extension and in charge. Burke knew that his own future depended on his performance: he would have to convince McNeil that the Society was fulfilling its mandate, that he as president was the right man in charge of its daily operations and the *Catholic Register*, and that any changes to the Society's manner of conducting its business in order to improve its finances and the effectiveness of its missionary endeavours should be done according to the president's suggestions. Burke had to sell his agenda to McNeil.

The "Report" itself has a four-part structure that is apparent only after several readings. Not surprisingly, the first part is Burke's excuse for not having the Society do more in the absence of a chancellor. It appears up front, in the third sentence of the opening paragraph: "During the year the Chancellorship of the Society has been vacant and nothing could be done to promote its work."[27] Three paragraphs later, he repeats the excuse: "Then as we said before, the Chancellor of the Society after a year's illness, died, and whilst the see [sic] was vacant for another year, little or nothing could be done in the matter of propagation [of the Society's work]."[28] This is Burke covering for the board and himself by conveniently laying the blame for their lack of collective ambition on the doorstep of McEvay's illness and death. By taking this tactic, however, Burke, whether he realized it, was handing McNeil a golden opportunity to exert his episcopal will on the governance and direction of Church Extension in ways that his predecessor had never done and that caught Burke and the board off guard.

The second part was a largely non-informative general description of the Society's accomplishments during the year 1912/13. Burke mentioned many things, such as chapels, altar plate, vestments, Mass Intentions and literature, but he gave no details on numbers. The two financial figures – the expenditure of $50,000 and the *Catholic Register*'s profit of $3,550 – while interesting and at least superficially impressive, are also so general in nature that in each instance they tell the reader practically nothing. It is only in the last paragraph of his "Report" that

Burke mentioned several items of real interest: that the Society's appeals for financial assistance convinced many people to donate directly to bishops and priests, thus bypassing Church Extension, and that the Society had secured the appointment of a priest in Austria to direct Ukrainian immigrants to Canada and had paid the passage of Bishop Nykyta Budka and his secretary from Galicia to Canada.[29]

Parts three and four reveal Burke's real motives behind the "Report." In the third part, he listed the Society's disbursements of money, goods and Mass Intentions over its first three years of existence. Oddly, Burke was mistaken in his calculation of the Church Extension's age. By 28 February 1913, it was four years and three months old.[30] But this slip-up does not take away from the fact that Burke wanted to demonstrate to McNeil that Church Extension had done wonders with "direct donations to churches to the extent of $28,000. Loans to the value of $12,000. Mass Intentions to the value of $50,000. Literature and Church goods to the value of $10,000, making in all $100,000 in cash directed and disbursed by the Society in the interests of the Home Missions."[31] "Value" was the operative word in his presentation. And that was not all. Subscriptions to the *Catholic Register* had increased from 3,000 to 17,000. Burke was very proud of this achievement. It justified his having given "his closest attention to the organ of Extension so that it might be a newspaper worthy of the Society and of first standing among the Catholic Journals of Canada."[32] But such boasting, even if the figures were not inflated, as was often the practice in the newspaper world, did not protect Burke from the criticism that he was spending far too much time as editor-in-chief of the newspaper, treating it as his personal bailiwick, and not enough as president of the Society. McNeil certainly thought so.

The fourth part of the report was Burke's agenda for taking the Society to the next level of achievement. He wanted to increase the number of subscriptions to the *Catholic Register* by recruiting Catholic pastors in a campaign to put the paper in the hands of every Catholic family. This grand game plan could be achieved, according to Burke, if parishes signed up for bulk subscriptions and distributed the paper for free. Also, the Society would have to convince far more Catholic businessmen to take out advertising in the *Register*, for it was revenue generated by advertising, and not by the one-dollar yearly subscription rate, that produced the paper's profits. Concerning the need to increase the missionary spirit of Church Extension throughout the country, Burke proposed the enlistment of priests to serve as diocesan directors and fundraisers for Church Extension. These priest promoters would be

> engaged first, in the collection of founders payments; secondly in visiting prospective founders etc. in different places so that contributions will be indiscriminate; in preaching and collecting in churches; in making use of a chapel car along railway lines; in aiding in the successful administration of the Society's Hostel for immigrants.[33]

Burke's agenda was not without merit. He wanted a more organized and aggressive priest-centred organization that would go directly to the Catholic faithful – those who would fund the Society's good works and those who would receive the Society's assistance. American Church Extension had been quite successful in taking this approach to raising and dispensing money.

The immediate response of Archbishop McNeil to Father Burke's "President's Report" was totally unexpected, as if he had not heard a word of what Burke had just said or had come armed with a response in advance of the meeting. McNeil suggested that Church Extension publish a monthly magazine instead of a weekly newspaper. He pointed out that this was the practice of the American Extension Society, which had turned its magazine into a fine paying proposition. The subtext of McNeil's response was his desire to remove Burke as editor-in-chief of the *Catholic Register*. The only way to achieve this outcome was to convince the board of governors to surrender control of its newspaper. Church Extension would have its magazine, and the archdiocese would have its newspaper. The entire board rejected McNeil's proposal and opted to develop the newspaper "along the lines of the President's Report, so as to make of it one of the Society's best assets."[34]

Burke won the opening skirmish, and he was to win the next one. At the adjourned Annual General Meeting, on 16 April 1913, which was called to give more members of the board an opportunity to attend, the board carried a motion by Sir Charles Fitzpatrick, seconded by Mr. Justice Kelly, that "a circular to the Bishops and public be issued at once by the Chancellor in conjunction with the president of the Society."[35] McNeil was confident that within three months he could convince the bishops of Ontario to back an Extension campaign, and promised to assist the president in the matter of the newspaper. Burke must have felt that his position as president of Church Extension was safe from the archbishop's meddling. It was not unreasonable for him to have felt this way. In the face of a united board, McNeil had backed down on control of the *Catholic Register*,[36] and pressured by Fitzpatrick, Burke's strongest ally on the board, committed himself to working with Burke on an official campaign to enlist episcopal support for the Society.

But McNeil was not McEvay. In his mind, agreeing to do something at the behest of a board determined to protect Burke was one thing; doing the board's bidding was an entirely different matter. Burke and the board failed to appreciate the archbishop's determination to oust Burke as president and make Church Extension his own enterprise.

CHAPTER 10

SHOWDOWN WITH ARCHBISHOP NEIL McNEIL, 1913–1915

N eil McNeil was sixty-one years old when he was enthroned as the archbishop of Toronto on 22 December 1912. It would be his final posting. Prior to his arrival in Canada's largest English-speaking city, his career in the Church was a succession of stellar accomplishments in a variety of pastoral, academic and literary capacities. McNeil was highly educated and well travelled and was fortunate not to have spent too much time inside a diocesan chancery. He was one member of the Canadian hierarchy who had lived the life of the Church on both coasts of the country, and he was that rare ecclesiastic who was immune to the poisonous and partisan bickering over language that would lead to so much unhappiness in the Canadian Church during the early decades of the twentieth century.

Born on 23 November 1851, in Hillsborough, Cape Breton, Nova Scotia, he was the eldest son of Malcolm McNeil, a blacksmith and merchant, and Ellen Meagher. McNeil was educated in the parish school and worked in his father's business for several years. From 1869 to 1873, he was enrolled in classics at St. Francis Xavier College (later University) in Antigonish, where his talents and his dedication to learning were obvious to his teachers and classmates. Recognizing McNeil's potential as a scholar, and appreciating his desire for the priesthood, Bishop John Cameron of Antigonish sponsored him at the Pontifical Urban College de Propaganda Fide in Rome for theology. McNeil would live up to Cameron's expectations and become something of a golden boy in the diocese. In 1879, McNeil earned a doctorate in philosophy and theology at the college, and on 12 April of that year he was ordained a priest at the age of twenty-eight, at the Basilica of St. John Lateran. One of the highlights of his student days in the Eternal City was seeing John Henry Cardinal Newman at the English College on 14 May 1879. McNeil spent another year in Europe, studying astronomy and mathematics at the University of Marseille, France, before his return to Canada.

Father McNeil spent the next fifteen years in his home diocese as a parish priest at Arichat, West Arichat and finally D'Escousse, an Acadian parish where his sympathetic understanding of French-speaking Catholics first took root, as vice-rector and then rector of St. Francis Xavier University, and as editor of two Catholic newspapers, the *Aurora* (1881–1885) and the *Antigonish Casket* (1890–1892). McNeil succeeded in every task assigned to him by Bishop Cameron. By the time he was forty-four years old, McNeil was one of the most accomplished and high-profile priests of his generation in Nova Scotia. He was what Church watchers call "bishop material."

It came as no surprise, then, that Neil McNeil was consecrated the vicar apostolic of St. George's, Newfoundland, a mission territory, on 20 October 1895. He was the titular bishop of Nilopolis until his appointment as the first bishop of St. George's on 18 February 1904. Six years later, on 19 January 1910, Rome transferred McNeil to the Archdiocese of Vancouver, which was also something of a mission territory, but in so many respects a world away from that of Newfoundland, at that time still a British colony and isolated from Canada.[1]

When Archbishop McNeil was a priest and bishop on the East Coast, he undoubtedly would have known Father Alfred E. Burke, at least by reputation. As president of Church Extension, Burke naturally would have followed the episcopal fortunes of Archbishop Neil McNeil. The two men probably met for the first time in Burke's Church Extension office during McNeil's stopover in Toronto while on his way to Vancouver in 1910. Church Extension donated a thousand dollars to the archdiocese, a gift that McNeil acknowledged in a letter published in the *Catholic Register*. He was thankful for the substantial sum of money and added: "Nor is this the only favor which makes me regard the Society as a source of encouragement to every missionary in Canada. Apart altogether from financial needs, the Society gives us a centre of information, a bond of union, and a developing agency of missionary zeal."[2] This was excellent copy for the Society. Burke could not have asked for a more ringing episcopal endorsement.

The next time that McNeil and Burke encountered each other was in Vancouver. That meeting took place sometime in October 1912, or shortly thereafter. The purpose of the cross-country trip, which Burke undertook at the urging of the board of governors, was to convince McNeil to take an interest in the Society's work, since he was about to assume the reins of the Archdiocese of Toronto and the chancellorship of the Society. No record of their conversation has survived, and likely none was ever made. It was a private matter that did not merit a memorandum. Neither man ever referred to it in any exchange of letters between themselves, from 1913 to 1915, or with other correspondents during the same period.

Knowledge of the trip is limited to a brief and tantalizing reference in 1915.[3] The timeline for the Burke/McNeil interview is based on the fact that although McNeil had been made archbishop of Toronto on 10 April 1912 – much to his surprise and consternation – news of his appointment was kept secret for six months, at his request. From several *Register* stories about the Archdiocese of Vancouver that were published in August 1912,[4] it appears that McNeil might have asked the apostolic delegate to withhold publishing the news of his appointment so as not to leave his successor to Vancouver unprepared to deal with an archdiocese plagued by problems and on the cusp of significant social change. Regardless, the clergy and laity of the Archdiocese of Toronto did not learn of McNeil's transfer until 6 October 1912, when the Papal Bull was finally read at St. Michael's Cathedral.[5] Thus, it is reasonable to conclude that as soon as Burke and the board heard the news, Burke left for Vancouver. It was incumbent upon him to have McNeil on side.

Archbishop McNeil's first two priorities, as enunciated in his reply to the address of welcome at his installation ceremony, were St. Augustine's Seminary and the Catholic Church Extension Society, both of which had been initiated by Archbishop McEvay.[6] The completion and opening of the seminary proved far easier than anything he had in mind for Church Extension. In one of the grandest ceremonies in archdiocesan history, St. Augustine's was dedicated on 28 August 1913, a mere eight months after McNeil's very low-key arrival in Toronto. Meanwhile, his intention to transform Church Extension into a more productive and disciplined Society that would be truer to its original mission – and into a Church organization free from unnecessary controversy – quickly disintegrated into a drawn-out contest of wills that lasted more than two and a half years. During that time, a protracted and acrimonious struggle ensued between McNeil, the chancellor, and Burke, the president, involving not only the board of governors, who found themselves obliged to take sides, but also the apostolic delegate in Ottawa, many Canadian bishops, several high-ranking Vatican officials, and Father Francis C. Kelley of the American Church Extension Society.

Archbishop McNeil had commenced his campaign to wrest control of Church Extension from Burke and his board allies months in advance of being rebuffed at the Annual General Meeting of 2 April 1913 (see Chapter Nine). It began, interestingly enough, with a letter from Archbishop Stagni, the apostolic delegate, to McNeil in January 1913. Stagni laid out for McNeil his own understanding of Church Extension's mandate and the prime reason why the Society had been unable to fulfill it:

> This Society was established for the avowed purpose of collecting material resources for the aid and increase of the Catholic missions of Canada. It has the strongest recommendation on the part of the Holy See. It is an organization which has already

done some good and which, if properly supported, is capable of doing very much more. It is to be deplored that it has not received the general support which it deserves, but frequently has encountered opposition and discouragement.[7]

According to Stagni, the Society's lack of success was due to a lack of general support. For the delegate, the question was this: Why did Church Extension not receive "general support" for its missionary work? Stagni's use of "general" in this instance pointed the finger of blame at the Catholic faithful. Why had the laity not rallied around Church Extension in Canada in sufficient numbers for it to realize its true potential?

McNeil used the above quote from the delegate in a circular letter of 17 January 1913 to his fellow bishops, and ended with this plea: "I beg you to help me understand the situation by stating somewhat fully, why, in your opinion, the Extension Society has not been successful, and what steps should be taken to make it serve the high purpose of its foundation."[8] This is not as innocuous as it appears in print. For McNeil, the question to be asked did not concern the discovery of reasons for Church Extension's lack of support and hence its lack of success. Rather, the question was all about the Society's lack of success, which in McNeil's way of thinking absolved the bishops from trying to ferret out the reasons for lay apathy towards Church Extension, or to explain why so many in the hierarchy were indifferent to the Society's work or even downright hostile to its very existence. By focusing on the Society's lack of success – and ignoring the Society's lack of support – McNeil in a roundabout way invited the bishops to tell him who in the Society might be to blame for its lack of success. McNeil's indirection produced the desired results.

As well as sending a circular to the bishops, McNeil brought up the subject of Church Extension with his episcopal colleagues at the funeral of Bishop Richard Alphonsus O'Connor of Peterborough on 28 January 1913. Attending O'Connor's Requiem Mass were Archbishop Gauthier of Ottawa, Archbishop Spratt of Kingston and the following bishops: Fallon of London, Scollard of Sault Ste. Marie, Émard of Valleyfield, Québec, McDonald of Alexandria, Ryan of Pembroke, and Budka of the Ukrainian Eparchy. Bishop Dowling of Hamilton, a Church Extension supporter from the very beginning, did not attend the funeral and thus did not have a chance to impress upon McNeil his own loyalty to the Society.[9]

Eight episcopal responses to McNeil's circular survive. There may have been more, but this is unlikely, considering the integrity and extent of McNeil's administrative archive. (He kept his papers, if not in order, at least in sight of his desk.) Bishop Albert Pascal, OMI, of Prince Albert, Saskatchewan, told McNeil that he was a recipient of Church Extension's generosity. On the one hand, he was unstinting in his support and approval of the Society; on the other, he did recognize the need to reorganize it on a sounder footing. Pascal proposed that the Society appoint an organizer "whose only business would be to travel the length and breadth of Canada preaching Extension."[10] In other words, Church Extension needed a full-time priest-publicist to promote the Society's unique mission to the Catholic people of Canada as an excellent way to heighten interest and increase funds. It was a good idea, long overdue. Bishop Olivier-Elzéar Mathieu of Regina wrote that Catholics were dispersed over the Prairies, which made it difficult to build and maintain new churches. But any work undertaken by Church Extension on their behalf had to be conducted under the direction of the diocesan bishops or else the work would be useless. Although Mathieu did not mention Burke by name, he was certainly criticizing the manner in which Church Extension had conducted its business under his presidency.[11] It was a mild diplomatic rebuke from a bishop whose appointment had aroused all sorts of hostile reaction from English-speaking Catholics. Mildness and diplomacy, however, were far from evident in the six other replies.

Bishop Élie-Anicet Latulipe, the vicar apostolic of Témiscamingue in northern Ontario since 1908, told McNeil that he had never asked Church Extension for help and did not know how it ran its affairs. But he did know that the president of the Society did not have the confidence and sympathy of the clergy. Latulipe went on to warn that the unhappy and inexplicable divisions between French-speaking and English-speaking Catholics could only exercise a disastrous influence on all Catholic works. The implication was that Burke's anti-French attitude was at fault for Church Extension's lack of success because he was part of the language debacle bedevilling Catholics. What the Church in Canada needed was peace and charity.[12]

In his reply, Archbishop Michael J. Spratt of Kingston made it clear that he had been in office for only a year, and because there was a $100,000 cathedral debt, he would be unable to do much for Church Extension. Also, he had met Burke only once or twice at Church functions. What he knew about the Society was admittedly conjecture, but he shared it with McNeil to help him in his inquiries. "I feel inclined to be of the opinion," Spratt wrote, "that such opposition is not so much to the Society itself, as to the director general, who, I believe, is not regarded favourably by many of the priests and a number of the bishops of this dominion."[13] Spratt then hinted in passing that there had been some "unpleasant history connected with the organization of the Society."[14] He did not elaborate, leaving one to wonder what he meant.

Bishop James Morrison of Antigonish was unsparing in his indictment of Father Burke. Morrison expressed his opinions for the good of religion and because McNeil had asked him "to speak plainly on the matter."[15] Although Morrison knew nothing about the Society's inner workings, as he described its management, not for a moment did he doubt that the cause of all the Society's troubles was Burke's disputatious and duplicitous personality:

> To my mind the management of the Society, as far as its outward expression goes, has been unfortunately tactless and without much good judgment. Indeed I think that I should at once say that the Reverend President of the Society is a man totally unfitted for the position, and, for that matter, for any position of responsibility where the progress of religion is concerned. When he lived in the East, he made more personal enemies than any other man I know of. When he was not in a quarrel over 'small politics', he was generally wrangling with someone else and mostly over imaginary issues. He was regarded as proud and overbearing with his equals; he had a good share of contempt for his inferiors, while towards his superiors[,]

at least towards his bishop, he was not only disrespectful, but even unjust, disloyal and disobedient. He had the reputation of being a mischievous and erratic intriguer, and one scarcely knew from one week to another what difficulty would be next forthcoming. In a word he generally kept the place either in turmoil or in dread of one. This reputation was not confined to his native province but extended fairly far and wide. The result of it all was that few who had intimate knowledge of him cared to have much to do with him.[16]

Bishop Morrison was not finished. Burke "was considerably narrow in his national feelings, and unsparing in his manner of giving expression to them," which would have been anathema to McNeil, who went out of his way to mend fences with the French. Morrison added that "while the 'Register' contains many good selections, its editorial comments are considered by many as rough and quite too belligerent."[17] Since Burke was the editor-in-chief of the *Register*, he was culpable for its editorial content. The man had to go. He was quarrelsome, contemptuous and disobedient; he was openly anti-French; he was ill suited to be the editor of a national Catholic newspaper.

The reply of Archbishop Adélard Langevin, OMI, of St. Boniface was a brief handwritten letter in English. The Catholic Church Extension Society, he wrote, should be supported by every Catholic since its end – its goal – was "so good and so high ... but the spirit in which it has been conducted, at least, as far as I know by my personal experience, is such that I could not give to it my confidence and my support."[18] Attached to this letter was a two-page typed memorandum in French consisting of six complaints against the conduct of Church Extension. Translated into English, and presented in condensed form, they are as follows:

1. It had tried to impose its own seminary on the Archdiocese of St. Boniface;

2. Although it has raised money for the Ruthenians and a Ruthenian newspaper and for several missionary priests and the Redemptorist Fathers, it had never disclosed the amount in a financial report, and regardless of the sum that the Society had expended on the

Ruthenians, it was only a fraction of the amount spent by his archdiocese;

3. Father Burke admitted that there were times when he did not inform him before the Society had sent money and religious goods to his priests;

4. Burke had encouraged Father Jules Pirot, a missionary in the Diocese of Regina, to work outside diocesan authority when he was still a member of the Archdiocese of St. Boniface;

5. The *Catholic Register* had blatantly ignored the work of the Western bishops on behalf of the Ruthenians and stridently proclaimed that the Society not only had discovered and but also had saved the Ruthenians; and

6. The Society sent two priests [Father Joseph T. Roche and Father Hugh J. Canning] to Winnipeg in 1909 to conduct a survey of the Ukrainians while he [Langevin] was at the Plenary Council of Québec.[19]

Langevin ended his memorandum by stating that if the Society wanted to assist the Ukrainians, it would have to work with Bishop Budka. The Society, of course, already had been working closely with Budka. Langevin's point was to tell Church Extension to leave him and his archdiocese alone. He asked McNeil not to make his notes public but to consider them as a contribution in McNeil's plan to alter Church Extension so that it would be more worthy of "the high approval that it has received."[20]

Bishop David Scollard of Sault Ste. Marie made three points and one recommendation. One, Church Extension "was not started in the proper way. All the Bishops, or at least all the archbishops of the Dominion should have been consulted, and a meeting of them called, so that the project might have the united support of the entire hierarchy. This was not done."[21] This criticism, given in the fifth year of the Church Extension's existence, sounded very similar to the objection of Archbishop Joseph-Thomas Duhamel, in October 1908, to the manner in which Church Extension had been established – without consulting the country's archbishops and bishops.[22] Two, "A complete and detailed statement of all receipts and disbursements should be made, at least once a year,"[23] for the benefit of the bishops and priests and perhaps for prominent Catholics who were supportive of the Society's work. Three, "The common opinion of the clergy of the Archdiocese of Toronto, who have, of course, occasion to know more of the Very Rev. President of the Extension Society, is that it can never be a success under his direction. The same opinion was expressed to me at the Quebec Plenary Council by some of the Maritime Province Bishops."[24] Reading this, McNeil must have felt that no imaginable compromise could save Burke's presidency of the Society.

But the last thing that Scollard wanted to see was the demise of Church Extension. Burke may not have been the right man to lead the Society, but his views on the need for it to produce English-speaking priests for the missions in the West remained valid:

> The crying need of Canada, it seems to me is priests of the English tongue. All priests should be fervently exhorted to work up and not allow vocations to be lost, and a fund through Catholic Extension should be on hand to educate these young men for the priesthood. If French-speaking Canada will not lend its co-operation and support to Catholic Church Extension, then let English-speaking Canada unite to further the scheme, because it is English-speaking Catholics of the west who need most to be looked after.[25]

Bishop Fallon of London, an ally of Scollard's on language matters, could not have said it better or more forcefully. And Burke would have agreed with both men – up to a point. The Western provinces definitely needed English-speaking priests, and Church Extension should have been the vehicle to provide them, but it was Ukrainian Catholics, by sheer force of numbers, and not English-speaking immigrants and settlers, who needed them the most. Regardless, in his capacity as president of Church Extension, and as editor-in-chief of the *Catholic Register*, Burke had been excoriated by the French hierarchy, priests and press for his opinions supporting English-speaking priests for the missions. Now that he was being blamed for the Society's second-grade performance, Scollard attributed that failure to Burke for not pursuing such an overtly Anglo-centric agenda more aggressively. Burke was caught in the classic paradox of damned if he did, and damned if he didn't. And Scollard was not the only bishop to scold Church Extension for allegedly ignoring the needs of English-speaking Catholic settlers in the West. Bishop Ryan was another critic in this regard.

Bishop Patrick Thomas Ryan, the auxiliary bishop of Pembroke, was the most perceptive in his comments, despite his disclaimer that what he had to say was drawn from casual conversations and newspaper stories. For starters, Church Extension was not popular in Québec or anywhere that Québec's influence prevailed in Ontario, because the Society "was regarded as an organized attempt to forward the interests of the English language, and English influence generally in the Canadian West."[26] Moreover, when Father Burke publicized the plight of the Ukrainians at the Plenary Council in 1909, many opinion makers in Québec regarded Burke as "simply trying to discredit the work of French Bishops and priests in the West, and exaggerating conditions with this subject in view."[27] Ryan had attended the Council but had not bothered to canvass his fellow bishops on their opinions of Father Burke. "For myself," he told McNeil,

> I thought, at the time, and the facts have but confirmed me in the same opinion since, that Father Burke was doing a necessary work; and I surmised that it was his exposition of conditions that determined the Fathers of the Council to ordain an annual subsidy for a number of years in favor of Ruthenian missions.[28]

Score one for Burke. But Québec antagonism to Burke and Church Extension, which was practically a given, was not the real issue for Ryan. He put it aside and asked this question, one that had yet to be aired: "Why could not the English-speaking Catholics of Ontario and other provinces adopt the work as their own and make it succeed?"[29] In essence, Ryan thought that Church Extension should drop any pretensions about being a national Catholic Society, since that was impossible due to the highly self-destructive debate over the relationship between language and faith that was currently plaguing the Church, and instead function solely as an English-speaking Society – independent of

French-speaking Québec – whose moral and material support came from the rest of Canada. So, why had it failed to accomplish what was possible? Ryan gave four reasons:

1. The bishops of Ontario, as a whole, were lacking in sympathy with an enterprise that had been launched more or less independently of them and under the control of Father Burke.

2. There was, and is, I do not know why, some prejudice or objection to Father Burke personally as president of the Extension Society or having any office in it. The root of this objection or prejudice I do not know. I am sure it is not anything unpriestly in Father Burke's life.

3. There is a feeling among English-speaking people that their brethren in the Canadian West are not getting fair play, and that there is nobody in a position there to see that they get it, or to avert the suspicion that they are not getting it; that effort enough is not made on the spot to attend to the religious wants of English-speaking immigrants into the West, whether from Ontario or the Old Country. I do not know what is behind talk of that kind, and I have not any means of verifying statements and rumors that tend to give this impression, but certainly such feeling is apt to beget lukewarmness in support of the "Church Extension" project.

4. No Statement of Receipts and Expenditure has ever been made public by the C.E. Society. How much has been subscribed; where, and to whom, and for what purposes did it go; are there any accounts, and has any audit ever been made of them; is there any effective control over expenditures? These are all questions that may be and are put; and to them there is not the ready answer that one expects to find in the case of an enterprise conducted upon business principles. Such a statement, if satisfactory, <u>might</u> inspire or restore confidence in the C.E. Society. It might set at rest doubts that have been expressed as to whether the Catholic Register is a necessary part of Ch. Extension, or a real asset of the Society. It might explain why the names of prominent men in Church and Country no longer appear in the columns of the Catholic Register as a Board of Governors.[30]

Ryan's letter was dated 26 February 1913. It confirmed McNeil's worst fears concerning Church Extension's tenuous future and sustained him in his judgment of Burke that he rendered to the apostolic delegate.

In addition to his circular to the bishops, McNeil wrote a letter to Father Kelley, Father Burke's closest friend and confidante. McNeil delivered a most discouraging assessment of the crisis:

> I am face to face with an Extension problem here. Bishops and priests throughout Canada have no confidence in Canadian Extension as at present conducted. One Bishop of Ontario expressed to me his opinion that it would be hopeless to try now to revive it, for the reason that its unpopularity had sunk too deep in the Catholic public. Possibly you know enough about matters here to be able to make useful suggestions, and if so I beg you to do so without reserve. I am not yet in a position to say whether the condition is hopeless. I do know that the Bishops and some prominent lay founders of the Society here see scarcely a prospect of revival.[31]

McNeil had been careful not to mention any names, but Kelley would have known immediately that McNeil was laying the blame squarely on Burke. Kelley replied, also not mentioning any names but obviously referring to his good friend in Extension: "I do not think that the situation is hopeless. The Society, itself, was popular from the beginning, and, in spite of everything, has done good work, though it had only half a chance. Any unpopularity that pertains to an individual only is not deep enough to destroy the work."[32] By admitting to McNeil that Burke *was* unpopular, Kelley realized that Burke was enough of a problem that the matter required his immediate attention. In answer, Kelley suggested to McNeil that he invite Fallon to meet the two of them in London on 17 February.[33] But it is not clear from the documentary evidence if that meeting ever took place.

It was now time for Archbishop McNeil to report on the prospects for Church Extension to Archbishop Stagni, the apostolic delegate. He did so in a letter of 24 February 1913, in which McNeil signalled his intention to remove Father Burke from the presidency of Church

Extension. Based on letters and interviews with bishops, and from his discussions with priests and laymen, none of whom are mentioned by name, McNeil constructed a carefully worded letter in which he passed final judgment on Burke's fitness to be president, conceded the constitutional difficulty of removing him from office, asked the delegate to find Burke a promotion, and suggested a solution to the selection of a new president. He wrote:

> With great regret I find that the resignation of the present president is an essential condition of success in any effort to make the Society an effective medium of Catholic action. He has done some very good work; he is able and energetic; his life is above reproach. All admit this. But he has succeeded in alienating most of those needed as co-operators. They simply will not listen to any proposition which does not exclude his presidency of the Society. There is no need to investigate the cause of this. Enough know that it is useless to try to change their attitude. This fact means death to the Society if he remains president. I do not intend to waste any effort in a hopeless task, and I know it is hopeless to try to rehabilitate the Society under present conditions. As he was appointed president by His Holiness [,] I can do nothing. Possibly Your Excellency can find some other position for him which he would accept as a promotion. The change would perhaps be more easily effected if all the Bishops of Ontario were added to the governing Board of the Society and one of them appointed president, having a secretary to do the work now done by the president. This secretary would be the appointee of the whole Board and very carefully selected.[34]

McNeil's letter failed to move Stagni into his camp. The delegate, in his reply of 27 February 1913, was perplexed by McNeil's proposal to oust Burke by means of a promotion and disappointed that the archbishop had not removed opposition to Burke from the ranks of his own clergy. (In this matter, neither McNeil nor Stagni wasted any time in replying to each other. The turnaround time for a response was two to three days.) Stagni did not agree with McNeil that Church Extension's present situation was hopeless. He wrote:

One thing is certain, that, as you fully recognize, Dr. Burke has done some very good work as the founder and organizer of the Society. The opposition which has been shown him, and which has been made a reason or pretext for not supporting the Society, is chiefly on the part of the clergy, high and low, and is only based, as far as I can gauge it, on little personal foibles. His conduct of the "Catholic Register", though perhaps not free from blemishes, has been most creditable, and, it is generally admitted, has done much to infuse life into what previously had been dead or dormant surroundings. He certainly does not merit a dismissal which could in any way be construed as a punishment, and I am glad to note that Your Grace also shares this view.[35]

Next, Stagni very cleverly put the onus on McNeil. Since he had been the one to propose a promotion for Burke as a way out of a perceived mess, and since the only kind of promotion that would not imply punishment would be a bishopric, would McNeil agree to recommend Burke for bishop? Stagni then played his trump card:

I recall a proposition made by Your Grace when Archbishop of Vancouver, and repeated verbally to me in Toronto, of dividing the Archdiocese of Vancouver and creating a new diocese in that jurisdiction. I do not know if Archbishop Casey is aware of this and how he would feel disposed towards the project. If Dr. Burke is considered worthy of a bishopric, do you not think that he would be peculiarly fitted for pioneer work of this kind?[36]

McNeil told Stagni in a letter of 1 March 1913 that now was not the time to divide the Archdiocese of Vancouver, even though the idea had merit, and that in any case he knew for certain that Archbishop Timothy Casey "would oppose the particular nomination suggested so strenuously that nothing would come of it."[37] But McNeil still wanted Burke out of Church Extension. So, he made two suggestions. One, McNeil could offer Burke a parish in Toronto and bestow upon him the much-coveted Protonotary Apostolic. Such an offer was within McNeil's power because Burke as a priest of the archdiocese was subject to McNeil's episcopal authority. It depended on Burke accepting an honour in exchange for a transfer to parish work. At the moment, however, there was no parish in the city available for Burke, and it was unlikely that he would accept one in the countryside.

Two, instead of keeping Burke close at hand in a Toronto parish, send him to the farthest and coldest corner of the country. McNeil proposed the separation of the Yukon Territory from the Prefecture Apostolic of Yukon and Prince Rupert and the erection of a new Prefecture Apostolic of Yukon with Dawson as its headquarters.[38] McNeil was confident that Burke would accept this office. But that was not the end of the matter. Having made his proposal, McNeil could not resist telling Stagni, "If he had not intrigued so much to obtain nomination or appointment to several Sees in Canada, one would have less hesitation in recommending for him the position of Bishop." On the sorry subject of Burke's foibles, as Stagni called them, McNeil charged Burke with a lack of consideration for others, "and when the co-operation of many people is to be secured a failing of that kind in the principal agent works havoc."[39] This was hardly a mere foible. Nor was the fact that Burke had a race problem – anti-French feelings. These feeling were so strong that "he has made it very difficult for his friends to be really of use to him."[40]

Stagni did not respond to McNeil's lecture on Burke's foibles. He stayed focused on the business at hand – enticing Burke to leave Church Extension without calling upon Rome's involvement in the affairs of the Society. In his letter of 4 March 1913, the apostolic delegate thought that the second of McNeil's two suggestions "offers the more satisfactory, though perhaps not easier, way."[41] But if the present Prefecture Apostolic of the Yukon and Prince Rupert were to be divided, and a new Prefecture of the Yukon created, Burke should be placed in charge of what Stagni, for the purpose of discussion, referred to as the Southern Prefecture, and Monsignor (later Bishop) Émile-Marie Bunoz, OMI, the current Prefect of the Yukon and Prince Rupert, should be transferred to the Northern Prefecture. Bunoz was an Oblate, as were all the missionaries in the Yukon, and there was no hope of having secular priests as missionaries there. It was pointless to have a secular priest placed in charge of a religious community in mission territory.

Stagni then addressed the division of the territory, a more challenging enterprise. He wanted the new Southern Prefecture to include the proposed Edmonton to Prince Rupert line of the Grand Trunk Pacific Railway. A Prefecture resident in Prince Rupert would best serve the new towns and settlements that undoubtedly would develop along the line. Stagni continued:

> Your Grace, by a mere look at the map, will easily see that this project would involve the cession on the part of the Archdiocese of Vancouver of one degree of latitude, the future limits being fixed at 53°. This new jurisdiction might for instance extend as far north as the 56°, leaving the other four degrees of Northern British Columbia to the Prefecture Apostolic of the North. As the 53° cuts the Queen Charlotte Islands in two, and as it would appear that they could be more easily served from Prince Rupert than Vancouver, they also might be annexed to the new Prefecture Apostolic of the South.[42]

The apostolic delegate ended by asking McNeil "to make the proposal in a definite form to me, suggesting briefly the reasons for the division, namely, the imminent development of the particular section of country traversed by the Grand Trunk Pacific, the immense jurisdictions now existing and the facility of administration which this new division would entail."[43] There was to be no mention, no hint, of Father Burke's character flaws and poor administration of Church Extension – the very reasons that had prompted their correspondence in the first place.

In all of this official back-and-forth, with each new letter sinking ever deeper into tedious detail, it was McNeil who would have to provide a solution, for it was McNeil who wanted to rid himself of Burke. Stagni, the diplomat, was comfortable in the knowledge that he had not initiated this increasingly bizarre crisis. McNeil did. Hence, Stagni saw his role as assisting McNeil in any petition to Rome in what would appear to officials at the Holy See as a reasonable request coming from Canada.

First, though, McNeil would have to accept the delegate's proposal to divide the Prefecture of the Yukon and Prince Rupert. He could not. It would not be fair to Monsignor Bunoz, he told Stagni, to be moved to Dawson with diminished jurisdiction. There were only 1,849 Catholics in the Yukon. And there was another problem: "the Vicariate Apostolic of Athabaska includes part of British Columbia, namely the triangle formed by the 60th parallel, the 120th degree of longitude, and the present boundary between the Yukon Prefecture and the said Vicariate."[44] McNeil, who knew his maps and ecclesiastical territories, made the very sensible suggestion that new dioceses in Canada should follow provincial boundaries. With that in mind, he made the following suggestions:

1. That a Vicariate, with head quarters at Prince Rupert and with Monsgr. Bunoz as Vicar Apostolic, be formed to include the Queen Charlotte Islands, the main land of British Columbia lying north of the 52nd parallel and west of the 126th degree of longitude and the Yukon Territory.

2. That the rest of British Columbia north of 52nd parallel be a Prefecture with head quarters at Fort George [now Prince George] or Quesnel. This proposed prefecture would include a large section of the Peace River District which only awaits railway communication to become really important. It will be noted that instead of the 53rd degree I have taken the 52nd. There are valleys and towns on the 53rd which it is not advisable to divide, and the Archbishop of Vancouver will never wish to go further north than the 52nd.[45]

McNeil contended that the administration of the new Prefecture would be viable if the Provincial of the Oblates would direct the Oblate Fathers in the Indian Missions, while the Prefect, assisted by one or two secular priests, would attend to all other Catholics.

Apparently, Archbishop McNeil's proposal, or some version there-of, was the one sent by Archbishop Stagni to Propaganda Fide and to Cardinal Martinelli, the cardinal protector of Church Extension.[46] Time passed. Rome dithered. Vatican authorities had given it a favourable reception, but "nothing could be done until the petition for division had been made by Archbishop Casey,"[47] reported Father Kelley from Chicago to Archbishop McNeil, in a letter of 5 February 1914. That would have been news to Archbishop Casey. Writing to McNeil, who had returned from his *ad limina* visit to Rome, just before the start of the First World War, Casey asked for

> any information as to what is to be done regarding the presidency of the Church Extension Society, or with the actual president. Is there any prospect of Dr. Burkes [sic] getting an appointment to a Vicariate, or anything like that out here in the West? There is some talk of a certain division of this archdiocese, and of course just now I cannot but be interested in such a matter. I would be very grateful if you could give me any information, especially as to the prospects of Dr. Burke.[48]

In the summer of 1914, McNeil was unable to give his successor in Vancouver any information about Burke's prospects. But Casey need not have worried. Kelley had told McNeil a lot more than just what he had heard about the proposed division of the Archdiocese of Vancouver. He let McNeil know that Burke had been under the impression that Kamloops would be the new ecclesiastical jurisdiction in British Columbia and had made up his mind to accept it. Informed that it was Fort George, and not the more southerly and built-up Kamloops, that was up for Rome's consideration, Burke was shocked, exclaiming that it would be impossible to make anything of the place. When pressed by the Roman authorities to speak about the suitability of Burke for Fort George, Kelley told them that Burke "would make a very good man to build up and colonize, on account of his influence." But he also had to tell Cardinal De Lai and Cardinal Merry de Val that Burke did not want to be a Prefect. He preferred an appointment as Vicar Apostolic. This did not sit well with the two cardinals. "Both of them," Kelley told McNeil, "said that if he [Burke] were appointed and showed good results in a few years that he would be made Vicar-Apostolic on his own representation."[49]

This put an end to a bishopric for Burke.[50] In any event, Kelley's letter to McNeil was not written until ten months after the AGM of 2 April 1913. It was too late to make a difference in Burke's future. As for McNeil, he found himself outnumbered and outmanoeuvred at the adjourned meeting of 16 April 1913. It was at that meeting that he lost his bid to assume control of the *Catholic Register* and, as a sop to his opponents on the board, promised to send a circular to the bishops and to assist Burke in improving the fortunes of the newspaper (see Chapter Nine). McNeil had no intention of living up to either promise. Unbeknownst to the board, he had already sent a circular to the bishops, on 17 January 1913, and from the responses that he received he had concluded that if Burke remained president, Church Extension had no chance of surviving.

An uneasy calm settled over the affairs of the Society in the wake of the two board meetings in April 1913. It ended in November when a frustrated and irate McNeil resumed his offensive. He called Burke into his office on Friday, 7 November, and demanded that he hand over control of the *Register* to the archdiocese. Burke refused and told McNeil that the board had decided otherwise. McNeil then requested him to ask the board members – formally and for a second time – for their opinions about changing the Society's publication from a weekly to a monthly and relinquishing the weekly to the Archdiocese of Toronto. This did not sit well with Burke. Two days after the meeting, Burke wrote to Kelley, describing the request as "a nice job. Breeds trouble anyway. If he gets the paper he gets everything; if he doesn't, he'll wreck us, if he can. God help us."[51] What passed for sarcasm on Burke's part was in reality a deep-seated fear of McNeil: he really believed that if he lost control of the *Register*, he would lose control of the Society. In a hastily written postscript, Burke remarked that McNeil had sent his own handwritten letter to board members, "asking for paper for Diocese."[52]

Burke wrote to the board members on 8 November 1913. His letter was reproduced in the "Minutes" of the AGM of 22 April 1914. After Burke quoted extracts from the "Minutes" of the previous year's AGM and the adjourned AGM – which demonstrated the will of the board to retain ownership of the *Register*, and McNeil's promise to assist Burke's efforts to strengthen the paper's viability – he told the board,

His Grace says that he is greatly in need of a Diocesan publication for his own Associated Charities. Of course, no legal action could be taken with regard to the paper except at a meeting of the Board specially called for this purpose, but His Grace is anxious to have your opinion on the matter before going any further.[53]

Burke also reproduced replies from four board members to his inquiry on behalf of the archbishop: George Lang, M.J. Haney, G.P. Magann and Archbishop Legal of Edmonton. All were in favour of Society ownership of the *Register*.[54]

There survives only one exchange between McNeil and a board member on the *Register* question. That board member was Sir Charles Fitzpatrick. McNeil opened his two-page typewritten letter of 8 November 1913 with a declaration: "The Catholic Extension Society of Toronto is at present doing a small part of the work it was organized to do. This does not mean that failure is to be the outcome. I expect in time the co-operation needed for success."[55] In the meantime, he wanted to present his case for having Church Extension give up its weekly newspaper to the Archdiocese of Toronto. He gave three reasons: a weekly took up too much of the Society's energies (this was a criticism of Burke); it antagonized and competed against other Catholic weeklies; and "This Archdiocese has many other large interests of its own. We feel the need of a weekly paper very much, and the special organ of a particular Society is found not to serve the purpose."[56] The Society's new publication could keep the title of *Catholic Register and Church Extension* and its list of subscribers. He offered to defray all expenses incurred by the Society in the changeover or, if preferred, to make a lump sum payment of $3,000.

Fitzpatrick replied three days later. He was brutally blunt in laying the blame on the bishops for the Society's lack of success:

I have your letter of Nov. 8th. I quite agree with you: "The Catholic Extension Society of Toronto is at present doing only a small part of the work it was organized to do."

I am not, however, of the opinion that the fact of the publication by the Society of a Catholic weekly paper is the chief cause of our failure. The reason for our lack of success lies deeper and must be sought in the want of co-operation by the Bishops in the work of the Society. They are the anointed leaders in all such work as we had in contemplation when the Society was incorporated and without their aid nothing effective can be accomplished. May I venture to suggest that Your Grace should send for Father Burke and explain your views to him? If the interests of the Church are not being served by the present organization why not dissolve and let others take our places? I would be heartily in favour of some such action as I am convinced that the position of the Society cannot be maintained if a radical change in our relations with the Episcopate does not take place.

I have asked Father Burke to come and see me here with Mr. Haney as it is impossible for me to go to Toronto. Before answering your enquiry about the transfer of the paper it is necessary for me to take counsel with them.[57]

McNeil wisely chose to ignore Fitzpatrick's bluff about letting the board dissolve itself and have a new slate of directors take over. He had no intention of allowing Church Extension to implode on his watch. And he already had talked to Burke, on 7 November. But McNeil did inform the apostolic delegate of his plans for the *Register*. In his response, Stagni said that he had no opinion on McNeil's proposal. Rather, he gave a full account of a conversation that he had had with Father Burke in Ottawa on 14 November 1913. Seeing that Burke and the delegate talked on a Friday evening, it is reasonable to assume that Burke consulted with Fitzpatrick prior to talking with Stagni. McNeil received this reply from Stagni:

I ... discussed with him the general situation of Church Extension, and I endeavored to show him as clearly as I could that he was considered the chief obstacle to its success. I was careful to point out to him that Your Grace had nothing against him, and that you readily recognized his energy, activity, irreproachable conduct, as well as the good work he had accomplished. I added, however, that after consulting bishops, clergy and laymen, you had come to the conclusion that the task of rehabilitating Church Extension under present management was a hopeless one. I thought it best to speak thus plainly to Dr. Burke, and to use the information which Your Grace had conveyed to me. In justice however I had to state that I was not prepared to say that opposition to him was justified or justifiable, – in fact I rather thought not – but, however that might be, the opposition itself was a fact which paralyzed the working and usefulness of the institution. Dr. Burke did not think that the opposition was so universal and seemed confident that if he only had half a backing, things would be very different. He repeatedly stated that he was not complaining of Your Grace, as he was fully aware of the numberless occupations which take up your time and attention.[58]

At the AGM of 22 April 1914, the board duly noted the correspondence concerning the issue of newspaper ownership, and by taking no action, one way or the other, it kept the *Register* in the Society's hands. McNeil was stymied. The board did appoint twelve new members to its ranks – ten from the episcopacy and two laymen. This was in keeping with McNeil's wish to add more members of the hierarchy to the board to be a counterweight to the influence of the laity. The bishops nominated to be governors were Bishop Henry J. O'Leary of Charlottetown; Archbishop Timothy Casey of Vancouver; Bishop Thomas J. Dowling of Hamilton; Bishop Nykyta Budka of the Ukrainian Eparchy; Bishop David Scollard of Sault Ste. Marie; Bishop Alexander MacDonald of Victoria; Bishop Olivier-Elzéar Mathieu of Regina; Bishop John Thomas McNally of Calgary; Bishop Richard M.J. O'Brien of Peterborough; and Bishop Gustave Blanche, CJM, Vicar Apostolic of the Gulf of St. Lawrence (Seven Islands, Québec). The new lay members were Thomas Long of Toronto and Charles Dalton of Tignish, Prince Edward Island.[59]

These nominations were the board's only concession to McNeil. It accepted Father Burke's President's Report, in which Burke faulted the economic downturn of 1913 as the principal culprit in the Society's admittedly lacklustre performance during the past year. Highlights from the past fiscal year included an increase of twenty percent in advertising sales for the *Register* and the purchase of modern machinery for the press, an efficiency that was intended to increase the number of printing contracts and thus revenues for the paper; a gift of $2,500 from the Catholic Order of Foresters in Ontario for five memorial chapels and a promise of an additional $15,000 from the Catholic Foresters when they met at their international convention in Toronto in August 1915; total disbursements of $21,765.97 for charitable work; a profit of almost $1,000 in the management of St. Philip Neri Hostel; and the wonderful work of the Women's Auxiliary.[60]

With Archbishop McNeil in mind, Burke once more asked for the active support of the clergy, beginning with McNeil himself:

> In conclusion, might I again urge the necessity for more help in the work of the Society from the Bishops and priests throughout the country, and especially in this Diocese, from our Most Reverend and worthy Chancellor, to take up the work in earnest, and help Extension with its many pressing needs, as well as effectually assist in the dissemination of our publication everywhere.[61]

Turning to the board of governors, Burke made an emotional plea:

> Do strengthen our hands, do place in them something wherewith to relieve the distress of the Home Missions, and thus enable us to fulfill the best of all charities, the spread of God's Kingdom on earth. We must have charity to save our souls, and with the needs of our own Missions who will say that charity does not begin at home.[62]

As the AGM was drawing to a close, Michael J. Haney asked Burke if the Most Reverend Chancellor had provided the assistance promised to him at last year's AGM. Burke answered no. In response to his answer, the board struck a three-man sub-committee consisting of Haney, George P. Magann and Justice Hugh T. Kelly "to secure action in the matter."[63]

In October 1914, not having advanced any further in his desire to remove Burke from the presidency, or, at the very least, to take control of the *Catholic Register*, Archbishop McNeil next decided to ask Stagni to intervene on his behalf, hoping now to have Burke dismissed from the presidency based on the Latin Constitution of 1910, the very same Constitution that had never been accepted by Pius X when he recognized Church Extension as a Papal Society in the Apostolic Brief *Allata nuper ad nos* (see Chapter Three).[64] As a tactical move, it was bound to fail, but McNeil, not having participated in the founding of Church Extension, did not understand the history of the origins of the Society's constitution to the same degree that Burke and Kelley did. McNeil may have understood that only Rome could oust Burke, but he did not know that the Latin Constitution, even if put in the hands of the right person in Rome, would be totally useless as a legal avenue to secure Burke's suspension and, in time, his dismissal.

McNeil also wrote to Cardinal Gaetano De Lai, the secretary of the Sacred Consistorial Congregation (now called the Congregation of Bishops), asking him to find a position in the Church for Burke. De Lai scouted around Rome and even wrote to the apostolic delegate in the United States, which must have seemed odd to the delegate in Washington, but the cardinal's inquiries proved fruitless. He suggested to McNeil that the delegate in Ottawa might be able to come up with a solution, an avenue that McNeil had been busily pursuing for months, and wondered what approach the Society might take to Burke's removal without causing serious consequences.[65]

While McNeil was busy writing to Ottawa and Rome, Burke fell seriously ill. He had had ptomaine poisoning, which was followed by pleurisy and then a bout of pneumonia. Father Roche relayed this news to Father Kelley, adding this claim: "The Archbishop is going to send him [Burke] to a parish as soon as he is able to take charge. Will oust him from the presidency of the society at the same time."[66] Roche was exaggerating for effect and Kelley knew it.[67] But the atmosphere at Church Extension headquarters definitely had turned sour, with no relief in sight. How sour can be gauged by Roche's reluctance to continue to work on the *Register*, even though McNeil had invited him to stay, and by his telling Kelley, again with exaggeration, that Europe, which had been at war since August, "was a much safer place than Toronto at the present time."[68]

Although Burke had yet to recover fully from his various illnesses, he felt that he had to plead his case in person with Archbishop Stagni in Ottawa. He did not see Stagni, but he did speak to Monsignor Sinnott, the delegate's secretary, on 26 November 1914. Sinnott then reported the gist of their conversation to Stagni, who immediately sent a written version of Sinnott's report to McNeil:

> The report brought back to me is that Dr. Burke is not disposed to tender his resignation and that he would feel aggrieved were he deprived of his office before the expiration of his term. Moreover, he declares that the supposed "Constitutions" were never approved by Rome and therefore are not worth the paper they are printed on. These "Constitutions," he maintains, were prepared and sent to Rome, but the Holy See refused to approve them, but instead issued a Brief granting the Society Canonical institution. The Brief, in short, is the only thing that has come from Rome.[69]

The word "resignation" appears for the first time in the correspondence concerning Burke's fate. McNeil must have asked him to resign, or Stagni may have brought up the idea at McNeil's prompting or on his own. Regardless, Burke was ready to confront such a demand by pointing out, in this case to Stagni, that the Latin Constitution did not give McNeil the right to force him to resign or even to ask him for his resignation. This was one of Burke's trump cards, and he played it at the right time. Yet for the first time, Burke began to buckle under the strain. He realized that another five-year term as president was highly unlikely. Cornered, and under pressure from not only McNeil, as was to be expected, but also Stagni, he asked the delegate that he be allowed to complete his term, which would have taken him to April 1916. This would be his second trump card.

The 1915 Annual General Meeting of the board of governors took place on three different dates. The AGM began on 14 April, but it did not last very long before it was adjourned. It was resumed on 26 April, which also ended in an adjournment, and finally came to a close on 12 August, at which time Father Burke and Sir Charles Fitzpatrick tendered their resignations. The board of governors was divided into two distinct camps: in one camp were Archbishop Neil McNeil, Monsignor Kidd and the bishops, and in the other were Father Burke and the lay members. Bitterness, contention and misunderstanding marred the first two meetings, and the board put on a brave face during the last one. Tired of all the unseemly infighting, the board closed the Father Alfred E. Burke chapter in the history of the Catholic Church Extension Society of Canada.

Four issues proved highly divisive. The first surfaced as a lead-up to the AGM of 12 August. Although it was resolved without the involvement of the board, it set the stage for a negative and hostile tone at the AGM, which made the resolution of the other three issues – the terna (three candidates for president), the qualification of governors, and the report of the sub-committee – all the more impossible for the board to settle in an amicable fashion. The first issue, then, concerned the determination of the end date of Burke's five-year term as president. This was a problem for McNeil and no one else. He was under the impression that since Pius X had nominated Burke as president on 10 December 1910, Burke's tenure would end on 10 December 1915. But there was one potential flaw to his seemingly simple calculation. The board had not confirmed the pope's choice of Burke until 14 April 1911. If this were to be counted as the date when his presidency commenced, Burke's term would not end until 14 April 1916. Burke insisted that the latter date was the correct one. The prospect of having to deal with Burke beyond 1915 was an unappetizing one for McNeil, to say the least, which is why McNeil asked Stagni to issue a ruling, in a letter probably written in February 1915.

When Burke got wind of McNeil's letter to the apostolic delegate, he immediately wrote to Kelley, on Good Friday, 2 April 1915. At one point in his letter, he referred to the archbishop as "Nilus of the Nine Hostages." This was a nasty pun on the names Neil, Nilus and Niall, in reference to "Niall of the nine hostages," the mythological ancestor of the Uí Néill kingship of Tara, Ireland. Burke accused McNeil not only of being on a rampage – "Quae regio terrae?" [Is he the king of the world?] – but also of antagonizing civil and religious authority by asking the delegate, who had no authority, to adjudicate on the matter of his term as president.[70] In Burke's mind, McNeil had acted rashly and wrongly.

Burke need not have worried. Stagni had already asked Cardinal De Lai, the secretary of state, for his advice on the question. As soon as the cardinal's response had arrived from Rome, Stagni informed McNeil on 9 April 1915, five days before the AGM, that the "'quinquennium' is to be computed from the time at which the appointment was notified officially to the Board, that is, in our case, from April 1911."[71] The ruling was in Burke's favour. However, that was not the end of the matter. Stagni closed his letter by reminding McNeil that it would be necessary at the next meeting of the board to draw up a terna of names for nomination to the presidency for the five-year term that would begin in April 1916. The board's failure to produce a list of three candidates for the pope's consideration became the second issue. When McNeil demanded at the adjourned AGM of 26 April 1915 that the board carry out the delegate's instructions to submit a terna, the board found itself deadlocked in a struggle over who should be in control of Church Extension: the clergy or the laity.

Before Burke was apprised of the delegate's ruling, he met McNeil at the latter's house on Easter Tuesday, 6 April 1915, on the advice of Monsignor Sinnott, the delegate's secretary and confidant of Burke. Also in attendance was Monsignor Kidd, the rector of St. Augustine's Seminary and a member of the board. According to Burke, who informed Sinnott, the meeting was cool but cordial. Perhaps the blessings of Easter had yet to dissipate. McNeil made the most of the occasion. He said that it had been a big mistake for the board of governors to have given Burke the added responsibility of editing the *Catholic Register*. He also told Burke that he had tried to find him a position in the curia in Rome, but that the death of Pius X (on 20 August 1914) had put an end to his inquiries. The upshot of the meeting was that nothing had changed. The two men remained on a collision course.[72]

The third issue involved the qualification of governors. This was Burke's revenge for McNeil having convinced the board at the AGM of 1914 to add ten bishops to the list of governors. They may have been nominated to become members of the board, but were they qualified to participate in the upcoming AGM, according to the Constitution? Attached to the notification of the AGM, sent out on 22 March 1915, was this:

> Section 4, Article 4, of the Constitution says: "Hereafter no person shall be added to the Board who has not taken out a Life Membership in the Society as provided for in Article 3, of the Constitution."

> Article 3. Life Members: "All those who pay into the Society's funds one thousand dollars either in one sum or in ten annual payments of one hundred dollars each, and those who guarantee to support one student in the Missionary College of the Society during ten years shall be considered a Life Member."

> As the Board has not passed any regulation respecting proxies it is desirable that qualified Governors attend the meeting in person.[73]

Burke's penchant for intrigue astonished McNeil[74] and prompted him to ask Burke, in a hand-delivered note of 22 March 1915, to send over to him the "Minutes" of the board meetings. We know from subsequent correspondence between McNeil and the law firm Foy, Knox & Monahan that McNeil wanted a legal opinion on qualification based on an examination of the "Minutes," in tandem with that of the Constitution and By-Laws.[75] It is impossible, however, to determine if Burke was aware of McNeil's intentions, because Burke never kept any of his incoming correspondence. In any event, Burke responded the same day: "although I felt at the moment that I could not legally let the minutes of the Society out of my hands, I have taken advice and am now confirmed in that opinion. This book and any other book in the Society's possession will be gladly put before Your Grace at these offices any time and for any time."[76] He then informed McNeil that a list of qualified governors would be drawn up and sent to him. As events transpired, the qualification issue came to the fore as a result of the board's failure to produce a terna.

Now to the fourth issue. On 5 March 1915, the special sub-committee of the board, comprised of Haney, Magann and Kelly, published its report – the Memo – in the form of an open letter to Archbishop McNeil. The Memo's purpose was to "see what could be done to remove the obstacles which now hinder the progress of the Society."[77] Largely drawn from the "Minutes," it was a capsule history of the Society from its founding in 1908 to the board meeting of 22 April 1914 and a careful recitation of the many and various accomplishments of the Society, including its assistance to Bishop Budka and the 200,000 Ruthenian Uniates under his care and the success of the *Register* in serving the Catholic faith in Canada, despite the handicaps and restrictions that the Society and its newspaper encountered in carrying out its missionary work. The Memo ended on this provocative note:

> In view of all this representation, we desire to approach Your Grace, as Chancellor of the Society, and respectively request that we be advised when Your Grace will take measures to aid us in the advancement of the Society, for notwithstanding all it has accomplished, as shown by the foregoing statement, we are convinced that without the full and sympathetic co-operation of the Most Rev. Chancellor of the Society, its beneficent objects can only be partially attained.[78]

In their eyes, McNeil was the problem. He was the main obstacle that was hindering the progress of the Society. Once again, the archbishop was put on the defensive. In a letter of 27 March 1915 to Judge Kelly, he wondered "whether it is with your consent that this Report is printed and circulated."[79] Kelley replied that he would give his reasons for publishing the document when they met[80] – which would have been the upcoming AGM on 14 April 1915.

The AGM did not last long. Archbishop McNeil was in the chair. Father Burke acted as secretary. The qualified governors in attendance were Bishop Scollard and Bishop O'Brien, Monsignor Kidd, Justice H.T. Kelly, M.J. Haney and G.P. Magann. Also present but apparently not voting was Thomas Long, who had been nominated to the board in 1914. Before the meeting commenced, both Scollard and O'Brien had paid the initial installment of $100 towards a Life Membership to qualify as governors with a right to vote. After the board approved the "Minutes" of the previous year's AGM, Burke read to the board two communications from Sir Charles Fitzpatrick: a special delivery letter of 12 April and a night lettergram dated the next day, in which Fitzpatrick asked for an adjournment until Monday, 26 April. He was undergoing medical treatment in Atlantic City, New Jersey, and would not be able to return to Canada until the Sunday before the day of the proposed adjournment. He promised to take a direct train from New York to Toronto.[81] The vote was four to three in favour of adjourning the meeting, with Burke and the three laymen voting yes and Kidd and the two bishops voting no.[82]

The adjourned AGM took place on 26 April 1915, as requested by Sir Charles Fitzpatrick. Present for the meeting were Archbishop McNeil in the chair, Father Burke as secretary and the following qualified governors: Bishop Scollard, Bishop O'Brien, Monsignor Kidd, Justice H.T. Kelly, M.J. Haney, G.P. Magann and George Lang. Also in attendance were Archbishop Timothy Casey of Vancouver and Bishop Alexander MacDonald of Victoria. The board approved the "Minutes" from the AGM of 14 April and unanimously adopted the President's Report and the Report of the Women's Auxiliary. That was the end of the unanimity.

The next item on the agenda was a motion moved by M.J. Haney and seconded by Bishop O'Brien that the sub-committee's Memo to the Chancellor be tabled and filed. McNeil, as chairman of the meeting, refused to put the motion, and during the ensuing discussion complained that he had been tried unheard. Haney, as chairman of the sub-committee, replied that the Memo "was a mere statement of fact in courteous language, terminating with one single question; it was a report of a sub-committee and should be received."[83] McNeil, however, refused to receive it. As a result, the Memo was not recorded in the "Minutes." It was as if it had never been commissioned and written.

One can easily imagine how Haney, Magann and Kelly must have felt when McNeil pushed aside their work.

McNeil now turned to the question of the terna. What follows is Burke's account in the "Minutes":

> The Chancellor then read a clause from a letter of the Apostolic Delegate declaring that the President's term ended in April, 1916, and saying that a terna be made for such a nomination. A very animated discussion took place, when Sir Charles Fitzpatrick rose and declared the whole thing to be in very bad taste and advised a conference from both sides of the Board for peace. The Chairman named Bishops O'Brien and Scollard to act with him and Sir Charles Fitzpatrick named Mr. Justice Kelly and Mr. M.J. Haney. The other members withdrew. The conference lasted quite a time, and in due course the Chancellor summoned those who had withdrawn, to return to the meeting. Nothing was effected by the conference.[84]

Burke, of course, knew nothing of what had transpired in conference. For that we turn to McNeil, who wrote his version of events in a letter of 30 April 1915 to Stagni, the apostolic delegate:

> Sir Charles Fitzpatrick asked for a special committee before which he wished to lay certain matters. He emphasized strongly his opinion that the Catholic Church Extension Society is a lay and civil society. The proposition as to the committee was agreed to. To this committee Sir Charles proposed that by arrangement the name of Dr. Burke be placed upon the terna to be sent to the Holy See for appointment as next President. By the constitution of the Society the term of the President is five years. Sir Charles was asked what position in the terna he wished Dr. Burke's name to occupy. He replied that it should be first place. He was then asked whether he would agree to second place if the Bishops on the committee also agreed to accept him as one of the terna. This he refused to agree to, and the Bishops were equally firm in refusing to allow Dr. Burke's name to stand first. Thus the committee failed in its purpose, and the general meeting resumed.[85]

We cannot determine if Burke knew beforehand that Sir Charles Fitzpatrick would insist on having his name appear first on the terna. But he must have been informed sometime afterwards of the bishops' united and firm opposition to his name appearing at the top of any terna, and because of that news he must have been convinced that his resignation from the presidency before his term expired was inevitable. All that was left, from a practical point of view, was to negotiate the best terms possible for a dignified departure. Recognition of his fate, soon after the adjourned meeting of 26 April, is the only plausible explanation for Burke's decision to see Stagni in Ottawa in May.

Upon reconvening the general meeting of the board, McNeil, under the "new business" section of the agenda, called for a vote on the terna for president, despite what had just occurred in conference. Strangely, the "Minutes" do not mention the names on the terna that McNeil was so anxious to put to a vote. The absence of such information might be understood by what followed his call for a vote. Again, we turn to Burke's version of events, recorded in his role as secretary of the meeting:

> Governor Haney asked the Secretary to declare whom of those present were qualified to vote. He read the list; but the Chancellor immediately objected; Mr. Haney then asked for a legal opinion, which the Secretary read to the Board. The Chancellor refused to accept any such opinion; and said that two Bishops had come all the way from British Columbia. Sir Charles Fitzpatrick replied by asking what they had come for; they should know the law. Finally the Chancellor declared – I will adjourn the meeting without further action on terna. Moved by Governor M.J. Haney, seconded by Governor G.P. Magann.[86]

Having a legal opinion to justify his selection of qualified governors was obviously a planned move on Burke's part, one made possible by McNeil's insistence that the board as a whole deal with the terna debacle. Burke's move was a clever one – but only by half. By shutting down the meeting without warning, McNeil quickly outflanked Burke and his board allies. Here is the archbishop's telling of the story to the apostolic delegate:

> To understand the next move, which was prepared in advance to defeat the object of the majority, it must be observed that, to have the right to vote at a meeting, a governor of recent appointment must be a Life Member. That is, he must make a first payment of $100 to the Society. On the 14th the Bishops of Sault Ste. Marie and of Peterborough paid that amount and exercised their right to vote. On the 26th the Archbishop of Vancouver and the Bishop of Victoria paid a like amount to the Society before the adjourned meeting was called to order. The money was accepted, and most of us assumed that their right to vote was unquestionable. After the failure of the committee, the President read a legal opinion secured from a firm of lawyers in the City to the effect that any governor who made his first payment after the 14th of April had no right to vote at the adjourned meeting. This would exclude the Archbishop of Vancouver and the Bishop of Victoria from the meeting. I refused to accept the legal opinion in question and the meeting adjourned sine die.[87]

The next move was up to Burke. While Church Extension was busy conducting its missionary work, and the *Register* was full of news every week about the Society's endeavours, Burke knew that he no longer had a place in the life of the Society that he had helped to found and the newspaper that he had edited and directed since 1908. He left for Ottawa on 7 May 1915.[88] Over the next several days, he conferred with Archbishop Stagni, Monsignor Sinnott and his closest friend on the board, Sir Charles Fitzpatrick.[89] Burke was under tremendous pressure to face the obvious. By 11 May, he had signalled to Stagni his intention to place "himself unreservedly in the hands of the Apostolic Delegate, through whom he intends to resign his office to the Holy See."[90] This was wonderful news to McNeil. Stagni thought that the resignation could take effect on 1 August and that Burke could take a leave of absence for the rest of the year before McNeil appointed him pastor of a city parish in the Archdiocese of Toronto. Also, Stagni recommended that Burke be promoted to a prelature. McNeil was only too happy to comply with Stagni's request:

> In view of the good work done in the past by the Very Rev. A.E. Burke, DD of this Diocese, and especially as proof that his resignation of the presidency of the Catholic Church Extension Society of Canada does not involve any blame or censure, I think it would be appropriate if the Holy See graciously consented to enroll him in the Roman prelature and thus give effect to the appreciation made in his behalf by my Predecessor in April 1910.[91]

Burke would finally receive the coveted Protonotary Apostolic, and he would be allowed to exit Church Extension with his head held high. But there remained two details to resolve. Burke pointed out to Stagni that in accordance with civil law, his resignation as president could not take effect until he tendered it to the board of governors and the board accepted it. Burke also mentioned the fact that he had no financial means to support himself, since he had never taken his $1,000 per year salary as president; he had only charged the Society for his expenses. For these reasons, Stagni recommended that the board reconvene and complete the AGM of 1915.[92]

The second (and final) adjourned meeting of the AGM of 1915 took place on 12 August. All was peace and harmony. Compromise and unity of purpose reigned. The board disposed of eleven motions without a whisper of debate:

1. Burke was owed a total of $6,561.68. Of this amount he kept $5,000 and donated the remainder to the Society.

2. The Memo produced by the three-man sub-committee, and dated 5 March 1915, was reproduced in its entirety in the "Minutes."

3. The board accepted the resignation of Father Burke, congratulated him on the Protonotary Apostolic and wished him all the best in his new role as a military chaplain.

4. The board accepted the resignation of Sir Charles Fitzpatrick and thanked him for his invaluable services to the Society.

5. Monsignor Kidd was appointed acting managing governor of the Society.

6. A new executive committee was formed and consisted of Archbishop McNeil, Monsignor Kidd and G.P. Magann.

7. Father J.B. Dollard, formerly associate editor of the *Register*, was appointed editor-in-chief at a salary of $1,000 per year.

8. The board composed the following terna for a new president: Bishop Michael F. Power of St. George's, Newfoundland, Dignissimus; Monsignor Arthur A. Sinnott, Dignior; Monsignor Émile Roy, Montréal, Dignus.

9. The board recommended that in future, the president of the Society be a bishop, and that since the Society was a Dominion-wide organization, it should be placed under the apostolic delegate and not under a diocesan bishop.

10. The board suggested that the executive committee make an effort to have a prominent French Canadian priest join the Society in some official capacity, such as vice-president.

11. The board accepted executive committee decisions made since April 1914.[93]

Father Burke was gone. Archbishop McNeil had triumphed. In a show of solidarity with their chancellor, the board of governors, now dominated by the bishops, voted at the Annual General Meeting of 3 May 1916 to remove from the "Minutes" of the adjourned AGM of 12 August 1915 the Memo of 5 March 1915 and the recommendation that Church Extension be placed under the Apostolic Delegate.[94] M.J. Haney, the chairman of the sub-committee that had written the Memo, seconded the motion. Both motions were crossed out. By eliminating the Memo as an official document in the administrative history of Church Extension, the board denied recognition of Father Burke's many accomplishments as the first president of the Society during its formative years. It was a harsh judgment.

••••

Father Alfred E. Burke spent the last years of his life as an itinerant priest. Stability was never one of his virtues, and controversy always trailed in his wake. He was a chaplain in the Canadian Expeditionary Forces in England from 1915 to 1917. He was appointed an Hon. Major and rose to the rank of Hon. Lieutenant Colonel, but he was unable to work with other chaplains and took his rank far too seriously. He was forced to resign his commission. On his return to North America, he lived with Father Francis C. Kelley for a year and became a thorn in his side. Kelley did not know what to do with him and asked Archbishop Neil McNeil, Burke's Ordinary, to put Burke on permanent leave of absence with the pay of a parish priest, which was $1,000 per year. McNeil complied.

This gave Burke considerable independence of a type that suited his wandering instincts. In 1919, Kelley sent him to Mexico to investigate the anti-clerical regime of President Venustiano Carranza, who had exiled the Mexican hierarchy to the United States. Although Burke went with the blessing of the United States Department of State and the Mexican bishops, and acted on behalf of American Church Extension, he managed to make a mess of his mission. He misrepresented himself, claiming incorrectly that he was working on behalf of the American bishops, thought that Carranza was fairly conservative within the volatile and violent context of Mexican politics, and then had the temerity to tell the truth about the alienation of the faithful from the Mexican clergy, in the pages of the Jesuit journal *America*. Kelley had to recall him and send him on his way.

Burke returned to Toronto. But McNeil, who judged him to be nothing more than a nuisance and a nightmare, was in no hurry to find him a post in a parish or in any other capacity. From Toronto, Burke travelled to Rome and delivered a report on the situation of the Church in Mexico to Pope Benedict XV and then returned to the United States, where he served for a brief spell as the representative of American Church Extension in California. Bored, he returned to Rome. Except for his attendance at the International Eucharistic Congress in Chicago in June 1926, Burke resided in the Eternal City, where he worked as a freelance journalist for the Knights of Columbus and regularly dunned McNeil for his stipend.[95]

Father Burke died on 15 December 1926 and was buried in the Campo Santo Cemetery in the vicinity of the Basilica of St. Paul-Outside-the-Walls in Rome. The Canadian Press and the *Canadian Annual Review of Public Affairs* ran notices of his death, and the *Charlottetown Guardian* published a lengthy obituary with a photograph.[96] Sadly, there was no mention of his passing in the *Catholic Register* or in the "Minutes" of the Society's Annual General Meeting of 1927. Time had demoted Monsignor Burke, the priest from Prince Edward Island, into Church Extension's forgotten founder.

CHAPTER 11

AN ASSESSMENT OF FATHER BURKE'S PRESIDENCY

F ather Alfred E. Burke was a paradox: he was the right man and the wrong man at the same time. In his role as the right man, he would accomplish many good things during the formative years of the Catholic Church Extension Society of Canada. Father Burke was the right man to kick-start the Society into operational life. He was Church Extension's foremost founder, its front man, its bagman, its voice, its presence. Decades before there was a permanent episcopal conference in Canada, he understood the need for a national Catholic organization to provide various and much-needed assistance for the pastoral care of new Catholic communities then springing up in numerous places in the West and British Columbia, and to provide the same kind of timely and consistent aid in the form of outright donations or loans to remote parishes and missions in northern Ontario, the Gulf of St. Lawrence and the Diocese of St. George's, Newfoundland. He also introduced the readership of the *Register* to missions in the Arctic.

Burke agreed to the formation of the Women's Auxiliary of Church Extension, which was probably the most effective administrative decision of his presidency. Starting in 1910, the Women's Auxiliary collected and distributed an enormous quantity of church goods – in particular, vestments, children's toys and clothing, and Catholic literature for numerous isolated and poor missions throughout the West. The Auxiliary helped to establish Rosary Hall and administer St. Philip Neri Hostel. Church Extension without the Women's Auxiliary would have been a rump of an organization.

And, most importantly, Burke was an early, ardent and passionate champion of the rights of Ukrainian Eastern Rite Catholics. He may have resorted to hysterical and inflammatory language when describing their plight and demonizing their enemies, but as an advocate of the preservation of the Ukrainian Catholic Church so recently transplanted to the Prairies, and as a priest who understood their plight, almost instinctively, no one among the clergy in Eastern Canada was his equal. Bishop Budka could not lavish enough praise and thanks on Church Extension.

For Father Burke, the Church was much more than one's local parish. Catholics had to emerge from their nineteenth-century ghettos and embrace a Church that was far more universal and diversified than previously imagined or experienced by Canadian Catholics. As Canada was changing, so, too, was the Catholic Church. To keep Catholics abreast of those changes and challenges to Church life, Burke purchased the *Catholic Register*. Within a short period of time, he increased its circulation and turned it into a modestly profitable weekly. He effectively used the paper's Church Extension pages as a reliable conduit not only for Society news, which was always plentiful and informative, but also as a convenient avenue to explain and justify the Society's evolving missionary mandate.

It is difficult to imagine Church Extension coming into existence in 1908 without the forceful personality of Father Burke. He helped to give birth to the Society and to nurture it through its infancy, despite the collective inexperience of the Society's founders in creating something as elusive as a home missionary spirit among the Catholic people. Burke and the board of governors also had to deal with a Catholic population whose means were modest at best and already supporting Propagation of the Faith, Peter's Pence, the China Mission Society, regular parish collections and special diocesan projects. To complicate the picture even further, following the Plenary Council of 1909, Canadian dioceses were committed to contributing to the welfare of Ukrainian Catholics on an annual basis, via the Archdiocese of St. Boniface. This arrangement lasted from 1910 to 1930. Many bishops, in particular those from Québec, used this collection as an excuse to ignore Church Extension's existence.

All in all, the absence of a sizeable and generous Catholic middle class made the early years of fundraising on behalf of Church Extension, aside from the initial windfall generated by wealthy founders, a frustrating exercise in begging for money one dollar at a time. It was an uphill struggle for Burke and Church Extension to convince Catholics to recognize the needs of the Canadian Church beyond the boundaries of their own parish and diocese. According to an official tabulation, from December 1908 to March 1915, the Society handed out $93,452.89 to home missions.[1] (This total excluded the money raised from 80,000 Mass intentions, which canonically could not be treated as donations but may have been regarded as such by many people who dutifully sent Mass intentions to Church Extension for missionary priests.) This was a fraction of the money raised by various Protestant home mission societies.[2] It was painfully obvious to Archbishop McNeil that Church Extension had failed to convince enough Catholics of the moral necessity of financially supporting the Society's missionary undertakings.

In his role as the wrong man, Father Burke would antagonize and alienate powerful members of the Catholic hierarchy with his sense of entitlement and self-importance, his extravagant and pompous style and his freewheeling and oftentimes inflammatory opinions on matters that had nothing directly to do with Church Extension. Burke was unable to put aside for the greater good of Church Extension his Imperialism, his English Canadian nationalism and his intense dislike of what he (and some others) thought was the inward-looking French Canadian element in the Church both inside and outside of Québec. He should never have been editor-in-chief of the *Catholic Register*, for it was as an editorialist and commentator on the pages of the Society's newspaper that he caused so much grief for himself and Church Extension, undermining his authority as president and the Society's standing in the larger Catholic community. In the end, Burke angered the wrong people, bishops foremost among them, and consequently undercut Church Extension's ability to cultivate a wider audience and a broader base of financial support. The death of Archbishop McEvay, on 10 May 1911, left Burke alone in a world of Catholic critics increasingly hostile to him and his style of leadership.

Of course, Burke did not create the French–English divide in Canadian society or in the Church. That unfortunate division, founded on language and culture, preceded his arrival in Toronto. As a Catholic priest and the ambitious president of a Catholic society, however, Burke did next to nothing to heal the wounds of this division. Instead, governed by an inflated ego, and a misguided righteousness about all things concerning the inevitable triumph of the English language, he provoked a French Canadian backlash against Church Extension with his campaign on behalf of English-speaking missionaries for the West, his unwillingness to understand Archbishop Langevin's point of view on the rights of an Ordinary in his own diocese, and his unapologetic approbation of Bishop Fallon's crusade against bilingual schools in Ontario. The Fallon episode was a political blunder from which there was no recovery.

Unnecessary and debilitating controversy was the predictable outcome. Soon, it strengthened an already existing perception among numerous French-speaking clergy and laity that Church Extension, headquartered in Protestant Toronto, was the vanguard of the English-speaking Church's plan to anglicize historic French-speaking dioceses in the West.[3] That perception may have been exaggerated, if not downright mistaken, but perceptions by their very nature are powerful instruments in the art of setting the tone of public discourse and as such are difficult to dislodge from the political arena. Indeed, so powerful was this perception of Church Extension, as an indictment of Burke, that it has led some historians to judge Church Extension's less than stellar performance during the years 1908 to 1915, at least in part, as a result of Burke's belligerent behaviour towards his French co-religionists. Without them, Church Extension could not claim to be a national society.

That is a true statement, but it is beside the point. There was nothing that Burke could have said or done that would have presented Church Extension as a trustworthy enterprise in the estimation of the French Canadian hierarchy and its apologists in the French Canadian press. From the outset, it was suspicion that informed their judgment of the motives that inspired the establishment of Church Extension, and it was suspicion that convinced first the archbishop of Montréal and then the archbishop of Ottawa to refuse Burke's invitation to host Church Extension's home office. If either prelate had been genuinely interested in Church Extension, or was concerned about influence or control over its activities, he would have welcomed the opportunity to have the Society operate in his episcopal city, where he could have kept a watchful eye on it. Church Extension did not become a national society because such a goal was impossible in the corrosive climate then governing Church politics in Canada. Burke's animus against the French, which definitely injured the fortunes of Church Extension, did not create that climate but certainly added to it.

So, a more precise failing should be attributed to Father Burke and, to no less extent, to the entire board of governors. The Society's real failure was not to become an English-speaking Catholic Church Extension Society in the rest of Canada, but primarily in Ontario, which was its base.[4] It was a goal that was both reasonable and well within the Society's reach and, moreover, one that would not have disturbed to any lasting degree the relative independence of the Church's two reigning solitudes. It was a missed opportunity.

How, then, are we to judge the success of Father Burke's eight-year presidency? One of the better ways is to measure the extent to which Church Extension, led by Burke, lived up to its aims or objects as listed in Article 2 of the 1908 Constitution:

a) **By cultivating a missionary spirit in the clergy and people**: There was very little or no home missionary spirit among the Catholic faithful until the advent of Church Extension. After the Society was up and running, the people demonstrated their spirit by making donations, sending in Mass intentions, purchasing subscriptions to the *Catholic Register*, joining in the work of the Women's

Auxiliary, and supporting St. Philip Neri Hostel. However, despite the best efforts of Burke, the board of governors, the *Register* and the missionaries in the field reporting to the paper, Church Extension did not become a national movement supported by the hierarchy.

b) **By the founding of a college for the education of missionaries**: This was Burke's biggest ambition for Church Extension. It went nowhere and caused nothing but hard feelings between Burke and Archbishop Langevin, who adamantly opposed it. Burke spoke about it at the First American Catholic Missionary Congress in Chicago in 1908 and held fast to his dream as late as 1914, a year after the opening of St. Augustine's Seminary in Toronto should have put an end to any idea about building St. Dunstan's Missionary College in Prince Edward Island.[5]

c) **By the building and equipping of chapels in pioneer districts**: The sub-committee report of 5 March 1915 claimed that Church Extension had financed the construction of forty-seven chapels at $500 each, for a total expenditure of $23,000, and helped to organize another 130 missions and parishes.[6] The Society also issued loans for new chapels or repairs to existing ones at interest rates no higher than four percent, and oftentimes at no charge. Although the *Register* published plenty of stories and photographs about new chapels, it is difficult to verify the sub-committee's number or if it included those chapels sponsored by the Women's Auxiliary. Regardless, the number was impressive.

d) **By contributing to the support of poor missions**: Church Extension existed to assist poor missions, and it did so in numerous ways, such as chapel building; making loans; sending out shipments of vestments, albs, surplices, altar linens, chalices, ciboriums, monstrances, altars, altar plate, crucifixes, statues and other church decorations; distributing Catholic literature; sponsoring Bishop Budka's episcopal ministry; and reporting on the state of the missions in the *Catholic Register*. Did the Society live up to its potential? No. Although it did commence a vibrant and glorious work of Catholic corporate charity under the day-to-day direction of Father Burke, the scope and reach of the Society's missionary mandate had little chance of expanding due to an unfortunate confluence of three factors: Burke's disruptive personality, the absence of a wide base of episcopal co-operation, and the Society's failure to convince a substantial number of the Catholic rank and file to embrace the home missions as *their* cause. Interestingly, after 1912, Burke replaced "contributing to the support of poor missions" with an entirely new and more specific object: "To aid the Bishop of the Ruthenians in his missionary work." Church Extension definitely fulfilled that promise.

e) **By the circulation of Catholic literature**: The Women's Auxiliary carried out this task, sending thousands of books and cards into the mission fields every year.

••••

From our history of the Catholic Church Extension Society of Canada, as presented in Chapters One to Ten, and from this chapter's assessment of Father Alfred E. Burke's stewardship of the Society, it is fair to conclude that while Father Burke was essential to the establishment and early success of the Society, he was also an impediment to its ability to mature into a well-managed grassroots organization working in alliance with the Catholic hierarchy. The history of Church Extension during the years of ambition and turmoil, from 1908 to 1915, is in essence a story of survival. The Society survived the vortex of Father Burke; it survived the death of Archbishop McEvay; it survived Archbishop McNeil's initial blundering to rid Church Extension of its first president. The Society's foundations were deep enough and strong enough on which to build a better organized and more reliable community of service to Catholic Missions in Canada.

Endnotes

Chapter 1

1   Archives of the Catholic Church Extension Society of Canada, Toronto, Ontario [hereafter Church Extension Archives], *Minute Book of the Catholic Church Extension Society of Canada*, two pages, handwritten, [1]. This *Minute Book* will be distinguished from any other document labelled *Minute Book* with the descriptive addition of "two pages, handwritten." The order of names is that given by Father Burke. Arthur Alfred Sinnott (1877–1954) became the first archbishop of Winnipeg in 1915 and remained in that post until his resignation in 1952. See Jean LeBlånc, "Sinnott, Arthur Alfred," *Dictionnaire biographique des évêques catholiques du Canada* (Ottawa: Wilson & LaFleur, 2002), 819. John Thomas Kidd (1868–1951) became the first rector of St. Augustine's Seminary in Toronto in 1913, bishop of Calgary in 1925 and bishop of London in 1931. See Michael Power and Daniel J. Brock, *Gather up the Fragments: A History of the Diocese of London* (London, Ont.: Diocese of London, 2008), 61–68.

2   *Catholic Register*, 19 November 1908, 1. This was not the newspaper's first story on Church Extension. That appeared on 17 September 1908, 4. Although the name of the newspaper was changed from *Catholic Register* to *Catholic Register and Canadian Extension* in January 1909, and in many documents is referred to as *Register-Extension*, in this volume the shorter form of *Catholic Register* or *Register* will be used, and in the endnotes the abbreviation *CR* will refer to both the *Catholic Register* and *Catholic Register and Canadian Extension*.

3   *CR*, 19 November 1908, 1.

4   Ibid., 7 January, 1909, 9.

5   Burke's handwriting was so appalling that Kelley told Burke he had to send his latest letter to an expert in Egyptian hieroglyphics in Philadelphia. See Archives of the Archdiocese of Oklahoma City [hereafter AAOC], Papers of Bishop Francis Clement Kelley [hereafter Bishop Kelley Papers], Kelley to Burke, 28 July 1910.

6   Church Extension Archives, *Minute Book of the Catholic Church Extension Society of Canada*, two pages, handwritten, [1] –[2].

7   Francis C. Kelley, *The Story of Extension* (Chicago: Extension Press, 1922), 159–68; Francis C. Kelley, *The Bishop Jots It Down: An Autobiographical Strain on Memories* (New York and London: Harper & Brothers Publishers, 1930), 143–52.

8   Kelley, *The Story of Extension*, 161–62.

9   Ibid., 162.

10 Ibid.

11 Division des archives de l'Université Laval, U506/24/4, Bureau du secrétaire general, Registres de réglementation et de nominations, deuxième volume, nos 810 (Kelley) and 811 (Burke), 197–98. This information was provided by James Lambert, archivist, in an e-mail communication to the author, 2 February 2010.

12 James P. Gaffey, *Francis Clement Kelley & the American Catholic Dream*, vol. 1 (Bensenville, Ill.: The Heritage Foundation, Inc., 1980), 82.

13 Ibid., 95–96.

14 Although "Ukrainian Catholic" is incorrect for this time period, it will be used for the sake of simplicity and modern sensitivity. See Chapter Five for a discussion on the use of "Ukrainian," "Ukrainian Catholic," etc. and historically related words such as "Ruthenian" and "Galician."

15 St. Boniface was erected into an archdiocese on 22 September 1871. Before that it was known as the District of the North-West (1820), the Vicariate Apostolic of the North-West (1844), Diocese of the North-West (4 June 1847) and the Diocese of St. Boniface. Langevin was consecrated archbishop on 19 March 1895. During the preceding seventy years, there had been only two episcopal predecessors to him: Joseph-Norbert Provencher (1820–1853) and Alexandre-Antonin Taché (1853–1894). For additional biographical information on Langevin, see Roberto Perin, "Langevin, Adélard," *Dictionary of Canadian Biography* (hereafter *DCB*), vol. 14 (Toronto: University of Toronto Press, 1998), 597–601; LeBlanc, "Langevin, Louis-Philippe-Adélard, O.M.I., 1855–1915," *Dictionnaire biographique des évêques catholiques du Canada*, 575–77.

16 Raymond Huel, "Legal, Émile-Joseph, *DCB*, vol. 14 (Toronto: University of Toronto Press, 1998), 639–40; LeBlanc, "Legal, Émile-Joseph, O.M.I., 1849–1920," *Dictionnaire biographique des évêques catholiques du Canada*, 604–5; LeBlanc, "Pascal, Albert," *Dictionnaire biographique des évêques catholiques du Canada*, 732–34.

17 Corporation archiépiscopale catholique romaine de Saint Boniface [hereafter CACRSB], Series Adélard Langevin, File Correspondance, L34262, Kelley to Langevin, 20 November 1907.

18 Ibid., Series Adélard Langevin, File Correspondance, L34263, Kelley to Langevin, 23 December 1907.

19 Raymond J.A. Huel, "*Gestae Dei Per Franos*: The French Canadian Experience in Western Canada," in *Visions of the New Jerusalem: Religious Settlement on the Prairies*, ed. Benjamin G. Smillie (Edmonton: NeWest Press, 1983), 48.

20 CACRSB, Series Adélard Langevin, File Correspondance, L34269, Langevin to Bégin, 21 August 1908. Regina became a diocese on 4 March 1910 and an archdiocese on 4 December 1915. Its first Ordinary was Olivier-Elzéar Mathieu. A native of Québec, Mathieu was Langevin's candidate and remained Ordinary until his death in 1929. He was the only Québec-born prelate of Regina. Many clergymen, including Burke, had an opinion about Regina. It was a hotly debated topic. See AAOC, Bishop Kelley Papers, Burke to Kelley, 20 July 1911: "By a telegram to me there you will have seen that Mgr. Mathieu has been made first Bishop of Regina. I have also a letter from the bishop-elect today acknowledging the truth of the statement, and informing me in the most pathetic terms that he is in the most terrible desolation because of it. I suppose the French had to get a concession, and if it must be a Frenchman at all you will easily see that Mgr. Mathieu is the most available person possible."

21 AAOC, Bishop Kelley Papers, Kelley to Sbarretti, 13 March 1908.

22 Kelley, *The Bishop Jots It Down*, 148.

23 AAOC, Bishop Kelley Papers, Burke to Kelley, 17 March 1908; Burke to Kelley, 17 March 1908 (second letter); Circular Letter, Burke to My Lord, 17 March 1908; Burke to Kelley, 18 March 1908; Burke to Kelley, 23 March 1908.

24 Roberto Perin and Gayle M. Comeau-Vasilopoulos, "Duhamel, Joseph-Thomas," *DCB*, vol. 13 (Toronto: University of Toronto Press, 1994), 296–301.

25 Archives of the Roman Catholic Archdiocese of Toronto [hereafter ARCAT], OC07. C001, Duhamel to Sinnott, 13 October 1908.

26 AAOC, Bishop Kelley Papers, Burke to Sbarretti, 13 April 1908, copied into Burke to Kelley, 14 April 1908.

27 Ibid., Bishop Kelley Papers, Burke to Kelley, 14 April 1908.

28 CACRSB, Series Adélard Langevin, File Correspondance, L34265, Lacoste to Sbarretti, 5 May 1908.

29 Ibid., Series Adélard Langevin, File Correspondence, L34264, Sbarretti to Langevin, 14 May 1908.

30 ARCAT, OC07.C001, Langevin to McEvay, 16 January 1909.

31 CACRSB, Series Adélard Langevin. File Correspondence, L34269, Langevin to Bégin, 21 August 1908.

32 Mark G. McGowan, "McEvay, Fergus Patrick," *DCB*, vol. 14 (Toronto: University of Toronto Press, 1998), 698; AAOC, Bishop Kelley Papers, Burke to Kelley, 17 March 1908 (first letter): "and Sunday was put in at London with Bp McEvay. A very pleasant occasion and one which gave me some news inside as the journals say."

33 *CR*, 18 June 1908, 1, 8.

34 McGowan, "McEvay, Fergus Patrick," 698.

35 Henry James Morgan, ed., *The Canadian Men and Women of the Time: A Hand-book of Canadian Biography of Living Characters*, 2nd ed. [hereafter Morgan, *Canadian Men and Women of the Time*] (Toronto: William Briggs, 1912), "Fitzpatrick, The Rt. Hon. Sir Charles," 400–01; David Evans, "Fitzpatrick, Sir Charles," *The Canadian Encyclopedia*, vol. 1 (Edmonton: Hurtig Publishers, 1985), 647.

36 ARCAT, OC07.C001, "First attempt at framing Constitution for the Catholic Church Extn Soc'y of Canada, Drafted in the Library of St. Dunstan's College July 1908."

37 Ibid., OC07.C001, Burke to McEvay, 8 July 1908.

38 Library and Archives Canada [hereafter LAC], Q4 51931, MG 27, Series II, C1, Vol. 82, Papers of Sir Charles Fitzpatrick, Burke to Fitzpatrick, 15 July 1908.

Chapter 2

1 Arthur O'Shea, *A.E. Burke* (Charlottetown, P.E.I.: 1993), 1, 3; Mark G. McGowan, "Burke, Alfred Edward," *DCB*, vol. 15 (Toronto: University of Toronto Press, 2005), 166. O'Shea and McGowan provide the two most extensive accounts of Burke's life.

2 For more information on Bishop McIntyre, see G. Edward MacDonald, "McIntyre, Peter," *DCB*, vol. 12 (Toronto: University of Toronto Press, 1990), 637–40.

3 Kelley, *The Bishop Jots It Down*, 143.

4 McGowan, "Burke, Alfred Edward," 167; O'Shea, *A.E. Burke*, 8–14.

5 Mark G. McGowan, *The Waning of the Green: Catholics, the Irish, and Identity in Toronto, 1887–1922* (Montreal & Kingston: McGill-Queen's University Press, 1999), 165–66.

6   "Grand Trustee, Rev. Father Burke," *The Canadian* (London, Ont.) 10, no. 12 (December 1904), 5.

7   Ibid.; McGowan, "Burke, Alfred Edward," 167; O'Shea, *A.E. Burke*, 24–31, 32–33.

8   "Rev. Dr. A.E. Burke," *Canadian Magazine* (June 1907), reprinted in James Donahue, *Prince Edward Island Priests* (Minneapolis, Minn.: [Webb Publishing Company, c. 1912]), 89. "Burke, Very Rev. Alfred Edward," *The Canadian Who's Who* (London: *The Times*, 1910; Toronto: Musson Book Company, [1910]), 30. The entry describes his publications this way: "A whole series of Monographs, Forestry, Agriculture, Horticultural, Historical, Religious, etc." Monographs should be understood to mean pamphlets and not books.

9   O'Shea, *A.E. Burke*, 29–30. O'Shea credits the University of Carolina with awarding Burke the honorary degree. This is incorrect. In an obituary for Burke, Biltmore University is mentioned. See *The Charlottetown Guardian* (P.E.I.), 20 December 1926, 3. The more correct name would have been Biltmore Forest College. Matthew Turi, e-mail communication to the author, 31 August 2010. In "Burke, Very Rev. Alfred Edward," *The Canadian Who's Who*, there is mention of an LLD. This must refer to his 1906 honorary doctorate.

10 For additional information on Archbishop O'Brien, see Terrence Murphy, "O'Brien, Cornelius," *DCB*, vol. 13 (Toronto: University of Toronto Press, 1994), 772–74.

11 Boyde Beck, "Howlan, George William," *DCB*, vol. 13 (Toronto: University of Toronto Press, 1994), 483.

12 Although Father Burke was often absent from his parish, records indicate that he did not have a curate. Neighbouring priests or friends in the clergy must have covered for him. Art O'Shea, e-mail communication to the author, 25 August 2010.

13 O'Shea, *A.E. Burke*, 36–38.

14 *The Summerside Journal* (P.E.I.), 29 June 1892, 3; *The Charlottetown Guardian* (P.E.I.), 20 December 1926, 3.

15 *The Daily Examiner* (Charlottetown, P.E.I.), 19 July 1893, 2.

16 Ibid., 11 July 1894, 2.

17 For a concise explanation of this thorny issue, see Paul E. Crunican, "Manitoba Schools Question," *The Canadian Encyclopedia*, vol. 2 (Edmonton: Hurtig Publishers, 1985), 1084. For a detailed study, see Paul Crunican, *Priests and Politicians: Manitoba Schools and the Election of 1896* (Toronto: University of Toronto Press, 1974).

18 *The Daily Examiner*, 11 July 1894, 2.

19 Ibid., 26 December 1894, 2.

20 Ibid., 16 August 1898, 2, 5; 24 August 1898, 2, 4; 17 September 1898, 2; 19 September 1898, 2.

21 Ibid., 19 September 1898, 2; O'Shea, *A.E. Burke*, 38.

22 *The Daily Examiner*, 12 November 1897, 2, 3; 16 November 1897, 3; 18 November 1897, 4. For more information on Archbishop Cleary, see Brian J. Price, "Cleary, James Vincent," *DCB*, vol. 12 (Toronto: University of Toronto Press, 1990), 198–200.

23 O'Shea, *A.E. Burke*, 18.

24 Diocese of Charlottetown Archives, Papers of Bishop James Charles McDonald, Letter Book [hereafter McDonald Letter Book], McDonald to Falconio, 31 August 1901, 283–85. McDonald's letter to the Apostolic Delegate reproduces excerpts from several of Burke's letters to *The Daily Examiner* and correspondence between McDonald and Burke and between McDonald and Archbishop Cornelius O'Brien. When McDonald is speaking directly to Falconio, the citation will read: McDonald Letter Book, McDonald to Falconio. When McDonald quotes a letter or correspondence, it will be identified as such in the citation. See also O'Shea, *A.E. Burke*, 18–21.

25 Diocese of Charlottetown Archives, McDonald Letter Book, 282: McDonald to Falconio.

26 For additional information on Bishop McDonald, see G. Edward MacDonald, "McDonald, James Charles," *DCB*, vol. 14 (Toronto: University of Toronto Press, 1998), 687–88.

27 O'Shea, *A.F. Burke*, 21–23.

28 *The Daily Examiner*, 25 May 1901, 1. *L'Impartial* was a Tignish, P.E.I., newspaper.

29 *The Daily Examiner*, 1 June 1901, 2.

30 Ibid., 31 May 1901, 8.

31 Ibid., 5 June 1901, 5.

32 Diocese of Charlottetown Archives, McDonald Letter Book, 287: McDonald to Burke, 7 June 1901.

33 Ibid., McDonald Letter Book, 288: O'Brien to McDonald, 15 June 1901.

34 Ibid., McDonald Letter Book, 289: McDonald to O'Brien, 19 July 1901.

35 Ibid., McDonald Letter Book, 290: O'Brien to McDonald, 22 August 1901.

36 Ibid., McDonald Letter Book, 288: McDonald to Falconio, 31 August 1901.

37 Ibid., McDonald Letter Book, 290–91: McDonald to Falconio, 31 August 1901.

Chapter 3

1 LAC, Q4 51931, MG 27, Series II, C1, Vol. 82, Papers of Sir Charles Fitzpatrick, Burke to Fitzpatrick, 15 July 1908.

2 Church Extension Archives, *Minute Book of the Catholic Church Extension Society of Canada*, two pages, handwritten, [2]. Louis-Nazaire Bégin (1840–1925) was a charter member of the Royal Society of Canada, bishop of Chicoutimi in 1888, coadjutor of Québec in 1891, with right of succession in 1892, archbishop of Québec in 1898 and cardinal in 1914. See Roberto Perin, "Bégin, Louis-Nazaire," *DCB*, vol. 15 (Toronto: University of Toronto Press, 2005), 71–77. Louis-Alexandre Taschereau (1867–1952) was a member of a prominent family of lawyers and jurists. He was premier of Québec from 1920 to 1936. See Bernard L. Vigod, "Taschereau, Louis-Alexandre," *The Canadian Encyclopedia*, vol. 3 (Edmonton: Hurtig Publishers, 1985), 1785.

3 Nive Voisine, "Archambeault, Joseph-Alfred," *DCB*, vol. 14 (Toronto: University of Toronto Press, 1998), 21–23. Voisine makes no mention of Archambeault's membership on the board of Church Extension.

4 LAC, Q4 51931, MG 27, Series II, C1, Vol. 82, Papers of Sir Charles Fitzpatrick, Burke to Fitzpatrick, 7 November 1908.

5   CACRSB, Series Adélard Langevin, File Correspondance, L34269, Langevin to Bégin, 21 August 1908.

6   "A letter of excardination without which a priest may not be permanently attached to a diocese other than his own." See Donald Attwater, ed., *A Catholic Dictionary*, 3rd ed. (New York: The Macmillan Company, 1961), 182.

7   ARCAT, Clergy Personnel file, Alfred E. Burke, Exeat; Clergy biographies, "Burke, Alfred Edward."

8   LAC, Q4 51931, MG 27, Series II, C1, Vol. 82, Papers of Sir Charles Fitzpatrick, [Circular], 31 July 1908, 1.

9   Ibid., 1–2.

10   Ibid., 1.

11   *CR*, 17 September 1908, 4.

12   Ibid., 7 January 1909, 4.

13   ARCAT, OC07.CG01, "Constitution of the Catholic Church Extension Society of Canada." The "By Laws" appear on the second page. A copy of the Society's 1908 "Constitution" can also be located in Church Extension Archives, *Minute Book of the Catholic Church Extension Society of Canada* [hereafter *Minute Book*], vol. 1, "Constitution of the Catholic Church Extension Society of Canada," 17–18.

14   *CR*, 22 December 1910, 5. This change was actually covered in the By-Laws.

15   Ibid., 22 December 1910, 1. "Constitution of the Catholic Church Extension Society of Canada."

16   Ibid.

17   Ibid.

18   *CR*, 17 September 1908, 4.

19   ARCAT, OC07.CG01, "Constitution of the Catholic Church Extension Society of Canada," 1.

20   Richard A. Willie, "Beck, Nicholas Du Bois Dominic," *DCB*, vol. 15 (Toronto: University of Toronto Press, 2005), 69–70.

21   Morgan, *Canadian Men and Women of the Time*, "Beck, Nicholas Du Bois Dominic," 79.

22   ARCAT, OC07.CG01, "Constitution of the Catholic Church Extension Society of Canada," 1.

23   Ibid., 1–2.

24   Ibid., 2.

25   A later version of the 1908 "Constitution" included the following sentence at the end of Article 5: "Any Officer of this Society may, for good and sufficient reasons, be removed from office at any time by the Board of Governors." It is impossible to determine the origin or date of this interpolation. See Church Extension Archives, *Minute Book*, vol. 1, "Constitution of the Catholic Church Extension Society of Canada," 18.

26   ARCAT, OC07.CG01, "Constitution of the Catholic Church Extension Society of Canada," "By Laws," 2–3.

27 Ibid., 2.

28 Ibid., OC07.C001, Burke to McEvay, 18 September 1908.

29 Church Extension Archives, *Minute Book*, vol. 1, "Minutes of the Meeting of the Board of Governors," 23 September 1908, 19.

30 Michael Power, "O'Keefe, Eugene," *DCB*, vol. 14 (Toronto: University of Toronto Press, 1998), 796–97.

31 Church Extension Archives, *Minute Book*, vol. 1, "Minutes of the Meeting of the Executive Board," 25 November 1908, 20.

32 Michael Power, *A History of Mount Hope Cemetery, Toronto, Ontario 1898–1998* (Toronto: Catholic Cemeteries, Archdiocese of Toronto, 1998), "Hugh Thomas Kelly," 48–49.

33 Church Extension Archives, *Minute Book*, vol. 1, "Minutes of the Meeting of the Board of Governors," 19 November 1910, 23.

34 *Statutes of Canada*, "An Act to Incorporate the Catholic Church Extension Society of Canada," 1909, 8–9 Edw. VII, c. 70.

35 LeBlanc, "Legal, Émile-Joseph," 604; Huel, "Legal, Émile-Joseph," 639–40.

36 Morgan, *Canadian Men and Women of the Time*, "O'Brien, Michael John," 860.

37 Ibid., "Haney Michael John," 496–97.

38 Ibid., "Magann, George Plunkett," 723.

39 *CR*, 25 June 1908, 4.

40 Information supplied by Karen Ball-Pyatt of the Kitchener Public Library, in an e-mail communication to the author, 1 June 2010. See also *CR*, 18 November 1909, 5.

41 *Statutes of Canada*, "An Act to incorporate the Catholic Church Extension Society of Canada," 1909, 8–9 Edw. VII, c. 90, "Objects."

42 *CR*, 14 April 1910, 5.

43 AAOC, Bishop Kelley Papers, Kelley to Burke, 5 January 1909.

44 Ibid., Bishop Kelley Papers, Burke to Kelley, 8 January 1909; Burke to Kelley, 10 January 1909.

45 Ibid., Bishop Kelley Papers, Kelley to Burke, 11 January 1909. William D. O'Brien, Emmanuel B. Ledvina, Alexander P. Landry and Edward L. Roe were priests involved in the administration of Church Extension in the United States.

46 Ibid., Bishop Kelley Papers, Kelley to Burke, 20 January 1909.

47 Ibid., Bishop Kelley Papers, 7 May 1909.

48 Church Extension Archives, *Minute Book*, vol. 1, "Minutes of the Meeting of the Board of Governors," 22 June 1909, 21.

49 Ibid., *Minute Book*, vol. 1, "Minutes of the Meeting of the Board of Governors," 6 April 1910, 22.

50 Although I cannot determine exactly when Sbarretti left for Rome, I do know that he did not attend the consecration of Bishop Michael Francis Fallon at St. Peter's Cathedral in London, on 25 April 1910. His name is absent from newspaper accounts of the

ceremony. Information supplied by Arthur G. McClelland, London Room Librarian, London Public Library, in an e-mail communication to the author, 20 August 2011.

51 AAOC, Bishop Kelley's Papers, 2 February 1910; 28 February 1910. In these two lengthy letters, Kelley reveals the extent of Falconio's hostility towards Church Extension. See also Gaffey, *Francis Clement Kelley*, vol. 1, 105–9.

52 AOCC, Bishop Kelley Papers, Kelley to Burke, 18 January 1910; 21 January 1910; 28 January 1910; 2 February 1910; 3 February 1910; 11 February 1910.

53 Ibid., Bishop Kelley Papers, Roche to Kelley, 19 January 1910.

54 Ibid., Bishop Kelley Papers, Kelley to Burke, 21 January 1910.

55 Ibid., Bishop Kelley Papers, Kelley to Burke, 11 February 1910.

56 ARCAT, OC07.HI02, "Ad Sanctitatem Suam Pium X." This was reproduced under the title "Institutiones Apostolicae – Societatis Diffundendae rei Catholicae" in *CR*, 29 December 1910, 5; 5 January 1911, 5. Unfortunately, the paper did not provide an English translation, although there was reference to one in *CR*, 22 December 1910, 2.

57 Shaughnessy's name was added to the board of governors at its 6 April 1910 meeting. See *CR*, 14 April 1910, 5.

58 Theodore D. Regehr, "Shaughnessy, Thomas George, 1st Baron Shaughnessy," *DCB*, vol. 15 (Toronto: University of Toronto Press, 2005), 925.

59 St. Catharines Public Library, Special Collections, McSloy Family History File.

60 His name, too, first appeared on the list of the board of governors at its meeting of 6 April 1910. See *CR*, 14 April 1910, 5.

61 Church Extension Archives, *Minute Book*, vol. 1, "Letters of Commendation of the Catholic Church Extension Society of Canada," 6–10.

62 ARCAT, ME AF0329, Merry del Val to McEvay, 3 December 1908.

63 *CR*, 19 January 1911, 5.

64 Ibid.

65 The Society for the Propagation of the Faith and the Association of the Holy Childhood were two of four principal pontifical missionary associations under the Congregation for the Propagation of the Faith. The other two associations were the Society of St. Peter for the Training of the Native Clergy and the Missionary Union of the Clergy. Pius X was anxious that the Catholic Church Extension Society, the home missions for Canada, would not compete against Propagation of the Faith and Holy Childhood, which solicited funds from Canadian Catholics for mission work overseas. St. Philip Neri (1515–1595) was a leading light in the Catholic Counter Reformation and the founder of the Oratorians. He is regarded as the patron saint of Catholic Missions in Canada. His feast day is 26 May.

66 AAOC, Bishop Kelley Papers, Kelley to Burke, 27 November 1914.

67 ARCAT, OC07.C0, Merry del Val to McEvay, 13 Giugno 1910.

68 *CR*, 26 January 1911, 5.

69 ARCAT, ME DS12.17, McEvay to Sbarretti, 25 July 1910; OC07.C001, McEvay to Merry del Val, 25 July 1910; OC07.C001, McEvay to Martinelli, 25 July 1910.

70 Ibid., ME DS12.17, McEvay to Sbarretti, 25 July 1910.

71 Ibid., OC07.C001, McEvay to Martinelli, 25 July 1910.

72 *CR*, 26 January 1911, 5.

73 Ibid.

74 LAC, Q4 51931, MG 27, Series II, C1, vol. 13, Burke to Fitzpatrick, 22 July 1910.

75 Church Extension Archives, *Minute Book*, vol. 1, "A Meeting of the Catholic Church Extension Society," 19 November 1910, 23.

76 *CR*, 22 December 1910, 5. The remaining six parts can be located in *CR*, 29 December 1910, 5; 5 January 1911, 5; 12 January 1911, 5; 19 January 1911, 5; 26 January 1911, 5; 2 February 1911, 5. The special meeting of the board of governors ended with a dinner in the Rosedale home of Michael J. Haney. In attendance were McEvay, Fitzpatrick, Burke, J.J. Foy, Monsignor John J. McCann, Thomas Long, Father Hugh J. Canning, Father James B. Dollard, Monsignor John T. Kidd, George P. Magann, Hugh T. Kelly, George C.H. Lang of Berlin and five other gentlemen identified only by their last names: Miller, Gough, Seitz, Dr. Dwyer and Professor Kiley. This may have been one of the happiest and most hopeful gatherings of the board of governors during Burke's presidency. A full account of the festivities can be found in *CR*, 2 February 1911, 5.

77 AOCC, Bishop Kelley Papers, Kelley to Burke, 27 November 1915.

78 *CR*, 22 December 1910, 5.

79 AAOC, Bishop Kelley Papers, Roche to Kelley, 12 December [1910]. Father Joseph T. Roche was in Rome, where he gathered inside information on the progress of the two ternas – one for the Canadian Society and one for the American Society – after talking to Cardinal Merry del Val, Cardinal Martinelli and a Monsignor O'Kelly. He also had a private audience with Pius X, on Sunday, 11 December. In Roche's opinion, it was Kelley who might have a problem being appointed president of Church Extension in the United States. He told Kelley that if his enemies in Chicago succeeded in blocking his appointment, Kelley would be offered a bishopric.

80 ARCAT, OC07.C001, Martinelli to McEvay, 19 December 1910.

81 Ibid., OC07. C001, Merry del Val to McEvay, 17 December 1910.

82 Ibid., Clergy Personnel File, A.E. Burke, McEvay to Burke, 2 January 1911.

83 Church Extension Archives, M.J. Haney, G.P. Magann and H.T. Kelley, "To the Most Reverend Neil McNeil, D.D., Archbishop of Toronto, Chancellor of The Catholic Church Extension Society of Canada" (Toronto: 5 March 1915), 3.

84 *CR*, 12 November 1908, 4.

85 Church Extension Archives, *Minute Book*, vol. 1, "A Meeting of the Executive Board," 25 November 1908, 20.

86 Father Joseph Thomas Roche was born in Iona, Prince Edward Island, on 31 January 1865. After studying at Ottawa College (University of Ottawa) and St. Mary's Seminary in Baltimore, Maryland, he was ordained on 17 December 1892 for the diocese of Lincoln, Nebraska. In 1909, he transferred to the Diocese of Rockford, Illinois. Father Burke met Roche at the First American Missionary Congress in Chicago in November 1908 and invited him to join the staff of the *Catholic Register*. Burke petitioned Archbishop McEvay

to incardinate Roche, but McEvay refused, one of the few times that the archbishop did not support Burke as president of Church Extension. Roche was a peripatetic priest. He lacked the virtue of stability and could not stay in any one place for too long. He became a headache for Father Burke and Father Kelley and the subject of numerous questions and comments in their correspondence, from 1909 to 1915. He ended up leaving the *Register*, probably in 1912, travelling extensively and submitting the occasional article to the paper. Apparently, he spent time at the front during World War One (1915), but he disappears from the Kelley/Burke correspondence after December 1915. See AAOC, Bishop Kelley Papers, Kelley to Burke, 2 July 1915; Kelley to Burke, 10 December 1915: "I have not heard a word about J.T.R. I don't know where he is." See also ARCAT, Clergy Biographies, "Roche, Joseph Thomas"; Personnel File, Joseph T. Roche. Additional information supplied by Father Art O'Shea, in a letter to the author, 23 March 2010.

87 LAC, Q4 51931, MG 27, Series II, C1, Vol. 82, Papers of Sir Charles Fitzpatrick, Burke to Fitzpatrick, 7 November 1908.

Chapter 4

1 Gaffey, *Francis Clement Kelley*, vol. 1, 98.

2 Francis C. Kelley, ed., *The First American Catholic Missionary Congress* (Chicago: J.S. Hyland & Company, 1909).

3 *CR*, 12 November 1908, 4.

4 ARCAT, OC07.C001, Kelley to McEvay, 17 August 1908.

5 Fergus P. McEvay, "Sermon," in Kelley, *The First American Catholic Missionary Congress*, 36.

6 Ibid., 414.

7 Ibid., 415.

8 Ibid.

9 Ibid., 450–51.

10 Ibid., 78–79. The quotation is from the story of the Good Samaritan, Luke 10:30-37.

11 Ibid., 83.

12 Ibid.

13 *CR*, 7 January 1909, 10.

14 "Howard, Henry Fitzalan-," *The Dictionary of National Biography 1912–1921*, ed. H.W.C. Davis and J.R.H. Weaver (Oxford: Oxford University Press, 1927), 273–74; "Norfolk, 15th Duke of," *Dod's Peerage, Baronetage and Knightage of Great Britain and Ireland* (London: Simpkin, Marshall, Hamilton, Kent, 1911), 769–70.

15 *Canadian Annual Review of Public Affairs 1908*, ed. J. Castell Hopkins (Toronto: The Annual Review Publishing Company, [1909]), 246.

16 LAC, Q4 51931 , MG 27, Series II, C1, Vol. 82, Papers of Sir Charles Fitzpatrick, Burke to Fitzpatrick, 6 April 1909. Attached to the letter is a copy of the undated memorandum from Burke to Norfolk, "Memo on Canadian Church Extension," 2.

17 *Canadian Annual Review of Public Affairs 1909*, ed. J. Castell Hopkins (Toronto: The Annual Review Publishing Company, [1910]), 239–43; "First Plenary Council," *America* 1, no. 1 (17 April 1909), 3; "Ecclesiastical News," *America* 1, no. 3 (1 May 1909), 81; A.T.S. [Anna T. Sadlier], "The First Plenary Council of Canada," *America* 1, no. 5 (15 May 1909), 117; "The First Plenary Council of Canada," *America* 1, no. 24 (25 September 1909), 634; "The Canadian Plenary Council," *America* 1, no. 25 (2 October 1909), 662; Anna T. Sadlier, "The Plenary Council of Canada," *America* 2, no. 2 (23 October 1909), 31; "Canada," *America* 2, no. 4 (6 November 1909), 84.

18 CACRSB, Series Adélard Langevin, L34292, Burke to Langevin, 3 October 1909; L34294, Langevin to Burke, 12 October 1909.

19 ARCAT, OC07.C001, Burke to Sbarretti, 12 October 1909.

20 Ibid., OC07.C001, Burke to McEvay, 23 October 1909; Burke to McEvay, 28 October 1909. Burke did write a laudatory but largely uninformative article about the Plenary Council. See A.E. Burke, "Canada's First Church Council," *The Catholic World* 90, no. 537 (December 1909), 382–85.

21 Ibid., OC07.C001, "Circular," 24 January 1910.

22 Ibid., OC07.C001, "Memorial presented to the First Plenary Council, on the Ruthenian Catholics of Western Canada, by Very Rev. Dr. Burke, President of the Catholic Church Extension Society of Canada," 1 October 1909.

23 Achiel Delaere, *Mémoire sur les tentatives de schisme et d'hérésie au milieu des Ruthènes de l'Ouest canadien* (Québec: L'Action sociale, 1908).

24 A. Delaere, *Memorandum on the Attempts of Schism and Heresy Among the Ruthenians (commonly called 'Galicians') in the Canadian Northwest* (Winnipeg: West Canada Publishing Company, 1909). On the Latin version, see Paul Laverdure, *Redemption and Ritual: The Eastern-Rite Redemptorists of North America, 1906–2006* (Yorkton, Sask.: Redeemer's Voice Press, 2007), 49–50.

25 Josef de Vocht, *Father Achiel Delaere (1868–1939): The First Eastern Rite Redemptorist & Canada's Ukrainian Catholic Church*, trans. Christian Roy (Yorkton, Sask.: Gravelbooks, 2005), 139–41.

26 ARCAT, OC07.C001, Boels to Burke, 13 October 1909, 1–2 (translated from the French).

27 Ibid., 2.

28 Ibid., OC01.C001, Burke to McEvay, 23 October 1909, 2.

29 Ibid., OC07.C001, "Circular," 24 January 1909.

30 Laverdure, *Redemption and Ritual*, 52, fn. 37.

31 On the discussion concerning the appointment of a Ukrainian bishop for Canada, see Vocht, *Father Achiel Delaere*, 144–45.

32 First Plenary Council of Canada, *Acta et decreta concilii plenarii quebecensis primi anno domini MCMIX* (Quebec: L'Action sociale, 1912), 74; ARCAT, OC07.C001, "Circular," 24 January 1910; Church Extension Archives, *Minute Book*, vol. 1, "Extract from a Pastoral Letter of Rt. Rev. Bishop Legal of St. Albert, Alta., to the Faithful of his Diocese," 11. Legal decided to replace the Pentecost Sunday collection for the schools of the Northwest with a collection for the Ruthenians.

33 ARCAT, Occ20.RC01, Kidd to Langevin, 1 December 1910.

34 Ibid., OC07.C001, Burke to McEvay, 23 October 1909; and a second letter that ran for three pages, from Burke to McEvay, 23 October 1909.

Chapter 5

1 *Winnipeg Free Press*, 5 June 1908.

2 Delaere, *Memorandum on the Attempts of Schism and Heresy Among the Ruthenians*, 41. The original French-language version was published in 1908. See footnote 185.

3 In 1911, Father Burke, in his regular column for the *Catholic Register*, tried mightily to prove that there were 120,000 to 150,000 Ruthenians (that is, Ukrainian Catholics) in Canada, in this matter agreeing with the Protestant press. In 1913, after the arrival of Bishop Nykyta Budka, Burke claimed that there were 215,000 Ruthenians in his diocese (eparchy). See *CR*, 17 August 1911, 5; 13 February 1913, 5.

4 For an interesting (and at times bewildering) discussion of the meaning of "Greek Catholic," see W.L. Scott, "The Privy Council and Greek Catholic," *Law Times* (April 1919), 1–7.

5 Paul Yuzyk, "Religious Denominations," in *A Statistical Compendium of the Ukrainians in Canada, 1891–1976*, ed. William Darcovich and Paul Yuzyk (Ottawa: University of Ottawa Press, 1980), 168–69; Ivan Tesla, "Immigration to Canada," in *A Statistical Compendium*, 483–85; O.W. Gerus and J.E. Rea, *The Ukrainians in Canada* (Ottawa: Canadian Historical Association, 1985), 3; John-Paul Himka, "The Background to Emigration: Ukrainians of Galicia and Bukovyna, 1848–1914," in *A Heritage in Transition: Essays in the History of Ukrainians in Canada*, ed. Manoly R. Lupul (Toronto: McClelland and Stewart, 1982), 11–12; Paul Yuzyk, "Religious Life," in *A Heritage in Transition: Essays in the History of Ukrainians in Canada*, ed. Manoly R. Lupul (Toronto: McClelland and Stewart, 1982), 144–45.

6 *A Statistical Compendium*, 501–2. The two-thirds and one-third ratio is from Gerus and Rea, *The Ukrainians in Canada*, 9. It sounds reasonable enough, given the fact that there were ten times more Ukrainians in Galicia than there were in Bukovyna. Complicating matters, however, are the results of the 1901 and 1911 Census returns, which listed 5,682 and 75,432 Ukrainians, respectively. One can explain the great disparity between the Census returns and the immigration figures by examining the process of self-identification. There were Ukrainians who identified themselves as Ukrainian, a term gaining popularity, and there were Ukrainians who identified themselves as Ruthenians, Galicians, Bukovynians, Austro-Hungarians, Austrians and even Hungarians, and consequently were placed in other groupings. For the Canadian Census returns, see Gerus and Rea, *The Ukrainians in Canada*, 8, and *A Statistical Compendium*, 26. For the distribution of Ukrainians in Canada according to various Census returns, beginning in 1901, see Gerus and Rea, *The Ukrainians in Canada*, 17.

7 Gerus and Rea, *The Ukrainians in Canada*, 7.

8 Vladimir J. Kaye (Kysilewsky) and Frances Swyripa, "Settlement and Colonization," in *A Heritage in Transition: Essays in the History of Ukrainians in Canada*, ed. Manoly R. Lupul (Toronto: McClelland and Stewart, 1982), 48–49; Michael H. Marunchak, *The Ukrainian Canadians: A History* (Winnipeg, Ottawa: Ukrainian Free Academy of

Sciences, 1970), 63 (for a detailed study of Ukrainian immigration from 1897 to 1914, see 41–64.); Paul Yuzyk, "The First Ukrainians in Manitoba," in *Papers Read Before the Historical and Scientific Society of Manitoba*, 3rd ser., no. 8, ed. J.A. Jackson, W.L. Morton and P. Yuzyk (Winnipeg: 1953), 30–39.

9   "Tikhon, Patriarch of Moscow," *New Catholic Encyclopedia* [hereafter *NCE*], vol. 14 (New York: McGraw-Hill Book Company, 1967), 154–55.

10 Paul Yuzyk, "Ukrainian Greek Orthodox Church of Canada (1918–1951)" (Ph.D. diss., University of Minnesota, 1951), 90–91.

11 Ibid., 90–91.

12 Ibid., 81.

13 Roberto Perin, *Rome in Canada: The Vatican and Canadian Affairs in the Late Victorian Age* (Toronto: University of Toronto Press, 1990), 165.

14 Yuzyk, "Ukrainian Greek Orthodox Church in Canada (1918–1951)," 82.

15 "Toth, Alexis," *NCE*, vol. 14 (New York: McGraw-Hill Book Company, 1967), 212–13.

16 Yuzyk, "Ukrainian Greek Orthodox Church in Canada (1918–1951)," 76, 79.

17 *Judgment of the Lords of the Judicial Committee of the Privy Council on the Appeal of Zacklynski and others v. Polushie and others, from the Supreme Court of Canada; delivered the 3rd December 1907*. A copy of this judgment is in ARCAT, OC20.RR01 and is stamped 17 December 07.

18 *Pioneer Bishop: The Story of Nicetas Budka's fifteen years in Canada*, ed. Michael Shykula and Bernard Korchinski (Regina, Sask.: Bishop Budka Council #5914 Knights of Columbus, [1990]), 15–16.

19 Athanasious D. McVay, "The Mystery of Father Damascene Polivka," *Annales Ecclesiae Ucrainae* (20 January 2010), 10.

20 Stella Hryniuk, "Pioneer Bishop, Pioneer Times: Nykyta Budka in Canada," Canadian Catholic Historical Association, *Historical Studies* 55 (1988), 26.

21 Himka, "The Background to Emigration: Ukrainians of Galicia and Bukovyna, 1848–1914," 13; Yuzyk, "Religious Life," 146.

22 Yuzyk, "Ukrainian Greek Orthodox Church of Canada (1918–1951)," 82–86; Yuzyk, "Religious Life," 148–49; Perin, *Rome in Canada*, 165–66.

23 O.W. Gerus, "Olesków, Jósef," *DCB*, vol. 13 (Toronto: University of Toronto Press, 1994), 784–86; Kaye and Swyripa, "Settlement and Colonization," 38–41; Marunchak, *The Ukrainian Canadians: A History*, 28–38.

24 Marunchak, *The Ukrainian Canadians: A History*, 36.

25 For a thorough examination of the work of Fathers Dmytriw, Tymkewicz, Polivka and Zaklinski, see Paul Yuzyk, "The History of the Ukrainian Greek Catholic (Uniate) Church in Canada" (master's thesis, University of Saskatchewan, 1948), 45–62.

26 Stella Hryniuk, "Genyk (Genik, Genyk-Berezovsky), Cyril (Kyrylo)," *DCB*, vol. 15 (Toronto: University of Toronto Press, 2005), 400–01.

27 Oleh W. Gerus, "Dmytriw, Nestor," *DCB*, vol. 15 (Toronto: University of Toronto Press, 2005), 290–91; Marunchak, *The Ukrainian Canadians: A History*, 39–40, 99–102; Yuzyk, "Religious Life," 147–48.

28 Joseph Jean, "S.E. Mgr. Adélard Langevin, Archevêque de St-Boniface, et les Ukrainiens," Canadian Catholic Historical Association, *Rapport* (1944–45), 102; Yuzyk, "Religious Life," 148; Yuzyk, "Ukrainian Greek Orthodox Church of Canada (1918–1951)," 78–79; Perin, *Rome in Canada*, 170; Marunchak, *The Ukrainian Canadians: A History*, 102.

29 McVay, "The Mystery of Father Damascene Polivka," 1–10; Perin, *Rome in Canada*, 170; Marunchak, *The Ukrainian Canadians: A History*, 103.

30 Yuzyk, "Ukrainian Greek Orthodox Church of Canada (1918–1951)," 79; Perin, *Rome in Canada*, 170.

31 ARCAT, OC07.C001, Stagni to Bégin, 16 Septembre 1911; OC20.RC01, "The Annual Meeting of the Archbishops of Canada," 2–3.

32 J. Skwarok, *The Ukrainian Settlers in Canada and Their Schools with Reference to Government, French Canadian, and Ukrainian Missionary Influences 1891–1921* (Toronto: Basilian Press, 1959), 41–44.

33 Archives of the Catholic Archdiocese of Edmonton [hereafter ACAE], *General Report of all the Monies Collected among the Catholics of the Latin Rite of Canada, Received, controlled and transmitted from 1910 to 1930 By the Procure of the Archbishop's Palace of St. Boniface, Manitoba in favour of the Ruthenian Greek Catholics of Canada* (St. Boniface: 1933).

34 Mark G. McGowan, "The Harvesters Were Few: A Study of the Catholic Church Extension Society of Canada, French Canada, and the Ukrainian Question, 1908–1925" (master's thesis, University of Toronto, 1983), 55.

35 Raymond J.A. Huel, "French-speaking Bishops and the Cultural Mosaic in Western Canada," in *Canadian Plains Studies 3: Religion and Society in the Prairie West*, ed. Richard Allen (Regina: Canadian Plains Research Center University of Regina, 1974), 57, 58.

36 Langevin went to Rome in 1896, to the Netherlands in 1898 and to Vienna in 1904; Pascal was in Vienna, Lviv and Rome in 1898; Legal was in Rome in 1898; Bishop Agustin Dontenwill, OMI, of New Westminster (Vancouver) was with Father Albert Lacombe in Rome in 1900. The following memoranda were written: Pascal to Cardinal Ledowchowski, Prefect of the Congregation of Propaganda Fide, 19 December 1898; Lacombe to Sheptytsky, 17 September 1900; Dontenwill and Lacombe to Leo XIII; Langevin to Emperor Franz Joseph, 2 July 1904. See, Bohdan Kazymyra, "Metropolitan Andrew Sheptyckyi and the Ukrainians in Canada," Canadian Catholic Historical Association, *Report* (1957), 78, 79, 81.

37 Raymond Huel, "Lacombe, Albert," *DCB*, vol. 14 (Toronto: University of Toronto Press, 1998), 576.

38 "Sheptyts'kyĭ, Andriĭ," *NCE*, vol. 13 (New York: McGraw-Hill Book Company, 1967), 170–71; Kazymyra, "Metropolitan Andrew Sheptyckyj and the Ukrainians in Canada," 75–86.

39 Yuzyk, "The History of the Ukrainian Greek Catholic (Uniate) Church in Canada," 64.

40 Ibid., 66–72.

41 Huel, "French-speaking Bishops and the Cultural Mosaic in Western Canada," 59.

Chapter 6

1　Also written as Nicetas or Nikita.

2　*CR*, 7 October 1909, 5.

3　ARCAT, OC07.C001, "Memorial presented to the First Plenary Council, on the Ruthenian Catholics of Western Canada, by Very Rev. Dr. Burke, President of the Catholic Church Extension Society of Canada," 1 October 1909, 2.

4　Ibid.

5　*CR*, 18 May 1911, 5.

6　Ibid., 16 September 1909, 5.

7　United Church of Canada Archives [hereafter UCCA], *Acts and Proceedings of the Thirty-First General Assembly of the Presbyterian Church in Canada* (Toronto: Murray Printing Company, 1905), 10; *Acts and Proceedings of the Thirty-Second General Assembly of the Presbyterian Church in Canada* (Toronto: Murray Printing Company, 1906), 4.

8　A.J. Hunter, *A Friendly Adventure: The Story of the United Church Mission Among New Canadians at Teulon, Manitoba* (Toronto: Board of Home Missions of the United Church of Canada, 1929), 3, 8–9, 32–33, 34–37.

9　UCCA, *Acts and Proceedings of the Thirty-Second General Assembly of the Presbyterian Church in Canada*, 4.

10　Ibid, 13–14. In 1906, there were seventeen ministers in Manitoba, seven in Alberta and five in Saskatchewan. Seventeen of these did double duty as colporteurs. See UCCA, *Acts and Proceedings of the Thirty-Third General Assembly of the Presbyterian Church in Canada* (Toronto: Murray Printing Company, 1907), 16–17. See also Yuzyk, "Ukrainian Greek Orthodox Church of Canada (1918–1951), 50–51. His figures are for 1907.

11　UCCA, *Acts and Proceedings of the Thirtieth General Assembly of the Presbyterian Church in Canada* (Toronto: Murray Printing Company, 1904), 13.

12　Ibid., 33–34.

13　Ibid., *Acts and Proceedings of the Thirty-First General Assembly of the Presbyterian Church in Canada*, 37–38.

14　Ibid., *Acts and Proceedings of the Thirty-Second General Assembly of the Presbyterian Church in Canada*, 4.

15　*CR*, 23 September 1909, 5.

16　*Toronto Daily Star*, 20 September 1909.

17　According to John Webster Grant, "'Canadianism' became a favourite word in Protestant circles, and it invariably implied both loyalty to British institutions and conformity to Victorian moral standards." He also contended, "To Roman Catholics the social assimilation of immigrants was of less importance than their harmonious integration into church life." See John Webster Grant, *The Church in the Canadian Era: The First Century of Confederation* (Toronto: McGraw-Hill Ryerson, 1972), 96, 97. For Ukrainian Catholics, the question was: Whose church life?

18　UCCA, *Acts and Proceedings of the Thirty-First General Assembly of the Presbyterian Church in Canada*, 10.

19 Yuzyk, "Ukrainian Greek Orthodox Church of Canada (1918–1951)," 92–99; Yuzyk, "The History of the Ukrainian Greek Catholic (Uniate) Church in Canada," 85–91.

20 UCCA, *Acts and Proceedings of the Thirty-Third General Assembly of the Presbyterian Church in Canada*, 7.

21 Reprinted in *CR*, 8 August 1912, 1.

22 UCCA, *Acts and Proceedings of the Thirty-Ninth General Assembly of the Presbyterian Church in Canada* (Toronto: Murray Printing Company, 1913), 7. See also Yuzyk, "The History of the Ukrainian Catholic (Uniate) Church in Canada," 92.

23 Delaere, *Memorandum on the Attempts of Schism and Heresy Among the Ruthenians*, 10–36.

24 ACAE, Catholic Church Extension Society File, Burke to Legal, 15 May 1909.

25 *CR*, 9 September 1909, 5.

26 Ibid., 23 September 1909, 7.

27 Ibid., 16 September 1909, 1.

28 Ibid.

29 Ibid.

30 Ibid.

31 Ibid., 30 September 1909, 5; 4 November 1909, 5; 11 November 1909, 5.

32 Ibid., 16 September 1909, 4.

33 Ibid., 5.

34 Quoted in the *Telegram* (Toronto), 20 September 1909.

35 *Telegram* (Toronto), 20 September 1909.

36 Ibid.

37 As quoted in *CR*, 30 September 1909, 5.

38 *CR*, 7 October 1909, 1.

39 Ibid.

40 Ibid.

41 Ibid., 7 October 1909, 4.

42 Ibid.

43 Ibid.

44 "Canadian Events," *America*, 2, no. 12 (1 January 1910), 301.

45 *Canadian Annual Review of Public Affairs 1909*, 243–44.

46 *CR*, 16 June 1910, 5.

47 Bernier: *CR*, 17 February 1910, 5; 14 July 1910, 5. Legal: *CR*, 24 February 1910, 5. Sabourin: *CR*, 14 October 1910, 5. Jan: 21 October 1910, 1. Boels: *CR*, 28 October 1909, 5. Hura: *CR*, 5 May 1910, 5 (additional story: *CR*, 28 March 1912, 5). Decamps: *CR*, 16 June 1910, 5 (additional stories: *CR*, 30 March 1911, 5; 9 May 1912, 5; 10 October 1912, 5; 18 December 1913, 5). See also reports from Father Delaere, *CR*, 9 February 1911, 5; 30 March 1911, 5.

48 *CR*, 21 October 1909, 5; 28 October 1909, 1.

49 ARCAT, OC20.RC01, Sebratowicz to McEvay, 23 April 1910.

50 Ibid., OC20.RC01, Kidd to Sembratowicz, 21 September 1911 (handwritten extract). After Archbishop McEvay's death on 10 May 1911, the priests of the Archdiocese of Toronto chose Kidd to act as administrator. This was the same Kidd who was present at the founding of Church Extension.

51 Ibid., OC20.RC01, Kidd to To Whom It May Concern, 14 November 1911 (handwritten extract).

52 Ibid., OC20.RC01, Kidd to Ortynsky, 25 January 1912.

53 Ibid., OC07.C001, Delaere to Bruchési, 7 May 1910. Delaere also tattled on another married priest.

54 Ibid., OC07.C001, "Memorandum on the Ruthenian Question by Rev. Leo I Sembratowicz Forwarded by Very Rev. A.E. Burke, D.D. President of Catholic Church Extension Society," 1. The letter of Leo I. Sembratowicz to A.E. Burke, 4 October 1909, is included in the "Memorandum."

55 Ibid., OC07.C001, "Memorandum on the Ruthenian Question," 7. The letter of Leo I. Sembratowicz to A.E. Burke, 18 October 1909 is included in the "Memorandum."

56 *CR*, 28 October 1909, 1.

57 ARCAT, OC07.001, Burke to McEvay, 23 October 1909 (first letter).

58 Ibid., OC07.C001, Burke to McEvay, 23 October 1909, 1 (second letter).

59 Ibid., OC07.C001, Sembratowicz to Burke, 27 October 1909.

60 *CR*, 30 December 1909, 4.

61 Ibid., 28 March 1912, 5; 20 February 1913, 5.

62 *Pioneer Bishop*, 7, 39.

63 ARCAT, OC07.C001, Burke to McEvay, 23 October 1909, 1–2 (first letter).

64 Ibid., OC07.C001, Burke to McEvay, 23 October 1909, 1 (second letter).

65 Ibid., OC007.C001, Burke to McEvay, 28 October 1909.

66 *CR*, 20 October 1910, 5; 3 November 1910, 2; 10 November 1910, 5–6; 17 November 1910, 1; 1 December 1910, 1.

67 Ibid., 14 October 1909, 5; 11 November 1909, 5; 3 February 1910, 3; 10 March 1910, 5; 21 April 1910, 5; 19 May 1910, 5; 19 June 1910, 5; 22 September 1910, 5; 6 April 1911, 5; 1 February 1912, 5. See also Father [Jules] Pirot, *A Year's Fight for the True Faith in Saskatchewan; The Hungarian Question in Canada in 1910* (Toronto: Catholic Register and Canadian Extension, 1911); M.L. Kovacs, "The Saskatchewan Era, 1885–1914," in N.F. Driesziger, M.L. Kovacs, Paul Body and Bennett Kovrig, *Struggle and Hope: The Hungarian-Canadian Experience* (Toronto: McClelland and Stewart, 1982), 80–81.

68 Woodsworth: *CR*, 14 October 1909, 5; James S. Woodsworth, *Strangers Within Our Gates: Or, Coming Canadians* (Toronto: The Missionary Society of the Methodist Church, Canada, 1909), 133–39, 305–11. Methodist Missionary Congress: *CR*, 16 June 1910, 5; 18 May 1911, 5; 13 February 1913, 5. See also C.W. Gordon, "Our Duty to the English-speaking and European Settlers," in *Canada's Missionary Congress: Addresses Delivered*

at the Canadian National Missionary Congress, Held in Toronto, March 31 to April 4, *1909, with Reports of Committees* (Toronto: Canadian Council of Laymen's Missionary Movement, [1909]), 101–9; G.N. Emery, "Methodist Missions Among the Ukrainians," *Alberta Historical Review* 19, no. 2 (1971), 8–19; Neil Semple, *The Lord's Dominion: The History of Canadian Methodism* (Montreal & Kingston: McGill-Queen's University Press, 1996), 302–3. Baptist Home Missions: *CR*, 16 September 1909, 1; 17 April 1913, 5.

69 *CR*, 1 December 1910, 1.

70 Ibid.

71 Ibid.

72 Ibid., 16 February 1911, 5; 16 March 1911, 5; 30 March 1911, 5; 27 April 1911, 5; 18 May 1911, 5; 20 July 1911, 5; 27 July 1911, 5; 17 August 1911, 5.

73 Ibid., 1 December 1910, 1; 9 February 1911, 5; 30 March 1911, 5.

74 Ibid., 16 March 1911, 5.

75 Ibid., 9 March 1911, 1.

76 Ibid., 17 August 1911, 5.

77 Ibid., 27 February 1914, 5.

78 Ibid., 19 January 1911, 5.

79 Andrey Sheptytsky, "Address on the Ruthenian Question to their Lordships the Archbishops and Bishops of Canada," in *Two Documents of the Ukrainian Catholic Church 1911–1976*, ed. M.H. Marunchak (Winnipeg: National Council of Ukrainian Organizations for the Patriarchate of the Ukrainian Catholic Church, 1977), 9.

80 Ibid., 10.

81 AAOC, Bishop Kelley Papers, Burke to Merry del Val, 27 December 1911 (copy).

82 *CR*, 26 June 1913, 5.

83 ARCAT, OC07.C001, "The Catholic Church Extension Society," 4.

84 *CR*, 3 October 1912, 1; 24 October 1912, 1. Budka was ordained a bishop on 13 October 1912, left for Canada on 12 November 1912 and arrived in Winnipeg on 22 December 1912.

85 Church Extension Archives, *Minute Book*, vol. 1, "Minutes of the Meeting of the Board of Governors," 2 April 1913, 30.

86 *CR*, 27 March 1913, 5.

87 Ibid., 19 March 1914, 1–2.

88 Ibid., 20 August 1914, 1, 5. Burke published English-language versions of both letters, 27 July 1914 and 6 August 1914. These letters can also be found in Bohdan S. Kordan and Lubomyr Y. Luciuk, *A Delicate and Difficult Question: Documents in the History of Ukrainians in Canada 1899–1962* (Kingston, Ont.: Limestone Press, 1986), 24–32, and *Pioneer Bishop*, 115–20. The episode is treated at length in *Pioneer Bishop*, 58–68. See also Hryniuk, "Pioneer Bishop, Pioneer Times," 34–35.

89 *CR*, 24 September 1914, 5.

90 Ibid., 22 October 1914, 5.

91 *Annual Report of the Catholic Church Extension Society of Canada 1918* (Toronto: 1918), 17.

92 ARCAT, OC07.001, "The Catholic Church Extension Society of Canada, Toronto. Donations sent to Dioceses from March 1ˢᵗ, 1919 to March 1ˢᵗ, 1928, including vestments, linens, etc" [one-page typewritten document].

93 *CR*, 16 September 1909, 5; 16 June 1910, 5; 28 July 1910, 5; 15 June 1911, 5; 14 March 1912, 5.

94 Ibid., 21 October 1909, 5.

95 Ibid., 14 October 1909, 5; ARCAT, OC07.C001, Legal to McEvay, 3 April 1909. See also ACAE, Catholic Church Extension Society File, Burke to Legal, 5 March 1909; Burke to Legal, 29 April 1909; Burke to Legal, 15 May 1909; Burke to Legal, 27 May 1909; Hirst to Legal, 23 June 1909.

96 ACAE, "The Catholic Church Extension Society of Canada: Contributions for Chapels and Churches 1909–1962," comp. Éloi DeGrâce (2010), 1.

97 *CR*, 15 June 1911, 5.

98 Ibid., 28 April 1910, 5–6; 29 December 1910, 5.

99 Ibid., 6 January 1910, 5; 7 April 1910, 5.

100 Ibid. 15 December 1910, 10. This particular acknowledgement came from Leon Korcaynski, a trustee of the Ukrainian Catholic congregation at Jasmin, Saskatchewan. He was seconded by Father Decamps, C.S.s.R., of Hubbard, Saskatchewan.

Chapter 7

1 Church Extension Archives. *Minute Book*, vol. 1, "Minutes of the Adjourned Meeting of the Catholic Church Extension Society," 26 April 1915, "President's Report for the Year Ending February 28ᵗʰ 1915," 46.

2 *CR*, 28 September 1911, 5.

3 ACAE, Catholic Church Extension Society File, Emile Legal to A.E. Burke, 28 April 1910.

4 McGowan, *The Waning of the Green*, 181.

5 *CR*, 5 May 1910, 5.

6 Ibid., 19 May 1910, 7.

7 Diocese of Calgary Archives, *Minute Book, Catholic Church Extension Society, Women's Auxiliary, Calgary Branch, 1910–1916.*

8 For Calgary: *CR*, 9 February 1911, 5; 16 March 1911, 5; 1 June 1911, 6; 7 November 1911, 5. For Edmonton: *CR*, 2 March 1911, 5; 22 February 1912, 5.

9 *CR*, 15 June 1911, 5.

10 Ibid., 31 August 1911, 5.

11 Ibid., 5 May 1910, 5.

12 Ibid., 12 May 1910, 5; 17 November 1910, 5: "To priests laboring in poor places."

13 Ibid., 12 May 1910, 5.

14 Church Extension Archives, Women's Auxiliary, *Scrapbook 1915–1921*, clippings from *CR*, "A Review of Five Years." This Review was also printed in Church Extension Archives, *Minute Book*, vol. 1, "Minutes of the Adjourned Meeting of the Catholic Church Extension Society," 26 April 1915. "Report of the Women's Auxiliary," 47–50.

15 *CR*, 18 May 1911, 5; 25 January 1912, 5; 1 February 1912, 5.

16 Ibid., 28 July 1910, 10.

17 Amy Day was the wife of James Edward Day and the grandmother of Father Thomas Joseph Day, a priest of the Archdiocese of Toronto. The Day family was one of Toronto's most prominent and wealthy Catholic families. Amy Day died on 8 August 1971, at the age of ninety-seven years. Information provided by Jeff Beattie of Mount Hope Cemetery, Toronto.

18 *CR*, 7 December 1911, 5.

19 Information supplied by Constance Lewin of the John M. Kelly Library, University of St. Michael's College, Toronto. Sources consulted were H. Francis Mallon, *The Mallons of Spadina Road* (Toronto: 1982), 6–7; *Mallon Family Memorabilia* (Pamphlet 1999, no. 1, University of St. Michael's College Archives). Additional information supplied by Jeff Beattie of Mount Hope Cemetery, Toronto.

20 *CR*, 22 December 1910, 5; 29 December 1910, 5; 19 January 1911, 5.

21 Ibid., 17 August 1911, 5.

22 Ibid., 29 June 1911, 5.

23 Ibid., 16 February 1911, 5; 2 March 1911, 5; 30 May 1911, 5.

24 Ibid., 21 March 1912, 5.

25 Ibid., 20 July 1911, 5.

26 Ibid., 12 January 1911, 5.

27 Ibid., 8 February 1912, 5.

28 Ibid., 19 September 1912, 5.

29 Church Extension Archives, Women's Auxiliary, *Scrapbook 1915–1921*, clipping from *CR*, "Golden Jubilee of a Conversion. The President of the Women's Auxiliary."

30 McGowan, *The Waning of the Green*, 100.

31 Church Extension Archives, Women's Auxiliary, *Scrapbook 1 December 1925 to 2 April 1934*, clipping from *CR*, "Notable Lady Closes Useful Life."

32 Information provided by Jeff Beattie of Mount Hope Cemetery, Toronto. Interestingly, the cemetery records show Mary Hoskin as a Religious Sister.

33 *CR*, 18 April 1912, 5.

34 Ibid., 1 December 1910, 5.

35 Ibid.

36 *Official Report of the Second American Catholic Missionary Congress: Delegates' Edition* (Chicago: J.S. Hyland & Co., 1914), 278–84. See also AAOC, Bishop Kelley Papers, Burke to Kelley, 5 August 1913; Kelley to Burke, 9 August 1913.

37 Hospital visitations: there are numerous and oftentimes lengthy references in *CR* to members of the sub-councils paying visits to Catholic patients in Toronto hospitals. Members visited every hospital on a regular basis and on occasion assisted destitute families. Mercer Reformatory for Women: *CR*, 11 April 1912, 5; 25 April 1912, 5; 9 May 1912, 5; 16 May 1912, 5. Night School: 15 June 1911, 5; 12 September 1912, 5; 10 October 1912, 5.

38 *CR*, 21 May 1912, 5: 301 members; 26 June 1913, 5: 420 members. The membership fee was one dollar a year, which many women found difficult to produce.

39 *CR*, 3 November 1910, 5; 10 November 1910, 5–6; 25 April 1915, 5.

40 Ibid., 3 November 1910, 5.

41 Ibid., 25 April 1912, 5.

42 Ibid., 14 December 1911, 5.

43 Ibid., 3 November 1910, 5.

44 Ibid., 25 April 1912, 5.

45 Ibid., 10 November 1910, 5.

46 Ibid., 25 April 1912, 5.

47 Ibid., 23 May 1912, 5.

48 Ibid., 1 December 1910, 5.

49 Ibid., 12 January 1911, 5.

50 Ibid., 26 January 1911, 5.

51 Ibid., 30 November 1939, 8.

52 Ibid., 6 April 1911, 5.

53 Ibid., 23 November 1911, 5.

54 Ibid., 16 November 1911, 5.

55 Ibid., 23 November 1911, 5.

56 Ibid., 30 November 1911, 5.

57 Ibid., 21 December 1911, 5.

58 In 1921, Rosary Hall moved to 264 Bloor Street East. *CR*, 3 December 1936, 3.

59 *CR*, 18 May 1911, 5; 25 May 1911, 5; 3 August 1911, 5; 21 September 1911, 5; 26 October 1911, 5; 9 May 1912, 5.

60 Church Extension Archives, Women's Auxiliary, *Scrapbook 1915–1921*, clipping from *CR*, "A Review of Five Years."

61 *CR*, 9 May 1912, 5; 20 June 1912, 5; 18 July 1912, 5; 15 August 1912, 5; 19 September 1912, 5.

62 Church Extension Archives, Women's Auxiliary, *Scrapbook 1915–1921*, clipping from *CR*, "A Review of Five Years."

63 *CR*, 14 March 1912, 5.

64 Ibid., 21 March 1912, 5.

65 Ibid., 18 July 1912, 5.

66 For additional information on Margaret Fletcher and the early years of the CWL in Great Britain, see Paula M. Kane, "'The Willing Captive of Home?': The English Catholic Women's League, 1906–1920," *Church History* 60, no. 3 (September 1991), 331–55.

67 *CR*, 10 October 1912, 5.

68 Ibid., 17 October 1912, 5; 24 October 1912, 5.

69 Ibid., 20 March 1913, 5; 26 June 1913, 5.

70 Ibid., 30 April 1914, 5.

71 Church Extension Archives, Women's Auxiliary, *Scrapbook 1915–1921*, clipping from *CR*, January 1916, "The Hostel."

72 Ibid., Women's Auxiliary, *Scrapbook 1915–1921*, clipping from *CR*, "A Review of Five Years."

73 Ibid., *Minute Book*, vol. 1, "Minutes of the Adjourned Meeting of the Catholic Church Extension Society," 26 April 1915. "Report of the Women's Auxiliary," 47–50.

74 *CR*, 15 April 1920, 5; Church Extension Archives, Women's Auxiliary, *Scrapbook 1 December 1925 to 2 April 1934*, clipping from *CR*, "Annual Report," 4 March 1930.

Chapter 8

1 LAC, Q4 51931, MG 27, Series II, C1, Vol. 13, Papers of Sir Charles Fitzpatrick, Burke to Fitzpatrick, 22 July 1910. The reference to "pernicious anaemia" is found in this letter. According to Burke, "all his trouble came from poisoning through dentistry. As you will remember, his teeth were troubling him even in Quebec [Plenary Council, 1909?]. An old bridge cut his mouth and tongue and there was [sic] a couple of teeth that were capped secreting pus at the roots. This pus poisoned the whole system, and when the doctors took the blood count, it was no wonder that they found white blood corpuscles dominating." Burke thought that the removal of the old bridge and the problem teeth, along with several months of fresh air at a cottage in Newport, Rhode Island, would revive the archbishop. McEvay did recover sufficiently to return to Toronto by September 1910, but he had a relapse in January 1911.

2 *CR*, 18 May 1911, 1.

3 Ibid., 7.

4 AAOC, Bishop Kelley Papers, Kelley to Burke, 6 May 1911.

5 Mark McGowan, "Toronto's English-Speaking Catholics, Immigration, and the Making of a Canadian Catholic Identity, 1900–1930," in *Creed and Culture: The Place of English-Speaking Catholics in Canadian Society, 1750–1930*, ed. Terrence Murphy and Gerald Stortz (Montreal & Kingston: McGill-Queen's University Press, 1993), 204–31.

6 A.E. Burke, "The Position of Prince Edward Island," in *Empire Club Speeches: Being Addresses Delivered Before the Empire Club of Canada During its Session of 1908–1909*, ed. J. Castell Hopkins (Toronto: William Briggs, 1910), 134–41.

7 LAC, Q4 51931, MG 27, Series II, C1, Vol. 82, Papers of Sir Charles Fitzpatrick, Burke to Fitzpatrick, 6 April 1909.

8 Ibid., Q4 51931, MG 27, Series II, C1, Vol. 82, Papers of Sir Charles Fitzpatrick, "Memo on Canadian Church Extension," 3.

9 ARCAT, OC07.C001, Burke to McEvay, 28 October 1909.

10 LAC, Q4 51931, MG 27, Series II, C1, Vol. 13, Papers of Sir Charles Fitzpatrick, Burke to Fitzpatrick, 22 July 1910.

11 ARCAT, ME AF0626, McEvay to Gauthier, 18 April 1911.

12 A.E. Burke, "Need of a Missionary College," in Kelley, *The First American Catholic Missionary Congress*, 77–84.

13 Kelley, *The First American Catholic Missionary Congress*, 109.

14 CACRSB, Series Adélard Langevin, File Correspondence, L34272, Burke to Langevin, 28 December 1908; L34273, Merry del Val to McEvay, 3 December 1908.

15 Ibid., Series Adélard Langevin, File Correspondence, L34269, Langevin to Bégin, 21 August 1908; Vol. 11, p. 872, Langevin to Duhamel, 19 October 1908; L34278, David to Langevin, 17 February 1909; L34280, Gravel to Langevin, 10 March 1909; Vol. 12, p. 580–82, Langevin to Vicar General of the Archdiocese of Québec, 2 April 1909; L34282, Larny (?) to Langevin, 12 September 1909; L34286, Béliveau to Langevin, 20 September 1909; Vol. 13, pp. 339–44, Langevin to Sabourin, 16 October 1909; L34296, Husson to Langevin, 7 March 1910.

16 ARCAT, OC07.C001, Langevin to McEvay, 16 January 1909.

17 Ibid., OC07.C001, McEvay to Langevin, 19 January 1909.

18 CACRSB, Series Adélard Langevin, File Correspondence, L34292, Burke to Langevin, 3 October 1909.

19 Ibid., Series Adélard Langevin, File Correspondence, L34294, Langevin to Burke, 12 October 1909.

20 Ibid., Series Adélard Langevin, File Correspondence, L34300, Burke to Langevin, 13 April 1910; L34302, Langevin to Burke, 16 April 1910.

21 CR, 27 January 1910, 5. For more on the bilingual schools controversy and Fallon's role in it, see Jack Cecillon, "Turbulent Times in the Diocese of London: Bishop Fallon and the French-Language Controversy, 1910–1918," *Ontario History* 87, no. 4 (December 1995), 381–87; Robert Choquette, *Language and Religion: A History of English–French Conflict in Ontario* (Ottawa: University of Ottawa Press, 1975); John K.A. Farrell (O'Farrell), "Michael Francis Fallon, Bishop of London, Ontario, Canada: The Man and His Controversies," Canadian Catholic Historical Association, *Study Sessions* (1968), 73–90.

22 Ibid., 10 September 1910, 1; 20 October 1910, 1.

23 Church Extension Archives, *Minute Book*, vol. 1, "Minutes of the Meeting of the Board of Governors," 19 November 1910, 23.

24 ARCAT, OC07.C001, McEvay to Bégin, 27 December 1910, 5 pages.

25 Ibid., OC07.C001, McEvay to Bégin, 27 December 1910, 4 pages.

26 Perin, "Bégin, Louis-Nazaire," 75.

27 ARCAT, OC07.C001, Archambeault to McEvay, 30 December 1910; McEvay to Fallon, 10 January 1911.

28 Ibid., OC07.C001, Burke to Martinelli, 29 December 1910.

29 *CR*, 18 September 1913, 1, 4.

30 ARCAT, OC07.C001, Stagni to McNeil, 18 September 1913, 3 pages; Stagni to McNeil, 18 September 1913, 2 pages.

Chapter 9

1 AAOC, Bishop Kelley Papers, Burke to Kelley, 20 July 1911; Kelley to Burke, 31 July 1911; Kelley to Burke, 3 August 1911.

2 Ibid., Bishop Kelley Papers, Kelley to Burke, 31 July 1911.

3 Gaffey, *Francis Clement Kelley*, vol. 1, 117, 135.

4 As quoted in Gaffey, *Francis Clement Kelley*, vol. 1, 135.

5 Ibid.

6 AOCC, Bishop Kelley Papers, Kelley to Burke, 17 August 1909. In this letter, Kelley told Burke that one day he would be an archbishop.

7 Ibid., Bishop Kelley Papers, Burke to Kelley, 16 October 1911.

8 Ibid., Bishop Kelley Papers, Burke to Kelley, 29 October 1911.

9 Ibid., Bishop Kelley Papers, Burke to Kelley, 23 November 1911.

10 AAOC, Bishop Kelley Papers, Burke to Merry del Val, 27 December 1911 (copy); Archivio Segreto Vaticano [hereafter ASV], Delegazione Apostolica del Canadà [hereafter DAC] 74.2.1, Burke to Merry de Val, 27 February 1912.

11 Terence J. Fay, *A History of Canadian Catholics: Gallicanism, Romanism, and Canadianism* (Montreal & Kingston: McGill-Queen's University Press, 2002), 140.

12 Ibid.

13 AOCC, Bishop Kelley Papers, Burke to Merry del Val, 27 December 1911 (copy).

14 Ibid.

15 ASV, DAC, 74.2.1/v, Burke to Merry del Val, 27 February 1912.

16 Fay, *A History of Canadian Catholics*, 142.

17 *CR*, 5 September 1912, 1, 7; 12 September 1912, 5; 10 October 1912, 5; 16 January 1913, 5.

18 O'Shea, *A.E. Burke*, 61. In the 1970s, the new ranks of monsignor were Chaplain to His Holiness (CHH), Prelate of Honour (PH) and Protonotary Apostolic de numero (PA) or Protonotary Apostolic supranumerary (PA).

19 "Monsignor," *NCE*, vol. 9 (New York: McGraw-Hill Book Company, 1967), 1070.

20 AAOC, Bishop Kelley Papers, Burke to Kelley, 26 July 1910.

21 Ibid., Bishop Kelley Papers, Kelley to Burke, 17 August 1909; Burke to Kelley, 26 July 1910; Kelley to Burke, 28 July 1910; Burke to Kelley, 2 August 1910; Kelley to Burke, 4 August 1910; Kelley to Burke, 5 November 1910; Burke to Kelley, 14 December 1910 (telegram); Burke to Kelley, 17 January 1911; Burke to Kelley, 30 January 1911; Kelley to Burke, 1 February 1911; Kelley to Burke, 3 March 1911; Burke to Kelley, 29 October 1911.

22 Ibid., Bishop Kelley Papers, Burke to Kelley, 28 July 1910; Kelley to Burke, 4 August 1910.

23 Ibid., Bishop Kelley Papers, Kelley to Burke, 4 August 1910.

24 Ibid., Bishop Kelley Papers, Kelley to Burke, 1 February 1911.

25 Ibid., Bishop Kelley Papers, Kelley to Burke, 3 March 1911.

26 Church Extension Archives, *Minute Book*, vol. 1, "Minutes of the Board of Governors," 17 April 1912, 25–26.

27 Ibid., *Minute Book*, vol. 1, "Minutes of the Board of Governors," 2 April 1913, 28.

28 Ibid., 29.

29 Ibid., 30.

30 *Annual Report of the Catholic Church Extension Society of Canada* (Toronto: 1918), 9.

31 Church Extension Archives, *Minute Book*, vol. 1, "Minutes of the Board of Governors," 2 April 1913, 29. It must be noted that from the point of view of Canon Law, Mass Intentions could not be treated as donations. They were offerings from the faithful.

32 Ibid.

33 Ibid., 30.

34 Ibid.

35 Ibid., 31.

36 The Archdiocese of Toronto did not take control of the *Catholic Register* until 1986. See Church Extension Archives, "Minutes of Executive Committee," 22 December 1986.

Chapter 10

1 LeBlanc, "McNeil, Neil," *Dictionnaire biographique des évêques catholiques du Canada*, 659–60. See also George Boyle, *Pioneer in Purple: The Life and Work of Archbishop Neil McNeil* (Montreal: Palm Publishers, 1951).

2 *CR*, 22 September 1910, 5.

3 Church Extension Archives, *Minute Book*, vol. 1, "Minutes of the Adjourned Meeting," 6 August 1915, 55.

4 *CR*, 8 August 1912, 1; 15 August 1912, 1. There was also an earlier story. See *CR*, 8 February 1912, 5.

5 ARCAT, MN AH26.01, Circular Letter, "Dear Reverend Father," 11 December 1912.

6 Boyle, *Pioneer in Purple*, 126.

7 ARCAT, OC07.C001, Circular Letter, McNeil to "My dear Lord," 17 January 1913.

8 Ibid.

9 *Evening Examiner* (Peterborough), 24 January 1913, 7, 9; 28 January 1913, 7, 11.

10 ARCAT, OC07.C001, Pascal to McNeil, 28 January 1913.

11 Ibid., OC07.C001, Mathieu to McNeil, 31 January 1913.

12 Ibid., OC07.C001, Latulipe to McNeil, 4 February 1913.

13 Ibid., OC07.C001, Spratt to McNeil, 18 January 1913.

14 Ibid.

15 Ibid., OC07.C001, Morrison to McNeil, 29 January 1913.

16 Ibid.

17 Ibid.

18 Ibid., OC07.C001, Langevin to McNeil, 1 February 1913.

19 CACRSB, Series Adélard Langevin, File Correspondence, L34309, "La Canadian Catholic Church Extension Society," 31 January 1913; trans. Philip J. Kennedy, 22 July 2011.

20 Ibid.

21 ARCAT, OC07.C001, Scollard to McNeil, 4 February 1913.

22 Ibid., OC07.C001, Duhamel to Sinnott, 13 October 1908.

23 Ibid., OC07.C001, Scollard to McNeil, 4 February 1913.

24 Ibid.

25 Ibid.

26 Ibid., OC07.C001, Ryan to McNeil, 26 February 1913.

27 Ibid.

28 Ibid.

29 Ibid.

30 Ibid.

31 AAOC, Bishop Kelley Papers, McNeil to Kelley, 31 January 1913.

32 Ibid., Bishop Kelley Papers, Kelley to McNeil, 4 February 1913.

33 Ibid., Bishop Kelley Papers, Kelley to Fallon, 11 February 1913.

34 ARCAT, OC07.C001, McNeil to Stagni, 24 February 1913.

35 Ibid., OC07.C001, Stagni to McNeil, 27 February 1913.

36 Ibid.

37 Ibid., OC07.C001, McNeil to Stagni, 1 March 2011.

38 A Prefecture Apostolic is "The first stage in the ecclesiastical organization of a missionary territory …. A Prefect Apostolic is not usually a bishop, but has wide powers …." See Attwater, *A Catholic Dictionary*, 3rd ed., 397. The next stage would be Vicariate Apostolic, with a titular bishop as Vicar Apostolic. The third stage is diocese, with its own diocesan bishop.

39 ARCAT, OC07.C001, McNeil to Stagni, 1 March 1913.

40 Ibid.

41 Ibid., OC07.C001, Stagni to McNeil, 4 March 1913.

42 Ibid.

43 Ibid.

44 Ibid., OC07.C001, McNeil to Stagni, 6 March 1913.

45 Ibid.

46 Ibid., OC07.C001, Stagni to McNeil, 7 December 1913.

47 AAOC, Bishop Kelley Papers, Kelley to McNeil, 5 February 1914.

48 ARCAT, OC07.C001, Casey to McNeil, 7 August 1914.

49 AAOC, Bishop Kelley Papers, Kelley to McNeil, 5 February 1914.

50 In a testament to the Roman bureaucracy's centuries-old predilection for never hurrying a decision, Bunoz did not become Vicar Apostolic of Yukon and Prince Rupert until 20 November 1916 and the Vicar Apostolic of Prince Rupert until 14 January 1944, the same day that the Vicariate Apostolic of Whitehorse was erected. Bunoz died in 1945 and never did become the bishop of his own diocese. The Diocese of Kamloops was erected on 22 December 1945. Prince George did not become a diocese until 31 July 1967, the same day that Whitehorse became a diocese.

51 AAOC, Bishop Kelley Papers, Burke to Kelley, 9 November 1913.

52 Ibid.

53 Church Extension Archives, *Minute Book*, vol. 1, "Minutes of the Annual Meeting of the Catholic Church Extension Society of Canada," 22 April 1914, 37.

54 Ibid., *Minute Book*, vol. 1, "Minutes of the Annual Meeting of the Catholic Church Extension Society of Canada," 22 April 1914, 38–40.

55 LAC, MG 27, Series II, C1, Vol. 15, Papers of Sir Charles Fitzpatrick, 8 November 1913.

56 Ibid.

57 ARCAT, OC07.C001, Fitzpatrick to McNeil, 11 November 1913.

58 Ibid., OC07.C001, Stagni to McNeil, 16 November 1913.

59 Church Extension Archives, *Minute Book*, vol. 1, "Minutes of the Annual General Meeting of the Catholic Church Extension Society of Canada," 22 April 1914, 36. See *CR*, 4 June 1914, 5; 18 June 1914, 5; 9 July 1914, 5.

60 Church Extension Archives, *Minute Book*, vol. 1, "Minutes of the Annual General Meeting of the Catholic Church Extension Society of Canada," 22 April 1914, 32–33. The President's Report was reprinted in *CR*, 30 April 1914, 5.

61 Church Extension Archives, *Minute Book*, vol. 1, "Minutes of the Annual General Meeting of the Catholic Church Extension Society of Canada," 22 April 1914, 34.

62 Ibid.

63 Ibid., 40.

64 AAOC, Bishop Kelley Papers, Burke to Kelley, 24 November 1914.

65 ARCAT, MN RC9704, De Lai to McNeil, 15 November 1914; trans. Philip J. Kennedy, 28 July 1911.

66 AAOC, Bishop Kelley Papers, Roche to Kelley, 11 November 1914.

67 Ibid., Bishop Kelley Papers, Kelley to Roche, 13 November 1914.

68 Ibid.

69 ARCAT, OC07.C001, Stagni to McNeil, 26 November 1914.

70 AAOC, Bishop Kelley Papers, Burke to Kelley, 2 April 1915. For additional informa-tion on Niall of the nine hostages, see Gearóid Mac Niocaill, *Ireland Before the Vikings* (Dublin: Gill and Macmillan Ltd., 1972), 9–12.

71 ARCAT, OC07.C001, Stagni to McNeil, 9 April 1915.

72 O'Shea, *A.E. Burke*, 55.

73 ARCAT, OC07.C001, Notice of Annual General Meeting, Neil McNeil, 19 March 1915.

74 Archives of the Catholic Diocese of Peterborough, Bishop Richard M. O'Brien Papers, McNeil to O'Brien, 10 April 1915.

75 ARCAT, OC07.C001, McNeil to Messrs. Foy, Knox & Monahan, 29 April 1915; A.W. Anglin to T.L. Monahan, 7 May 1915; A.W. Anglin to T.L. Monahan, 12 May 1915. Anglin examined the *Minute Book* at Church Extension headquarters. His interpreta-tion of the Constitution and By-Laws on the business of the qualification of governors was not only inconclusive but also confounding. He admitted: "I confess I do not know what to think."

76 Ibid., OC07.C001, Burke to McNeil, 22 March 1915.

77 Church Extension Archives, Haney, Magann and Kelly, "To the Most Reverend Neil McNeil, D.D.," 1.

78 Ibid., 7.

79 ARCAT, OC07.C001, McNeil to Kelly, 27 March 1915.

80 Ibid., OC07.C001, Kelly to McNeil, 31 March 1915.

81 Church Extension Archives, *Minute Book*, vol. 1, "Minutes of the Annual Meeting of the Board of Governors of the Catholic Church Extension Society of Canada," 14 April 1915, 41.

82 ARCAT, OC07.C001, McNeil to Stagni, 30 April 1915.

83 Church Extension Archives, *Minute Book*, vol. 1, "Minutes of the Adjourned Annual General Meeting of the Catholic Church Extension Society of Canada," 26 April 1915, 44.

84 Ibid.

85 ARCAT, OCC07. C001, McNeil to Stagni, 30 April 1915.

86 Church Extension Archives, *Minute Book*, vol. 1, "Minutes of the Adjourned Meeting of the Catholic Church Extension Society of Canada," 26 April 1914, 44.

87 ARCAT, OC07.C001, McNeil to Stagni, 30 April 1915.

88 AAOC, Bishop Kelley Papers, Burke to Kelley, 7 May 1915.

89 Ibid., Bishop Kelley Papers, Burke to Kelley, ca. 10–11 May 1915.

90 ARCAT, MN DS 17.03, Stagni to McNeil, 11 May 1915.

91 Ibid., OC07.C001, McNeil to Stagni, 16 May 1915.

92 Ibid., MN DS 17.06, Stagni to McNeil, 29 July 1915.

93 Church Extension Archives, *Minute Book*, vol. 1, "Minutes of the Adjourned Meeting of the Catholic Church Extension Society of Canada," 12 August 1915, 51–59. On 15 November 1915, Monsignor Kidd relinquished his post as acting president of the Society

to Bishop Michael Power of St. George's, with the approval of the board. However, Bishop Power, on the advice of his doctors, moved to a warmer climate for the winter. In any event, the terna of 12 August 1915 had been rejected. See Archives of the Catholic Diocese of Peterborough, Bishop Richard M. O'Brien Papers, McNeil to "My Lord," 29 November 1915.

94 Ibid., *Minute Book*, vol. 1, "Minutes of the Annual Meeting of the Catholic Church Extension Society of Canada," 3 May 1916, 61.

95 Information for the Postscript was taken from three sources: McGowan, "Burke, Alfred Edward," 168–69; O'Shea, *A.E. Burke*, 69–84; Duff Crerar, *Padres in No Man's Land: Canadian Chaplains and the Great War* (Montreal & Kingston: McGill-Queen's University Press, 1995), 36, 42, 50–51, 53, 61–62, 64; ARCAT, Clergy File, Alfred Edward Burke.

96 *The Charlottetown Guardian*, 16 December 1926, 1, 20 December 1926, 3, 21 December 1926, 3; *Canadian Annual Review of Public Affairs 1926–27* (Toronto: The Canadian Review Company Limited, [1928]), 657.

Chapter 11

1 *Annual Report of the Catholic Church Extension Society of Canada* (Toronto: 1918), 9. Another and much higher figure was given in the sub-committee report of March 1915: "the Society has collected $287,000 over and above any contribution to St. Augustine's Seminary; that of this amount $133,917.92 went to the Home Missions of Canada." See Church Extension Archives, Haney, Magann and Kelly, "To the Most Reverend Neil McNeil, D.D.," 6.

2 Mark McGowan, "'Religious Duties and Patriotic Endeavours': The Catholic Church Extension Society, French Canada and the Prairie West, 1908–1916," Canadian Catholic Historical Association, *Historical Studies* 51 (1984), 100–11.

3 Ibid., 111–16; McGowan, "Toronto's English-Speaking Catholics, Immigration, and the Making of a Canadian Catholic Identity, 1900–30," 219–20; Mark McGowan, "A Watchful Eye: The Catholic Church Extension Society and Ukrainian Catholic Immigrants, 1908–1930," in *Canadian Protestant and Catholic Missions, 1820s–1960s: Historical Essays in Honour of John Webster Grant*, ed. John S. Moir and C.T. McIntire (New York: Peter Lang, 1987), 231; Fay, *A History of Canadian Catholics*, 166–69.

4 This was Bishop Ryan's very astute perception. See ARCAT, OC07.C001, Ryan to McNeil, 26 February 1913.

5 Burke, "Need of a Missionary College," 77–84; G. Edward MacDonald, *The History of St. Dunstan's University 1855–1956* (N.p.: Board of Governors of St. Dunstan's University and Prince Edward Island Museum and Heritage Foundation, 1989), 256–60.

6 Church Extension Archives, Haney, Magann and Kelly, "To the Most Reverend Neil McNeill, D.D.," 6.

BIBLIOGRAPHY

Archives

Archives of the Archdiocese of Oklahoma City (AAOC)

Archives of the Catholic Archdiocese of Edmonton (ACAE)

Archives of the Catholic Church Extension Society of Canada
    (Church Extension Archives)

Archives of the Catholic Diocese of Peterborough

Archives of the Roman Catholic Archdiocese of Toronto (ARCAT)

Archivio Segreto Vaticano (ASV), Delegazione Apostolica del Canadà (DAC)

Corporation archiépiscopale catholique romaine de Saint Boniface (CACRSB)

Diocese of Calgary Archives

Diocese of Charlottetown Archives

Division des archives de l'Université Laval

Library and Archives Canada (LAC)

United Church of Canada Archives (UCCA)

University of St. Michael's College Archives

Newspapers, Journals and Magazines

America
Canadian Magazine
Catholic Register (*Catholic Register and Church Extension)*
Evening Examiner (Peterborough, Ontario)
Globe (Toronto)
L'Impartial (Tignish, P.E.I.)
Telegram (Toronto)
The Charlottetown Guardian (P.E.I.)
The Daily Examiner (Charlottetown, P.E.I.)
The Summerside Journal (P.E.I.)
Toronto Daily Star
Winnipeg Free Press

Secondary Sources: Theses, Books, Chapters in Books, Articles, Reports

Annual Report of the Catholic Church Extension Society of Canada 1918. Toronto: 1918.

Attwater, Donald. Ed. *A Catholic Dictionary.* 3ʳᵈ Ed. New York: The Macmillan Company, 1961.

Boyle, George. *Pioneer in Purple: The Life and Work of Archbishop Neil McNeil.* Montreal: Palm Publishers, 1951.

Burke, A.E. "Canada's First Church Council." *The Catholic World* 90, no. 537 (December 1909): 382–85.

———. "The Position of Prince Edward Island." In *Empire Club Speeches: Being Addresses Delivered Before the Empire Club of Canada During Its Session of 1908–1909.* Ed. J. Castell Hopkins. Toronto: William Briggs, 1910.

Canadian Annual Review of Public Affairs 1908. Ed. J. Castell Hopkins. Toronto: The Annual Review Publishing Company [1909].

Canadian Annual Review of Public Affairs 1909. Ed. J. Castell Hopkins. Toronto: The Annual Review Publishing Company [1910].

Canadian Annual Review of Public Affairs 1926–27. Toronto: The Canadian Review Company Limited [1928].

Canadian Encyclopedia. 3 vols. Edmonton: Hurtig Publishers, 1985.

Canadian Who's Who. London: The Times, 1910. Toronto: Musson Book Company [1910].

Cecillon, Jack. "Turbulent Times in the Diocese of London: Bishop Fallon and the French-Language Controversy, 1910–1918. *Ontario History* 87, no. 4 (December 1995): 381–87.

Choquette, Robert. *Language and Religion: A History of English–French Conflict in Ontario.* Ottawa: University of Ottawa Press, 1975.

Crerar, Duff. *Padres in No Man's Land: Canadian Chaplains and the Great War.* Montreal & Kingston: McGill-Queen's University Press, 1995.

Delaere, Achiel. *Mémoire sur les tentatives de schisme et d'hérésie au milieu des Ruthènes de l'Ouest canadien.* Québec: L'Action sociale, 1908.

———. *Memorandum on the Attempts of Schism and Heresy Among the Ruthenians (commonly called 'Galacians') in the Canadian Northwest.* Winnipeg: West Canada Publishing Company, 1909.

Dictionary of Canadian Biography. 15 vols. Toronto: University of Toronto Press, 1966–2005.

Dictionary of National Biography 1912–1927. Ed. H.W.C. Davis and J.R.H. Weaver. Oxford: Oxford University Press, 1927.

Dod's Peerage, Baronetage and Knightage of Great Britain and Ireland. London: Simpkin, Marshall, Hamilton, Kent, 1911.

Donahue, James. *Prince Edward Island Priests*. Minneapolis, Minn. [Webb Publishing Company, c. 1912].

Emery, G.N. "Methodist Missions Among the Ukrainians." *Alberta Historical Review* 19, no. 2 (1971): 8–19.

Farrell (O'Farrell), John K.A. "Michael Francis Fallon, Bishop of London, Ontario, Canada: The Man and His Controversies." Canadian Catholic Historical Association, *Study Sessions* (1968): 73–90.

Fay, Terence J. *A History of Canadian Catholics: Gallicanism, Romanism, and Canadianism*. Montreal & Kingston: McGill-Queen's University Press, 2002.

Gaffey, James P. *Francis Clement Kelley & the American Catholic Dream*. Vol. 1. Bensenville, Ill.: The Heritage Foundation, Inc., 1980.

Gerus, O.W. and J.E. Rea. *The Ukrainians in Canada*. Ottawa: Canadian Historical Association, 1985.

Gordon, C.W. "Our Duty to the English-speaking and European Settlers." In *Canada's Missionary Congress: Addresses Delivered at the Canadian National Missionary Congress, Held in Toronto, March 31 to April 4, 1909, with Reports of Committees*. Toronto: Canadian Council of Laymen's Missionary Movement, [1909].

Grant, John Webster. *The Church in the Canadian Era: The First Century of Confederation*. Toronto: McGraw-Hill Ryerson, 1972.

Himka, John-Paul. "The Background to Emigration: Ukrainians of Galicia and Bukovyna, 1848–1914." In *A Heritage in Transition: Essays in the History of Ukrainians in Canada*. Ed. Manoly R. Lupul. Toronto: McClelland and Stewart, 1982.

Hryniuk, Stella. "Pioneer Bishop, Pioneer Times: Nykyta Budka in Canada." Canadian Catholic Historical Association, *Historical Studies* 55 (1988): 21–41.

Huel, Raymond J.A. "French-speaking Bishops and the Cultural Mosaic in Western Canada." In *Canadian Plains Studies 3: Religion and Society in the Prairie West*. Ed. Richard Allen. Regina: Canadian Plains Research Center University of Regina, 1974.

———. "*Gestae Dei Per Francos*: The French Canadian experience in Western Canada." In *Visions of the New Jerusalem: Religious Settlement on the Prairies*. Ed. Benjamin G. Smillie. Edmonton: NeWest Press, 1983.

Hunter, A.J. *A Friendly Adventure: The Story of the United Church Mission Among New Canadians at Teulon, Manitoba.* Toronto: Board of Home Missions of the United Church of Canada, 1929.

Jean, Joseph. "S.E. Mgr. Adélard Langevin, Archevêque de St-Boniface, et les Ukrainiens." Canadian Catholic Historical Association, *Rapport* (1944–45): 101–10.

Kane, Paula M. "'The Willing Captive of Home?' The English Catholic Women's League, 1906–1920." *Church History* 60, no. 3 (September 1991): 331–55.

Kaye (Kysilewsky), Vladimir J. and Frances Swyripa. "Settlement and Colonization." In *A Heritage in Transition: Essays in the History of Ukrainians in Canada.* Ed. Manoly R. Lupul. Toronto: McClelland and Stewart, 1982.

Kazymyra, Bohdan. "Metropolitan Andrew Sheptyckyj and the Ukrainians in Canada." Canadian Catholic Historical Association, *Report* (1957): 75–86.

Kelley, Francis C. *The Bishop Jots It Down: An Autobiographical Strain on Memories.* New York and London: Harper & Brothers Publishers, 1930.

———. Ed. *The First American Catholic Missionary Congress.* Chicago: J.S. Hyland & Company, 1909.

———. *The Story of Extension.* Chicago: Extension Press, 1922.

Kordan, Bohdan S., and Lubomyr Y. Luciuk. *A Delicate and Difficult Question: Documents in the History of Ukrainians in Canada 1899–1962.* Kingston, Ont.: Limestone Press, 1986.

Kovacs, M.L. "The Saskatchewan Era, 1885–1914." In N.F. Drieziger, M.L.

Kovacs, Paul Body and Bennett Kovrig. *Struggle and Hope: The Hungarian-Canadian Experience.* Toronto: McClelland and Stewart, 1982.

LeBlanc, Jean. *Dictionnaire biographique des évêques catholiques du Canada.* Ottawa: Wilson & LaFleur, 2002.

Mac Niocaill, Gearóid. *Ireland Before the Vikings.* Dublin: Gill and Macmillan Ltd., 1972.

Mallon, H. Francis. *The Mallons of Spadina Road.* Toronto: 1982.

Marunchak, Michael H. *The Ukrainian Canadians: A History.* Winnipeg & Ottawa: Ukrainian Free Academy of Sciences, 1970.

McGowan, Mark G. "A Watchful Eye: The Catholic Church Extension Society and Ukrainian Catholic Immigrants, 1908–1930." In *Canadian Protestant and Catholic Missions, 1820s–1960s: Historical Essays in Honour of John Webster Grant.* Ed. John S. Moir and C.T. McIntire. New York: Peter Lang, 1987.

_____. "'Religious Duties and Patriotic Endeavours': The Catholic Church Extension Society, French Canada and the Prairie West, 1908–1916." Canadian Catholic Historical Association, *Historical Studies* 51 (1984): 100–11.

_____. "The Harvesters Were Few: A Study of the Catholic Church Extension Society of Canada, French Canada, and the Ukrainian Question, 1908–1925." Master's Thesis, University of Toronto, 1983.

_____. *The Waning of the Green: Catholics, the Irish, and Identity in Toronto, 1887–1922*. Montreal & Kingston: McGill-Queen's University Press, 1999.

_____. "Toronto's English-Speaking Catholics, Immigration, and the Making of a Canadian Catholic Identity, 1900-1930." In *Creed and Culture: The Place of English-Speaking Catholics in Canadian Society, 1750-1930*. Ed. Terrence Murphy and Gerald Stortz. Montreal & Kingston: McGill-Queen's University Press, 1993.

McVay, Athanasius D. "The Mystery of Father Damascene Polivka." *Annales Ecclesiae Ucrainae*. 20 January 2010: 1–10.

Morgan, Henry James. *The Canadian Men and Women of the Time: A Hand-book of Canadian Biography of Living Characters*. 2nd Ed. Toronto: William Briggs, 1912.

New Catholic Encyclopedia. New York: McGraw-Hill Book Company, 1967–.

Official Report of the Second American Catholic Missionary Congress: Delegates' Edition. Chicago: J.S. Hyland & Co., 1914.

Perin, Roberto. *Rome in Canada: The Vatican and Canadian Affairs in the Late Victorian Age*. Toronto: University of Toronto Press, 1990.

Pioneer Bishop: The Story of Nicetas Budka's Fifteen Years in Canada. Ed. Michael Shykula and Bernard Korchinski. Regina, Sask.: Bishop Budka Council #5914 Knights of Columbus [1909].

Pirot, Father [Jules]. *A Year's Fight for the True Faith in Saskatchewan: The Hungarian Question in Canada in 1910*. Toronto: Catholic Register and Church Extension, 1911.

Power, Michael. *A History of Mount Hope Cemetery, Toronto, Ontario 1898–1998*. Toronto: Catholic Cemeteries, Archdiocese of Toronto, 1998.

Power, Michael and Daniel J. Brock. *Gather up the Fragments: A History of the Diocese of London*. London, Ont.: Diocese of London, 2008.

Semple, Neil. *The Lord's Dominion: The History of Canadian Methodism*. Montreal & Kingston: McGill-Queen's University Press, 1996.

Sheptytsky, Andrey. "Address on the Ruthenian Question to their Lordships the Archbishops and Bishops of Canada." In *Two Documents of the Ukrainian*

Catholic Church 1911–1976. Ed. M.H. Marunchak. Winnipeg: National Council of Ukrainian Organizations for the Patriarchate of the Ukrainian Catholic Church, 1977.

Skwarok, J. *The Ukrainian Settlers in Canada and their Schools with Reference to Government, French Canadian, and Ukrainian Missionary Influences 1891–1921.* Toronto: Basilian Press, 1959.

Statues of Canada. 1909.

Tesla, Ivan. "Immigration to Canada." In *A Statistical Compendium of the Ukrainians in Canada, 1891–1976.* Ed. William Darcovich and Paul Yuzyk. Ottawa: University of Ottawa Press, 1980.

Vocht, Josef de. *Father Achiel Delaere (1868–1939): The First Eastern Rite Redemptorist & Canada's Ukrainian Catholic Church.* Trans. Christian Roy. Yorkton, Sask.: Gravelbooks, 2005.

Woodsworth, James S. *Strangers Within Our Gates: Or, Coming Canadians.* Toronto: The Missionary Society of the Methodist Church, Canada, 1909.

Yuzyk, Paul. "Religious Denominations." In *A Statistical Compendium of the Ukrainians in Canada 1891–1976.* Ed. William Darcovich and Paul Yuzyk. Ottawa: University of Ottawa Press, 1980.

————. "Religious Life." In *A Heritage in Transition: Essays in the History of Ukrainians in Canada.* Ed. Manoly R. Lupul. Toronto: McClelland and Stewart, 1982.

————. "The First Ukrainians in Manitoba." In *Papers Read Before the Historical and Scientific Society of Manitoba.* 3rd ser. No. 8. Ed. J.A. Jackson, W.L. Morton and P. Yuzyk. Winnipeg: 1953.

————. "The History of the Ukrainian Greek Catholic (Uniate) Church in Canada." Master's Thesis, University of Saskatchewan, 1948.

————. "Ukrainian Greek Orthodox Church of Canada (1918–1951)." Ph.D. diss., University of Minnesota, 1951.

INDEX

Note: CCES = Catholic Church Extension Society

L'Action sociale, 167

Alexandroff, Vladimir, 87, 88

"Allata nuper ad nos" (Apostolic Brief), 63–68, 126–26, 137, 205

"An Act to incorporate the Catholic Church Extension Society of Canada (1909), 54, 56, 63

Archambeault, Joseph-Alfred, 46, 155; officer of CCES, 52; resignation from board of governors (CCES), 165, 166–67

Archdiocese of St. Boniface (1911): Ukrainian Catholics, 96, 112

Arthur, George, 103

Austro–Hungarian Empire, 11, 82, 89

Bacynski, Alexander, 107

Baker, George, 33

Baptists, 100

Basilian Fathers (monks), 78, 95, 97. *See also* Order of St. Basil the Great (OSBM)

Beck, Nicholas: board of governors (CCES), 51

Bégin, Louis–Nazarre, 20, 28, 155; board of governors (CCES), 47, 165, 166–67; correspondence with McEvay, 165–66

Behan, E.M., 112

Benedict XV, 217

Bernier, August, 119

Blanche, Gustave, 203

Blumberger, S., 104

board of governors (CCES), 11, 12; Annual General Meeting (1910), 57; Annual General Meeting (1914), 203; Annual General Meeting (1915), 206–16; new members (1908), 51, 54–55, 62; provisional (1908), 47; special meeting (19 November 1910), 66–67

Bodrug, Ivan (John), 107, 108

Boels, Hendrik, 77–78, 97, 119

Borden, Robert Laird, 171

Bowell, Mackenzie, 38

Breyant, Gabriel: Ukrainian Catholics, 93

Bruchési, Paul, 22, 26, 27, 65, 171

Budka, Nykyta, 93, 95, 97, 99, 123, 126–28, 203, 210

Bukovyna, 83–84, 85

Bunoz, Émile-Marie, 196–97

Burke, Alfred Edward, 12; agricultural societies, 34; "Allata nuper ad nos" (Apostolic Brief), 65–66; Annual General Meeting (CCES, 1915), 206–16; appointed first president

(CCES), 67–68; assessment of his presidency, 13, 52, 219–23; Biltmore Forest College (North Carolina), 35; birth, 32; bishopric, 196–99; board of governors (CCES), 47; Catholic Mutual Benefit Association (CMBA), 33, 37, 45; character, 31–32; clashes with McDonald, 40–45; controversialist, 39–45; correspondence with Duke of Norfolk, 74–75; correspondence with Kelley, 25–26; correspondence with Langevin, 163–65; *The Daily Examiner*, 39, 40, 41, 42, 43; death, 218; Diocese of Charlottetown, 32–33; editor-in-chief of the *Catholic Register*, 53; education, 32; English–French relations, 154–57, 222–23; European travels (1911, 1912), 169–72; final years, 217–18; First American Catholic Missionary Congress (1908), 72–74; First Plenary Council of Canada (1909), 76–79; founder (CCES), 16, 17–22; General Managing Director (CCES), 54; illness, 205; immigration and colonization, 38; inter-colonial conference (1894), 38–40; invited to Chicago, 24; journalism, 39, 68; keeps control of the *Catholic Register*, 200–203; "Manitoba's Recent Immigrants," 112–13; McLaren, 104, 109, 113–19, 125–26; meets McNeil (1910, 1912), 183; "Memorial to the Ruthenian Catholics of Western Canada," 76–77, 98, 104; monsignorship, 168, 172–75, 215; officer (CCES), 53; ordination, 53; Pius X, 127; Pontifical Society (CCES), 57–58; Prefecture Apostolic of Yukon and Prince Rupert, 196–99; President's Report (1913), 176–79;

President's Report (1914), 203–4; rail tunnel under Northumberland Strait, 35–37; reforestation of Prince Edward Island, 35; relationship with McEvay, 152–53; resignation, 207; Sembratowicz, Leo I., 120–23; steamer navigation, 35; St. Philip Neri Hostel, 148–49; temperance, 33–34; traveller, 37–39; *The Tunnel Between Prince Edward Island and the Mainland*, 30; Women's Auxiliary of Toronto (CCES), 131–32, 133–35

Cameron, John, 182
Canadianization, 106
Canning, Hugh J., 67, 100–13, 115, 129, 189
Carmichael, J.A., 116, 117, 118
Carranza, Venustiano, 217
Casey, Timothy, 195, 199, 203, 211
Catholic Church Extension Society in the United States, 12, 16, 20, 22, 23
Catholic Church Extension Society of Canada (CCES): achievements, 14, 175–76, 221; "Allata nuper ad nos" (Apostolic Brief), 63–68; "An Act to incorporate the Catholic Church Extension Society of Canada" (1909), 54; assessment of its work under Burke, 223–25; board of governors, 11, 12, 47, 51, 54–55, 57, 60, 62, 203, 206–16; By-Laws, 49, 52–53; English–French relations, 154–57, 222–23; English-language Constitution, 30, 49–52, 53; executive committee, 54; First Plenary Council of Canada (1909), 76–79; founders, 16, 17–22; founding, Chapter 1; "French Foundership," 47; Latin Constitution, 59–63, 64–65, 66–67, 206; officers, 53;

organization, Chapter 3; Pontifical Society, 57–68; primary mandate, 10; purchase of the *Catholic Register*, 68; Women's Auxiliary of Toronto, Chapter 7

Catholic Church Extension Society of Germany, 172

Catholic Congress of Germany, 172

Catholic ideal of religious and social progress, 49

Catholic Missions in Canada, 14, 15

Catholic Register, 13, 17, 18, 19, 75; Burke's President's Report (1913), 177, 178–79; purchase by CCES, 68; Ukrainian Catholics, 102–3

Catholic Women's League, 133, 141, 149, 173

chapels, 224; for Ukrainians, 129

Chekkoustev, Arseniy, 88

China Missin Society, 220

Chomlak, Mary, 129

Chomliak, Ksenia, 129

Chomtak, Krenia, 129

Church Extension. *See* Catholic Church Extension Society of Canada

Claveloux, Désiré, 97

Cleary, James Vincent, 40

Cloutre, E., 171

Congregation of Propaganda Fide, Oriental Affairs, 90

Congregation of St. Josaphat, 97

Cormie, J.A., 103

Curran, T., 30

Dalton, Charles, 203

Danylchuk, John, 107

Davis, Michael Patrick: board of governors (CCES), 51

Day, Mrs. J.E. (Amy), 136, 145

Decamps, Noel, 97, 119, 125, 136, 148

Delaere, Achiel, 77, 80, 97, 109–10, 126, 160

De Lai, Gaetano, 157, 199, 205, 208

Desmarais, Arthur, 97

Diocese of Prince Albert: Ukrainian Catholics, 96

Diocese of Regina: Ukrainian Catholics, 96

Dmytriw, Nestor, 92

Dollard, James B., 135, 216

Dominion Alliance for the Total Suppression of the Liquor Traffic, 34

Dontenwill, Augustin, 26

Dowling, Thomas J., 203

Le Droit, 167

Duhamel, Joseph-Thomas, 26, 27

Duke of Norfolk, 74–75, 155, 156–57, 171. *See also* Howard, Henry Fitzalan

Dydyk, Sozont, 78, 97

Ea semper (papal bull, 1907), 90

Edna-Star (Vegreville), Alberta, 84, 87, 91; Judicial Committee of the Privy Council decision (1907), 88

Eleniak, Wasyl, 93

English-French relations, 154–67, 186–87, 190–92, 222–23

English-language Constitution (CCES), 30, 49–52, 53

Eucharistic Congress (1910), 122

Falconio, Diomede, 61, 94

Fallon, Michael Francis, 21, 165, 190, 222

Filias, Platonidas, 77, 97

First American Catholic Missionary Congress (1908), 17, 70–75

First Plenary Council of Canada (1909), 76–79, 122; pledge of financial assistance for Ukrainian Catholics, 79

Fitzpatrick, Charles, 12, 13, 47, 53, 66, 67, 68, 170, 180; "Allata nuper ad nos" (Apostolic Brief), 66; Annual General Meeting (1915), 211, 213, 214; board of governors (CCES), 47; career, 29–30; correspondence with McNeil, 201–2; English–French relations, 115–56, 156–57; First American Catholic Missionary Congress (1908), 71, 72; founder (CCES), 16, 17–22; resignation, 207

Fletcher, Margaret, 19

Franz Joseph (Emperor), 96

French-Canadian Congress for Ontario (l'Association canadienne-française d'éducation d'Ontario), 166

Gaffey, James P., 169

Gagnon, Joseph, 97

Galicia, 83–84, 85

Gauthier, Charles-Hugues, 157–58

Genyk, Cyril, 92, 109

Gill, Luvonka, 129

Grandin, Vital-Joseph, 55; Ukrainian Catholics, 93

Grouard, Émile, 78, 93

Haney, Michael John, 25, 67, 204, 210, 211, 213, 216; board of governors (CCES), 55, 68; Catholic Register, 201

Hébert, Eugène, 171

Hirst, Anthony A., 129

Holy Childhood, 64

Hoskin, Mary, 131, 136–38, 143, 145, 148; "Dorothy" column in Catholic Register, 137; president of Women's Auxiliary of Toronto (CCES), 138–41

Howard, Henry Fitzalan, 74. See also Duke of Norfolk

Howlan, George, 35–36, 41

Hughes, Cornelia, 133

Hughes, Katherine, 133, 143

Hunter, A.J., 103–4; A Friendly Adventure, 104

Hura, Miron, 119

Independent Greek Church, 95, 100–101, 102, 103–9, 115, 116, 118, 126, 129

Ireland, John, 84

Jan, Alphonsus, 96, 119

Jean, Joseph, 97

Judicial Committee of the Privy Council decision (1907), 88

Kalpoushok, Emilia, 97

Kameneff, Dimitri, 87, 88

Kanadiyskaya Farmer (Canadian Farmer), 95, 109

Kanadiyskaya Niva (Canadian Field), 88

Kanadiyskaya Nyva, 95

Kanadyiskyi Rusyn (Canadian Ruthenian), 95

Karpec, Pawlo, 129

Kelley, Francis Clement, 12, 159, 219; Annual General Meeting (1915), 207–8; Constitution and By-Laws (CCES), 49; correspondence with Burke, 25–26; correspondence with McNeil, 193; European travels, 169–72; founder (CCES), 16, 17–22; Latin Constitution (CCES), 60–62; lobbies on behalf of CCES, 22–25; missionary college, 161–62; monsignorship, 172–75; Pontifical Society (CCES), 57–62; writings about Burke, 32–33

Kelly, Hugh T., 54, 56, 180, 204, 210, 21

Kidd, John Thomas, 12, 71, 120, 176, 207, 210, 211, 216; board of governors (CCES), 47; founder (CCES), 16, 17–22

Kneil, Mrs. Robert, 133
Knights of Columbus (Winnipeg), 110
Korchinski, Jacob, 88

Lacombe, Albert, 71
Lacoste, H., 28
Lang, George C.H., 66, 211; board of governors (CCES), 55, 56; *Catholic Register*, 201
Langevin, Adélard, 16, 26, 28 76, 222; correspondence with Kelley, 22–24; correspondence with McEvay, 159–62; English-French relations, 156, 157; First Plenary Council of Canada (1909), 78; McLaren, 106; opposition to CCES, 27–28, 47, 65, 103, 158–62, 188–89; Ukrainian Catholics, 93, 94–95
Latin Constitution (CCES), 59–63, 64–65, 66–67, 206
Latulipe, Élie-Anicet, 186–87
Laurier, Wilfrid, 35, 36
Laval University, 20
Legal, Émile-Joseph, 22, 27, 119, 156; board of governors (CCES), 55; *Catholic Register*, 201; Edna-Star controversy, 88; First American Catholic Missionary Congress, 71, 72; Ukrainian Catholic clergy, 95–96; Ukrainian Catholics, 93, 110; Women's Auxiliary (CCES), 132–33
Lenkevich, Ambrosia, 97
Long, Thomas, 203, 210
Lynch, John Joseph, 33

MacDonald, Alexander, 203, 211
MacDonald, Dugald, 41
Magann, George Plunkett, 68, 204, 210, 211, 213, 216; board of governors (CCES), 55–56; *Catholic Register*, 201

Mallon, Margaret ("Grettie"), 136, 140, 142, 145
Manitoba College, 107, 116
Manitoba Schools Question, 38
Martinelli, Sebastian, 63, 65, 67, 166–67, 169, 198
Mathieu, Olivier-Elzéar, 93, 157, 203; correspondence with McNeil, 186
McDonald, James Charles, 24, 33; board of governors (CCES), 47–48; clashes with Burke, 40–45
McEvay, Fergus Patrick, 12, 66, 76, 77, 122, 123, 129, 135, 174; "Alata nuper ad nos" (Apostolic Brief), 65; bishop of London, 25; board of governors (CCES), 47; correspondence with Bégin, 165–68; correspondence with Langevin, 159–62; death, 13, 57, 152–53, 177, 222; English-French relations, 154–55, 157; First American Catholic Missionary Congress (1908), 71–72; founder (CCES), 16, 17–22; installation as archbishop of Toronto, 28–29; officer (CCES), 53; Ruthenian Collection (1910), 79
McIntyre, Peter, 32–33
McLaren, E.D. (Ebenezer Duncan), 104; Burke, 104, 109, 113–19, 125–26; Langevin, 106; Roche, 124–25
McNally, John Thomas, 203
McNeil, Neil, 13, 57, 59, 167, 168, 221; Annual General Meeting (1915), 206–16; biography, 181–83; bishopric for Burke, 196–99; Burke and his allies on the board of governors (CCES), 184–85; circular letter of 13 January 1913, 185; correspondence with Stagni, 184–85, 193–98, 202–3, 205, 206, 212, 214, 215; correspondence with the hierarchy concerning Burke

and CCES, 186–93; failure to win control of the *Catholic Register*, 179, 180; meets with Burke (1910, 1912), 183; reaction to Burke's President's Report (1913), 177, 179

McSloy, Hugh: board of governors (CCES), 62–63

McSloy, James: board of governors (CCES), 62–63

Memorandum on the Attempts of Schism and Heresy Among the Ruthenians (commonly called 'Galicians') in the Canadian Northwest, 109

Mercer Reformatory for Women, 140

Merry de Val, Raphael, 59, 61, 65, 67, 159, 169, 170, 171, 173, 174, 199

Methodists, 100, 162

Meunier, J.E., 71

Minutes of the Catholic Church Extension Society of Canada, 18–19

missionary college, 48, 158, 162, 209, 224. *See also* St. Dunstan's College (PEI)

Morrison, James, 187–88

Muldoon, Peter J., 60

Munro, C.H., 103

Murphy, J.T., 30

Murphy, P.C., 42

Negrych, Ivan (John), 107, 108

Neri, St. Philip, 64

Ne Temere, 171–72

Novak, Wasyl, 107

Nyzankiwsky, Ostap, 91

O'Brien, Cornelius, 35, 43–44

O'Brien, Michael John, 68; board of governors (CCES), 55

O'Brien, Richard M.J., 203, 219, 211

O'Connor, Denis, 28

O'Connor, Richard Alphonsus, 185

O emigratsii (About Emigration), 91

Oeuvre Protectrice des Immigrants Catholiques (Catholic Immigration Association of Canada), 166

O'Keefe, Eugene: officer (CCES), 53–54

O'Leary, Henry J., 203

Oleskiw, Joseph, 91–92

Orange Sentinel, 114–15

Order of Saint Basil the Great (OSBM), 90, 121. *See also* Basilian Fathers (monks)

Ortynsky, Soter, 90–91, 120

Pascal, Albert, 22, 26, 27, 156; correspondence with McNeil, 186; First Plenary Council of Canada (1909), 78; Ukrainian Catholic clergy, 95–96; Ukrainian Catholics, 93

Peter's Pence, 220

Petty, Ambrose, 60

Pillipiw, Ivan, 93

Pius X, 60, 63, 67, 127, 148, 159, 195; death, 208

Platon, Archbishop, 85

Polivka, Damascene, 92–93

Pontifical Society (CCES), 57–58

Power, Michael F., 216

Prefecture Apostolic of Yukon and Prince Rupert, 196–99

Presbyterian, 108

Presbyterian Home Mission Society, 100–102, 103–19

Propagation of the Faith, 64, 220

Pro vilni zemli (About Free Lands), 91

Quigley, James Edward, 57, 174, 175

Ranok (The Dawn), 95, 109, 110, 113, 114, 115, 116, 117, 161,

Redemptorists (Belgian), 97

Reid, J.T., 103

Riel, Louis, 29

Roche, Joseph T., 68, 71, 110–13, 115, 129, 135, 189, 205–6; McLaren, 124–25

Rosary Hall, 140, 145–46, 220; Advisory Board, 146; Association, 146

Roy, Émile, 216

Russian Orthodox Church (diocese of the Aleutians and Alaska), 85–86; missionaries in Western Canada, 87–89

Ruthenians, 73, 83; "Address on the Ruthenian Question," 127; definition, 81–83; "Memorial on the Ruthenian Catholics of Western Canada," 76–77, 98, 104; population in Canada, 80–81, 83–84; Ruthenian Collection (1910), 79; support given by CCES, 163; support given by Langevin, 160–61. *See also* Ukrainian Catholics

Ryan, Patrick Thomas, 191–93

Ryan, Stephen, 33

Sabourin, Adonis, 97, 111–12, 119, 161

Sbarretti, Donato, 12, 28–29, 153; "Allata super ad nos" (Apostolic Brief), 65; board of governors (CCES, 1908), 47; correspondence with Burke, 27; correspondence with Kelley, 24–25; First Plenary Council of Canada (1909), 78; founder (CCES), 16, 17–22; Latin Constitution (CCES), 61–63; officer (CCES), 53

Scollard, David, 189–90, 203, 210, 211

Scott, R.G., 103

Second American Catholic Missionary Congress (1913), 140

Sembratowicz, Joseph, 119

Sembratowicz (Sembratowich), Leo I., 119–23

Seraphim, 106, 107

Shaughnessy, Thomas, 61

Sheptytsky, Andrey, 90, 96–97, 119, 122, 123–24, 125; "Address on the Ruthenian Question," 127

Shipovsky, Isidora, 97

Simituk, Hania, 129

Sinnott, Alfred Arthur, 12, 67, 206, 214, 216; board of governors (CCES), 47; founder (CCES), 16, 17–22

Sisters Servants of Mary Immaculate, 95, 96, 97

Society, the. *See* Catholic Church Extension Society of Canada

"Society of Ruthenian Congregations in the United States and Canada, The," 90

Spratt, Michael J., 187

St. Dunstan's College (PEI), 159, 160. *See also* missionary college

St. Josaphat Ukrainian Catholic Church, 129

St. Patrick's Church (Montreal), 141

St. Philip Neri Hostel, 140, 148–50, 176, 220

St. Philip Neri Ruthenian Chapel (1912), 148

Stagni, Pellegrino Franceso, 153, 167, 214; correspondence with McNeil, 184–85, 193–98, 202–3, 205, 206, 212, 214, 215

Stanton, George Lynch, 112

Strangers Within Our Gates, 124

Strotsky, Anton, 97

Svoboda, 92

Tadoussac (steamer), 15, 18, 20, 29, 30, 45

Taschereau, Alexandre, 47, 155
Taschereau, Elzéar-Alexandre, 32
Têcheur, Charles, 97
Thompson, Annie, 39
Thompson, John, 39
Tikhon, Archbishop, 85, 88
Toth (Tovt), Alexis, 86–87
Treaty of Brest-Livovsk (1596), 82
Tymkewicz, Paul, 92
Tymoczko, John, 129

Ukrainian Catholic clergy, 85; early history in Canada, 89–98; married priests, 87, 90
Ukrainian Catholics, 22, 38, 62, 69–70; Archdiocese of St. Boniface, 96; *Catholic Register*, 102–3; chapels, 129; correspondence of Burke to Duke of Norfolk, 75; definition, 81–83; Diocese of Prince Albert, 96; Diocese of Regina, 96; First American Catholic Missionary Congress (1908), 73–74; First Plenary Council of Canada (1909), 76–79; Independent Greek Church, 95, 100–101, 102, 103–9; Latin Rite bishops, 93–96; population in Canada, 80–81, 83–84; Presbyterian Home Mission Society, 100–102; settlement patterns in Canada, 84–85. *See also* Ruthenians
Ukrainian Orthodox Church, 82–83
Ukrainian Orthodox clergy, 85
Ustvolsky, Stefan. *See* Seraphim

Vegreville (Alberta). *See* Edna-Star (Alberta)
Vincent, Charles, 138
Vladimir, Bishop, 79

Walsh, John, 33, 65
Winnipeg Free Press, 80, 84
Women's Auxiliary of Toronto (CCES), Chapter 7; board of governors, 143; Burke, 131–32, 133–35; By-Laws, 144; chapels, 148; committees, 145; Constitution, 141–44; five-year report (1911–1915), 150–51; Hoskin, 138–41; Mallon, 136; Supreme Council, 145; Toronto Council, 140; work, 140–41
Women's Auxiliary Society (Calgary), 133, 141
Women's Auxiliary Society (Edmonton), 133, 141
Woodsworth, James S., 124
Wrublevsky, Taida, 97

Yanishevsky, Jeremiah, 97

Zaklinski, Ivan, 92, 93
Zholdak, Basil, 96